AUTO-BIOGRAPI

This page enable...
to compile a list of
useful data on your
car, so that whether
you're ordering spares
or just checking the tyre
pressures, all the key
information - the infor-
mation that is 'personal'
to your car - is easily
within reach.

Registration number: ....

Model: ....

Body colour: ....

Paint code number: ....

Date of first registration: ....

Date of manufacture (if different): ....

VIN (or 'chassis') number: ....

Engine number: ....

Ignition key number: ....

Door lock key/s number/s: ....

Fuel locking cap key number (if fitted): ....

Alarm remote code (if fitted): ....

Alarm remote battery type: ....

Radio/cassette security code (if fitted): ....

Tyre size

Front: ....Rear: ....

Tyre pressure (normally laden)

Front: ....Rear: ....

Tyre pressure (fully laden)

Front: ....Rear: ....

Insurance

    Name and address of insurer:...

    ....

    Policy number:...

Modifications

    Information that might be useful when you need to purchase parts:..

    ....

    ....

Suppliers

    Address and telephone number of your garage and parts suppliers:...

    ....

    ....

First published in 1995 by Porter Publishing Ltd.

Porter Publishing Ltd.
The Storehouse
Little Hereford Street
Bromyard
Hereford HR7 4DE
England

British Library Cataloguing in Publication Data.

A catalogue record for this book is available from the British Library.

ISBN 1-899238-10-7

Series Editor: Lindsay Porter
Design: Martin Driscoll, Lindsay Porter and Lyndsay Berryman
Layout and Typesetting: Pineapple Publishing, Worcester
Cover photography: Jeremy Gale
Printed in England by The Trinity Press, Worcester.

Every care has been taken to ensure that the material contained in this Service Guide is correct. However, no liability can be accepted by the authors or publishers for damage, loss, accidents, or injury resulting from any omissions or errors in the information given.

 Copyright in all line drawings supplied by The Ford Motor Company remains the property of The Ford Motor Company.

Titles in this Series:

Absolute Beginners' Service Guide
Caravan Owner's Manual & Service Guide
Classic 'Bike Service Guide
Diesel Car Engines Service Guide
Ford Escort (Front Wheel Drive) & Orion Service Guide
Ford Sierra (All models) Service Guide
Land Rover Series I, II, IIA & III Service Guide
Land Rover Defender, 90 & 110 Service Guide

Metro (1980-1990) Service Guide
Mini (all models 1959-1994) Service Guide
MGB (including MGC, MGB GT V8 and MG RV8) Service Guide
Vauxhall Astra & Belmont (All models-1995) Service Guide
Vauxhall Cavalier Service Guide
VW Beetle Service Guide

- With more titles in production -

Ford Fiesta
Service Guide
& Owner's Manual
by
Lindsay Porter
& Peter Wallage

OIL AND WATER DON'T MIX

It is important to remember that even a small quantity of oil is harmful to water and wildlife. And tipping oil down the drain is as good as tipping it into a river. Many drains are connected directly to a river or stream and pollution will occur.

Each year the National Rivers Authority deals with over 6,000 oil related water pollution incidents. Many of these are caused by the careless disposal of used oil.

The used oil from the sump of just one car can cover an area of water the size of two football pitches, cutting off the oxygen supply and harming swans, ducks, fish and other river life.

OIL POLLUTES WATER
USE YOUR BRAIN-
NOT THE DRAIN!

Follow the Oil Care Code

◆ *When you drain your engine oil - don't oil the drain!* Pouring oil down the drain will cause pollution. It is also an offence.

◆ Don't mix used oil with other materials, such as paint or solvents, because this makes recycling very difficult.

◆ Take used oil to an oil recycling bank. Telephone FREE on 0800 663366 to find the location of your nearest oil bank, or contact your local authority recycling officer.

OIL CARE

FOLLOW THE CODE

This book is produced in association with Castrol (U.K.) Ltd.

"Cars have become more and more sophistated. But changing the oil and brake fluid, and similar jobs are as simple as they ever were. Castrol are pleased to be associated with this book because it gives us the opportunity to make life simpler for those who wish to service their own cars. Castrol have succeeded in making oil friendlier and kinder to the environment by removing harmful chlorine from our range of engine lubricants which in turn prolong the life of the catalytic convertor (when fitted), by noticeably maintaining the engine at peak efficiency. In return, we ask you to be kinder to the environment too... by taking your used oil to your Local Authority Amenity Oil Bank. It can then be used as a heating fuel. Please do not poison it with thinners, paint, creosote or brake fluid because these render it useless and costly to dispose of."

Castrol (U.K.) Ltd

CONTENTS

Introduction

Peter Wallage

Over the years, I have run any number of cars, from superb classic cars and modern cars, to those with one foot in the breakers yard. And I know only too well that any car is only enjoyable to own if it's safe, reliable and basically sound - and the only way of ensuring that it stays that way is to service it regularly. That's why we have set about creating this book, which aims to show the owner interested in DIY car servicing that there's nothing to fear; you really can do it yourself!

Making It Easy! Porter Publishing Service Guides are the first books to give you all the service information you might need, with step-by-step instructions, along with a complete Service History section for you to complete and fill in as you carry out regular maintenance on your car over the months ahead. Using the information contained in this book, you will be able to:

◆ see for yourself how to carry out every Service Job, from weekly and monthly checks, right up to longer-term maintenance items.

◆ carry out regular body maintenance and rustproofing, saving a fortune in body repairs over the years to come.

◆ enhance the value of your car by completing a full Service History of every maintenance job you carry out on your car.

I hope you enjoy keeping your car in trim while saving lots of money by servicing your car yourself, with the help of this book. Happy motoring!

Lindsay Porter
Porter Publishing Ltd

Lindsay Porter

Acknowledgements

No book like this could possibly be a solo effort and my thanks are due to numerous people who have helped to make its final production possible. First to Lindsay Porter for the long hours he spent laying down the basic format for the series which arranges the jobs necessary in a logical, straight-forward sequence which makes it easy to follow, even for the as-yet inexperienced enthusiast.

We are grateful to Ford dealer, Moff Motors of Castle Cary, Somerset who were more than helpful in giving us their time and for the expertise of Andrew Smith who was willing to hand over the sort of tips that only a true professional can offer. Some of his gems are in the INSIDE INFORMATION paragraphs. Seatons of Yeovil, Somerset also made a vehicle and one of their workshop lifts available for a photo session. Colin Heath and Darren Oliver also provided their cars for some of the photos.

The rustproofing was expertly carried out by Roger McNickle of Dinol (GB) Limited. More assistance came from Dunlop SP Tyres, from Sykes-Pickavant who kindly supplied almost all the high quality tools used here, and to David's Isopon who kindly supplied the expertise on body repair and finishing, and, of course, my thanks to Richard Price at Castrol whose advice and extensive knowledge of lubrication we value, and whose products we can unhesitatingly recommend.

Lastly my thanks to my wife Valerie for taking most of the photographs in this book and for the hours she spent at the computer putting coherence into my masses of notes and, of course, to anyone else who I might inadvertently have left out.

Peter Wallage

SPECIAL THANKS
The Publisher would like to thank - Andrew MacQuillan for contributing much of Chapter 3 - Robert Iles for taking some of the photographs for Chapter 3, carrying out the research for Chapter 8 and for taking the rustproofing photographs - Ford Motor Company for their generous and thorough assistance - John Bishop of Ford Agent, Bishop's Garage of Bromyard - Kathleen Young, Rachel Cross and Sharon Davies for allowing their cars to be photographed for the front cover and to Mark Berryman for his assistance - Gunsons for equipment and advice - and our good friends at Castrol for their continuing support, assistance and advice.

CHAPTER 1 - SAFETY FIRST!

You must always ensure that safety is the first consideration in any job you carry out. A slight lack of concentration, or a rush to finish the job quickly can easily result in an accident, as can failure to follow the precautions outlined in this Chapter. Whereas skilled motor mechanics are trained in safe working practices you, the home mechanic, must find them out for yourself and act upon them.

Remember, accidents don't just happen, they are caused, and some of those causes are contained in the following list. Above all, ensure that whenever you work on your car you adopt a safety-minded approach at all times, and remain aware of the dangers that might be encountered.

Be sure to consult the suppliers of any materials and equipment you may use, and to obtain and read carefully any operating and health and safety instructions that may be available on packaging or from manufacturers and suppliers.

PART I: IMPORTANT POINTS

Vehicle Off Ground

ALWAYS ensure that the vehicle is properly supported when raised off the ground. Don't work on, around, or underneath a raised vehicle unless axle stands are positioned under secure, load bearing underbody areas, or the vehicle is driven onto ramps, with the wheels remaining on the ground securely chocked to prevent movement.

ALWAYS ensure that the safe working load rating of any jacks, hoists or lifting gear used is sufficient for the job, and that lifting gear is used only as recommended by the manufacturer.

NEVER attempt to loosen or tighten nuts that require a lot of force to turn (e.g. a tight oil drain plug) with the vehicle raised, unless it is safely supported. Take care not to pull the vehicle off its supports when applying force to a spanner. Wherever possible, initially slacken tight fastenings before raising the car off the ground.

ALWAYS wear eye protection when working under the vehicle and when using power tools.

Working On The Vehicle

ALWAYS seek specialist advice unless you are justifiably confident about carrying out each job. The safety of your vehicle affects you, your passengers and other road users.

DON'T lean over, or work on, a running engine unless it is strictly necessary, and keep long hair and loose clothing well out of the way of moving mechanical parts. Note that it is theoretically possible for fluorescent striplighting to make an engine fan appear to be stationary - double check whether it is spinning or not! This is the sort of error that happens when you're really tired and not thinking straight. So...

...DON'T work on your car when you're over tired.

ALWAYS work in a well ventilated area and don't inhale dust - it may contain asbestos or other harmful substances.

REMOVE your wrist watch, rings and all other jewellery before doing any work on the vehicle - and especially when working on the electrical system.

DON'T remove the radiator or expansion tank filler cap when the cooling system is hot, or you may get scalded by escaping coolant or steam. Let the system cool down first and even then, if the engine is not completely cold, cover the cap with a cloth and gradually release the pressure.

NEVER drain oil, coolant or automatic transmission fluid when the engine is hot. Allow time for it to cool sufficiently to avoid scalding you.

ALWAYS keep antifreeze, brake and clutch fluid away from vehicle paintwork. Wash off any spills immediately.

TAKE CARE to avoid touching any engine or exhaust system component unless it is cool enough not to burn you.

Running The Vehicle

NEVER start the engine unless the gearbox is in neutral (or 'Park' in the case of automatic transmission) and the hand brake is fully applied.

NEVER run catalytic converter equipped vehicles without the exhaust system heat shields in place.

TAKE CARE when parking vehicles fitted with catalytic

converters. The 'cat' reaches extremely high temperatures and any combustible materials under the car, such as long dry grass, could be ignited.

Personal Safety

NEVER siphon fuel, antifreeze, brake fluid or other such toxic liquids by mouth, or allow contact with your skin. There is an increasing awareness that they can damage your health. Best of all, use a suitable hand pump and wear gloves.

BEFORE undertaking dirty jobs, use a barrier cream on your hands as a protection against infection. Preferably, wear thin gloves, available from DIY outlets.

WEAR GLOVES for sure when there is a risk of used engine oil coming into contact with your skin. It can cause cancer.

WIPE UP any spilt oil, grease or water off the floor immediately, before there is an accident.

MAKE SURE that spanners and all other tools are the right size for the job and are not likely to slip. Never try to 'double-up' spanners to gain more leverage.

SEEK HELP if you need to lift something heavy which may be beyond your capability. Don't forget that when lifting a heavy weight, you should keep your back straight and bend your knees to avoid injuring your back.

NEVER take risky short-cuts or rush to finish a job. Plan ahead and allow plenty of time.

BE METICULOUS and keep the work area tidy - you'll avoid frustration, work better and lose less.

KEEP children and animals right-away from the work area and from unattended vehicles.

ALWAYS tell someone what you're doing and have them regularly check that all is well, especially when working alone on, or under, the vehicle.

PART II: HAZARDS

Fire!

Petrol (gasoline) is a dangerous and highly flammable liquid requiring special precautions. When working on the fuel system, disconnect the vehicle battery earth (ground) terminal whenever possible and always work outside, or in a very well ventilated area. Any form of spark, such as that caused by an electrical fault, by two metal surfaces striking against each other, by a central heating boiler in the garage 'firing up', or even by static electricity built up in your clothing can, in a confined space, ignite petrol vapour causing an explosion. Take great care not to spill petrol on to the engine or exhaust system, never allow any naked flame anywhere near the work area and, above all, don't smoke.

Invest in a workshop-sized fire extinguisher. Choose the carbon dioxide type or preferably, dry powder but never a water type extinguisher for workshop use. Water conducts electricity and can make worse an oil or petrol-based fire, in certain circumstances.

DON'T disconnect any fuel pipes on a fuel injected engine while the ignition is switched on. The fuel in the line is under very high pressure - sufficient to cause serious injury. Remember that many injection systems have residual pressure in the pipes for days after switching off. Consult the workshop manual or seek specialist advice before carrying out any work.

Fumes

In addition to the fire dangers described previously, petrol (gasoline) vapour and the types of vapour given off by many solvents, thinners, and adhesives are highly toxic and under certain conditions can lead to unconsciousness or even death, if inhaled. The

risks are increased if such fluids are used in a confined space so always ensure adequate ventilation when handling materials of this nature. Treat all such substances with care, always read the instructions and follow them with care.

Always ensure that the car is out of doors and not in an enclosed space when the engine is running. Exhaust fumes contain poisonous carbon monoxide, even when the car is fitted with a catalytic converter, since 'cats' sometimes fail and don't function when the engine is cold.

Never drain petrol (gasoline) or use solvents, thinners adhesives or other toxic substances in an inspection pit as the extremely confined space allows the highly toxic fumes to concentrate. Running the engine with the vehicle over the pit can have the same results. It is also dangerous to park a vehicle for any length of time over an inspection pit. The fumes from even a slight fuel leak can cause an explosion when the engine is started. Petrol fumes are heavier than air and will accumulate in the pit.

Mains Electricity

Best of all, avoid the use of mains electricity when working on the vehicle, whenever possible. For instance, you could use rechargeable

tools and a DC inspection lamp, powered from a remote 12V battery - both are much safer. However, if you do use mains-powered equipment, ensure that the appliance is wired correctly to its plug, that where necessary it is properly earthed (grounded), and that the fuse is of the correct rating for the appliance is fitted. For instance, a 13 amp fuse in lead lamp's plug will not provide adequate protection. Do not use any mains powered equipment in damp conditions or in the vicinity of fuel, fuel vapour or the vehicle battery.

Also, before using any mains powered electrical equipment, take one more simple precaution - use an RCD (Residual Current Device) circuit breaker. Then, if there is a short, the RCD circuit breaker minimises the risk of electrocution by instantly cutting the power supply. Buy one from any electrical store or DIY centre. RCDs fit simply into your electrical socket before plugging in your electrical equipment.

The Ignition System

You should never work on the ignition system with the ignition switched on, or with the engine being turned over on the starter, or running.

Touching certain parts of the ignition system, such as the HT leads, distributor cap, ignition coil etc, can result in a severe electric shock. This is especially likely where the insulation on any of these components is weak, or if the components are dirty or damp. Note also that voltages produced by electronic ignition systems are much higher than those produced by conventional systems and could prove fatal, particularly to people with cardiac pacemaker implants. Consult your handbook or main dealer if in any doubt.

An additional risk of injury can arise while working on running engines, if the operator touches a high voltage lead and pulls his or her hand away on to a sharp, conductive or revolving part.

The Battery

Never cause a spark, smoke, or allow a naked light near the vehicle's battery, even in a well ventilated area. Highly explosive hydrogen gas will be given off as part of the charging process.

Battery terminals on the car should be shielded, since a battery contains energy and a spark can be caused by any metal object which touches the battery's terminals or connecting straps.

Before working on the fuel or electrical systems, always disconnect the battery earth (ground) terminal. (But before doing so, read the relevant **FACT FILE** in *Chapter 3* regarding saving computer and radio settings.)

When using a battery charger, care should be taken to avoid causing a spark by switching off the power supply before the battery charger leads are connected or disconnected. Before charging the battery from an external source, disconnect both battery leads before connecting the charger. If the battery is not of the 'sealed-for-life' type, loosen the filler plugs or remove the cover before charging. For best results the battery should be given a low rate trickle charge overnight. Do not charge at an excessive rate or the battery may burst.

Always wear gloves and goggles when carrying or when topping up the battery. Even in diluted form (as it is in the battery) the acid electrolyte is extremely corrosive and must not be allowed to contact the eyes, skin or clothes.

Brakes and Asbestos

Obviously, a car's brakes are among its most important safety related items. ONLY work on your vehicle's braking system if you are trained and competent to do so. If you have not been trained in this work, but wish to carry out the jobs described in this book, we strongly recommend that you have a garage or qualified mechanic check your work before using the car.

Whenever you work on the braking system's mechanical components, or remove front or rear brake pads or shoes: i) wear an efficient particle mask; ii) wipe off all brake dust from the brakes after spraying on a proprietary brand of brake cleaner (never blow dust off with compressed air); iii) dispose of brake dust and discarded shoes or pads in a sealed plastic bag; iv) wash your hands thoroughly after you have finished working on the brakes and certainly before you eat or smoke; v) replace shoes and pads only with asbestos-free shoes or pads. Note that asbestos brake dust can cause cancer if inhaled.

Brake Fluid

Brake fluid absorbs moisture rapidly from the air and can become dangerous resulting in brake failure. Castrol (U.K.) Ltd. recommend that you should have your brake fluid tested at least once a year by a properly equipped garage with test equipment and you should change the fluid in accordance with your vehicle manufacturer's recommendations or as advised in this book if we recommend a shorter interval than the manufacturer. You should buy no more brake fluid than you need, in smaller rather than larger containers. Never store an opened container of brake fluid. Dispose of the remainder at your Local Authority Waste Disposal Site, in the designated disposal unit, not with general waste or with waste oil.

Engine Oils

Take care to observe the following precautions when working with used engine oil. Apart from the obvious risk of scalding when draining the oil from a hot engine, there is the danger from contamination contained in all used oil.

Always wear disposable plastic or rubber gloves when draining the oil from your engine. i) Note that the drain plug and the oil are often hotter than you expect. Wear gloves if the plug is too hot to touch and keep your hand to one side so that you are not scalded by the spurt of oil as the plug comes away; ii) There are very real health hazards associated with used engine oil. In the words of one manufacturer's handbook "Prolonged and repeated contact may cause serious skin disorders, including dermatitis and cancer." Use a barrier cream on your hands and try not to get oil on them. Always wear gloves and wash your hands with hand cleaner soon after carrying out the work. Keep oil out of the reach of children; iii) NEVER, EVER dispose of old engine oil into the ground or down a drain. In the UK, and in most EC countries, every local authority must provide a safe means of oil disposal. In the UK, try your local Environmental Health Department for advice on waste disposal facilities.

Plastic Materials

Work with plastic materials brings additional hazards into workshops. Many of the materials used (polymers, resins, adhesives and materials acting as catalysts and accelerators) contain dangers in the form of poisonous fumes, skin irritants, and the risk of fire and explosions. Do not allow resin or 2-pack adhesive hardener, or that supplied with filler or 2-pack stopper, to come into contact with skin or eyes. Read carefully the safety notes supplied on the can, tube or packaging and always wear impervious gloves and goggles when working with them.

Jacks and Axle Stands

Throughout this book you will see many references to the correct use of jacks, axle stands and similar equipment - and we make

SAFETY FIRST!

no apologies for being repetitive. This is one area where safety cannot be overstressed - your life could be at stake!

Special care must be taken when any type of lifting equipment is used. Jacks are made for lifting the vehicle only, not for supporting it while it is being worked on. Never work under the car using only a jack to support the weight. Jacks must be supplemented by adequate additional means of support, positioned under secure load-bearing parts of the frame or underbody. Axle stands are available from most auto. parts stores. Drive-on ramps are limiting because of their design and size but they are simple to use, reliable and offer the most stable type of support. We strongly recommend their use.

Full details on jacking and supporting the vehicle will be found near the beginning of *Chapter 3*.

Fluoroelastomers

MOST IMPORTANT! PLEASE READ THIS SECTION!

If you service your car in the normal way, none of the following may be relevant to you. Unless, for example, you encounter a car which has been on fire (even in a localised area), subject to heat in, say, a crash-damage repairer's workshop or a vehicle breaker's yard, or if any second-hand parts have been heated in any way.

Many synthetic, rubber-like materials used in motor cars contain a substance called fluorine. These materials are known as fluoro-elastomers and are commonly used for oil seals, wiring and cabling, bearing surfaces, gaskets, diaphragms, hoses and 'O' rings. If they are subjected to temperatures greater than 315 degrees C, they will decompose and can be potentially hazardous. Fluoroelastomer materials will show physical signs of decomposition under such conditions in the form of charring of black sticky masses. Some decomposition may occur at temperatures above 200 degrees C, and it is obvious that when a car has been in a fire or has been dismantled with the assistance of a cutting torch or blow torch, the fluoroelastomers can decompose in the manner indicated above.

In the presence of any water or humidity, including atmospheric moisture, the by-products caused by the fluoroelastomers being heated can be extremely dangerous. According to the Health and Safety Executive, "Skin contact with this liquid or decomposition residues can cause painful and penetrating burns. Permanent irre-versible skin and tissue damage can occur". Damage can also be caused to eyes or by the inhalation of fumes created as fluoro-elastomers are burned or heated.

After a vehicle has been exposed to fire or high temperatures:

1. Do not touch blackened or charred seals or equipment.

2. Allow all burnt or decomposed fluoroelastomer materials to cool before inspection, investigations, tear-down or removal.

3. Preferably, don't handle parts containing decomposed fluoro-elastomers, but if you must, wear goggles and PVC (polyvinyl chloride) or neoprene protective gloves whilst doing so. Never handle such parts unless they are completely cool.

4. Contaminated parts, residues, materials and clothing, including protective clothing and gloves, should be disposed of by an approved contractor to landfill or by incineration according to national or local regulations. Oil seals, gaskets and 'O' rings, along with contaminated material, must not be burned.

PART III: GENERAL WORKSHOP SAFETY

1. Always have a fire extinguisher of the correct type at arm's length when working on the fuel system.

If you do have a fire, DON'T PANIC. Use the extinguisher effectively by directing it at the base of the fire.

2. NEVER use a naked flame anywhere in the workplace.

3. KEEP your inspection lamp well away from any source of petrol (gasoline) such as when disconnecting a carburettor float bowl or fuel line.

4. NEVER use petrol (gasoline) to clean parts. Use paraffin (kerosene), white spirits, or a proprietary degreaser.

5. NO SMOKING. There's a risk of fire or of transferring dangerous substances to your mouth and, in any case, ash falling into mechanical components is to be avoided.

6. BE METHODICAL in everything you do, use common sense, and think of safety at all times.

CHAPTER 2 - BUYING GUIDE

In this Chapter, we show you how to go about buying a second hand car. We also look at which parts wear out, and we explain when they are likely to need replacement, so that whether you are giving your own car the once-over, or you're looking at a prospective purchase, you'll know what to expect; and we examine the best ways of buying parts for your pride and joy.

PART I: BUYING A SECOND-HAND CAR

In general, the safest - but also the most expensive - way of buying second hand is through a main dealer: NOT the same as a general second-hand dealer, whose standards are almost certain to be lower! We *strongly* recommend the use of HPI Autodata checks mentioned on page 110, because even main dealers can make 'mistakes', but once you've done that, and selected the main-dealer car you want, it's better to have an AA or RAC inspection carried out rather than carry out your own checks. But for many people, it's a question of saving money and buying privately, and that's what this Chapter is mainly about. But don't find yourself with the *worst* of both worlds...

Spot The Rogue Trader

One of the biggest dangers with buying privately is that you might encounter a real cheat: a trader masquerading as a private seller. Cars offered by such people are likely to be among the worst on offer, they may have had their mileometers tampered with and deep seated faults may have been cleverly concealed. Here's how to spot them:

• take note of the way traders often word their advertisements. Key phrases include: "a very clean car", "very straight", "a beautiful motorcar" and other glib phrases.

• when you telephone in response to an ad., *always* say, "I'm calling about the car..." If the person on the other end asks, "Which car?", put the 'phone down before the spiel starts.

• if you get past the telephone stage, take careful note of the attitude of the seller. Part-time, 'black economy' dealers often seem blase, even bored by the whole thing, and slicker than most private sellers.

• insist on looking at the Registration Document. If the seller isn't the registered keeper, why not?

How To Inspect A Used Vehicle

STAGE ONE: Even if you know very little about cars, you can root out the obvious no-hopers before arranging for a local main agent, AA or RAC inspection. The text in italics explains the problems.

• catch the light along all sides of the car. Can you see any ripples? Check for overspray inside wheel arches, inside engine bay and on tyres and trim. Does all the paint match? *All indicate poorly carried out crash repairs.*

• Look at the gaps between panels. Also, look very carefully inside the engine bay and inside the boot for evidence of rippling in the metal. Look low down, mainly in the vicinity of structural members. *Tell-tale signs of crash damage.*

STAGE TWO: If your car passes Stage One, look more closely at the bodywork - the most expensive part to repair.

• check the sills by lifting the carpets just inside the doors and also check the footwells, especially around the edges. *Rust!*

• look inside the engine bay especially at the tops of struts. *Check for corrosion.*

• check the bottoms of wings, the 'skirts' beneath front and rear bumpers and the tops of wing panels for corrosion. *Rust covered with filler will quickly burst through again.*

SPECIALIST SERVICE: It's hardly worth trying to check beneath a car without the use of a hoist. Leave it to the pro. inspection mentioned earlier, or see if you can persuade a local garage to lend or hire their hoist:

• check around spring mountings, the joints between floors and sills, all box-section 'chassis' members and anywhere that suspension components are fixed to the car's body structure.

• check all brake pipes and hoses. *Look for rubbing or corrosion.*

BUYING GUIDE

• look at the shock absorbers. *Fluid leakage means failure.*

• check the exhaust. *Look for rust, holes or patches.*

• examine each tyre carefully for bulges or splits. *Tyres worn more on one side than the other might mean that the car's tracking needs checking - easily adjustable - or it might indicate suspension damage, maybe from an accident.*

 If you are buying an older car which needs work doing to it, try making the owner an offer 'subject to MoT test'. Then, you can have the car tested as an inexpensive (though not necessarily complete) condition check.

Mechanical Components

• before starting up, remove the oil filler cap. *Grey sludge around the cap is a certain indicator that the engine is on its last legs.*

• pull out the dipstick. Is the oil level very low? Is the oil a dirty black and does it feel gritty between finger and thumb? *Not a well maintained car! Does it have droplets of water on it? Big problems! Probably a blown head gasket.*

• check inside the radiator cap (ONLY if the engine is cold!). Do you see anti-freeze colour? *Good!* Do you see rust? *Bad!* Do you see droplets of oil? *Disastrous! See previous paragraph.*

• start the car and note whether the starter motor sounds lively or whether it is struggling to keep up. *Could be duff battery; or tired starter motor.*

• undo and remove the oil filler cap again. (N.B. Most engines spray oil around in *copious* quantities. Ensure that you don't get covered!) *If oil mist chugs out, the engine bores are badly worn. Also...*

• ...look at the exhaust. Steam (especially in colder weather) and even water dripping out is no problem, although it should go away after the car has been driven. 'Rev' the engine, hard and several times. *If you see puffs or even clouds of black smoke (not grey steam), the engine is probably on the slippery slope.*

• does the oil pressure warning light flicker with engine cold? *Low oil pressure equals an engine rebuild?*

• bonnet open. Does the 'top' of the engine rattle on start up? *Mechanical tappets: adjustment needed.* If the rattle continues after 30 seconds, *the engine may need an expensive replacement camshaft.* Hydraulic tappets: *noise is always expensive!*

• rev the engine. Does it rattle in a deep, growly way, low down in the engine? *The big end and/or main bearings are gone - replacement engine time!*

Static Checks

• are the carpets wet? *water is leaking in. Windscreen seal leaks can often be cured easily. But if the car is old the screen surround may have corroded, requiring expensive welding. Alternatively, water coming in from beneath suggests that the car's lower structure has as much future as an old car park ticket. If water is leaking from the heater, remember that it can be expensive and tricky to replace.*

• seat rips can be a pain and devalue the car. *It can be difficult to find the right colour match on second hand seats.* Do your knees come up as your backside goes down. *The seat springing has gone.*

• can you live with headlining rips or severe discolouration? *It's difficult to clean easily and replacement is usually expensive.*

• take a *close* look at seat belts and mountings. *Life saver - and quite expensive to replace.*

• check that the heater works properly. *Or you'll end up hating the car!*

• take time to check every switch, accessory and electrical fitting on the car. *Replacements can be expensive.* Check that the stereo works - *and check that it's included with the car!*

• don't accept lame excuses when things don't work! *If things are so easy to fix, why haven't they been done already?*

• check the spare wheel and the condition (existence?) of the jack and toolkit. *More expense!*

• open and close windows and sunroof. *(Also look for stains around sunroof aperture - they can leak!)*

Finally, but perhaps most important of all, make sure that the person who is selling the car actually owns it!

• ask to see the Registration Document. *If it's not available it could be: the 'owner' has a) lost it; b) has it but it doesn't show the 'owner's' name because he is a trader; c) the car doesn't belong to the seller. If you can't see the Registration Document, walk away!*

• ask to see the owner's original purchase receipt and check that the car is owned by the 'owner' and is not subject to a finance agreement. See below. *IMPORTANT NOTE: You may be amazed to learn that, if you pay for a car that is subsequently found to belong to someone else, you will lose the car and the money!*

• check that the VIN (Vehicle Identification Number) shown on the Registration document is the same as those on the VIN plate riveted to the car. See "Fact File" later in this chapter for the precise location of these numbers. *If any of the numbers in these three locations are different, missing, or have obviously been tampered with, then under no circumstances consider buying the car unless the seller can provide an explanation, in writing, satisfactory to a third party, such as an AA or RAC inspector, or the Police!*

Spot The Rogue Car

Before buying *any* used car, check it out with HPI Autodata. (See Page 110.) A postal or telephone enquiry (cheques or credit card payments accepted) will (i) confirm that the vehicle details shown (make, model, colour, engine size, fuel type) are all correct, (ii) tell you if the vehicle is reported as stolen, or subject to an outstanding finance agreement, (iii) tell you if the vehicle has been logged as having a major insurance claim (not foolproof; many don't show up), (iv) identify vehicles which have had a registration plate change.

PART II: WHAT WEARS, AND WHEN

The following list provides a great way of checking what is *likely* to be worn on your Ford Fiesta, and at what stage it is likely to need replacement - useful when checking your own car, or when buying another. Please bear in mind that the mileages shown are only intended as an approximation of the lifespan of each component. In real life, some will wear out faster and some slower, of course but the chart below provides a useful rough guide.

> **SAFETY FIRST!**
> **Read and take note of Chapter1, Safety First! and the Safety information in Chapter 3 before carrying out any of these checks.**

COMPONENT:	COULD NEED REPLACEMENT AT:	CHECKS OR SYMPTOMS:
Alternator	80,000 miles	Fails without warning or the ignition warning light could glow dimly for a few miles.
Battery	4 to 7 years (original); 1 to 5 (non-original)	Goes flat, even though disconnected.
Brake Pads - Front	15 - 20,000 miles	See Job 75.
Brake Shoes - Rear	Check linings at 12 - 24,000 miles	See Job 76.
Cambelt	36,000 miles	Should be renewed - check your car's service history - renew if unsure.
Clutch	Up to 75,000 normally	Check for slipping when pulling away, hill climbing
Diesel Glowplugs	72,000 miles	Engine reluctant to start from cold and smokes (battery in good condition). See Jobs 87 and 109.
Diesel Injectors	75,000 miles	Excessive smoke; engine misfires
Exhaust mountings	Rears go every year or two	Examine visually; twist manually. See Job 34.
Exhaust pipe (Ford parts) (non-original parts)	Up to 4 years 1 to 3 years	Examine visually; listen for blowing. See Job 34.
Shock absorbers (front)	40,000 miles	Clean off and look for oil leaks. Grasp and twist, looking for wear in bushes top and bottom. See Job 74 and 96.
Shock absorbers (rear)	50,000 miles	
Starter motor	150,000 miles	Turns engine slowly *when battery and connections in good condition*.
Tyres (most models)	15 - 20,000 miles	
Tyres (XR2, XR2i and other high performance models)	7 - 10,000 miles	Check visually, especially inside tyre walls and spare.

PART III - BUYING SPARES

One of the great advantages of DIY servicing is that you can choose which parts you buy, where you buy your parts, and how much you pay for them, whereas if the dealer services your car you buy their parts at their prices!

Of course, you must take care not to buy poor quality parts, but it's worth bearing in mind that many of the car makers' parts are the same as those available from 'independents'.

Buying The Right Parts

All manufacturers change the parts they use on the production line, often with startling frequency. The only way of ensuring that the parts you buy are the right ones for your car is to take your car's Vehicle Identification Number (VIN) and engine number with you when buying spares.

Main Dealers

Main dealers more than anyone else should be able to match your car's VIN number to the precise part you need, so have it to hand. This can also be the key to a more helpful approach by some Parts Department staff! Also, try to avoid calling on the parts department in the early mornings and other busy periods, and you may find that staff have more time to help you. Consumable items are almost certain to be too expensive from your main dealer. Try high street auto accessory stores or out-of-town Superstores for best prices.

Auto Accessory Stores

Local parts factors and big-name motor accessory shops can be extremely useful for obtaining servicing parts at short notice - many 'accessory' outlets open late in the evening, and on both days at weekends. You'll find that the high-street shops and Superstores will usually be open when you need them, their prices are usually the keenest of all, because they can buy-in in great quantities, and the quality of the parts is excellent from the best-known shops, since they use the same big-name manufacturers as many of the original car makers.

Buying Second-Hand

Purchasing any safety-related items second-hand - such as braking, steering or suspension parts - is something to avoid. That's not to decry buying second-hand altogether. Replacing a worn out distributor or carburettor, for instance, with a second-hand component that you know to be 'low mileage' can make a lot of sense. Equally, non-performance related items, such as wheel trims, interior trim and other interior parts can often be obtained at a fraction of the 'new' cost.

Reconditioned Parts

These are best obtained from reputable retail suppliers. When buying, always enquire about the terms of the guarantee. Don't buy if there isn't a good one! 'Exchange' alternators and starter motors are good value - but only buy from a reputable source.

Steering racks are invariably available as exchange items. Ensure that you rotate the operating shaft fully from lock to lock, feeling for any undue free play, roughness, stiffness, or 'notchiness' as you do so. Reject any units showing signs of any of these problems.

Tyres

We recommend buying only good quality radial ply tyres. Cheaper tyres rarely perform as well as top brands, even when they are the cheaper brand of a top manufacturer. Your car may steer more erratically, have less grip on cornering and braking and be noisier than if you pay the small extra amount required for top brand tyres - and they usually last longer, too. Remould tyres are available at lower initial cost, but life expectancy is not as long as with new tyres and we don't recommend them.

Shopping Around

If you want to buy good quality parts *and* save money, you must be prepared to shop around. Ring each of your chosen suppliers with a shopping list to hand, and your car's personal data, from the Auto-Biography at the front of this book, in front of you. Keep a written note of prices - including VAT, delivery etc - whether the parts are proper 'brand name' parts or not and - most importantly! - whether or not the parts you want are in stock. Parts expected 'soon' have been known never to materialise. A swivel pin in the hand is worth two in the bush. (Bad pun!)

FACT FILE: IDENTIFICATION NUMBERS

1. There are three main numbers you will need to know in order to buy parts and touch-up paint for your car. The VIN is your car's internationally unique number and tells your parts supplier exactly which model and year the car is. (On older vehicles, you will find the maker's own 'chassis number'.) Quote the VIN whenever you buy spares for your car. The VIN plate position is on the bulkhead, near the wiper motor on some models, but more often, it's on the front closing plate, visible when the bonnet is open, and on a plate visible through the bottom corner of the windscreen on vehicles from 1994. On those models it's also stamped on the body, inside the right-hand door opening under a flap.

2. The engine number may also be shown on the VIN plate; it should certainly be on the engine. When viewed from standing in front of the car, it's on:

a) OHV engines, on front-right side, near the radiator.

b) CVH engines, front-left, near the alternator bracket.

1

Diesels, front-right (viewed from in front of the car), near the gearbox.

INSIDE INFORMATION: If you need an exact paint colour match, you'll need the car's paint code number. See the VIN plate (again!), or a paint code plate inside the fuel filler cap, the tailgate or some other place depending on model - see your handbook.

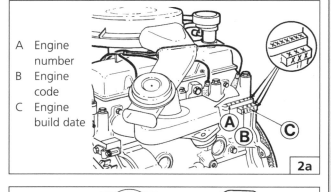

A   Engine number
B   Engine code
C   Engine build date

2a

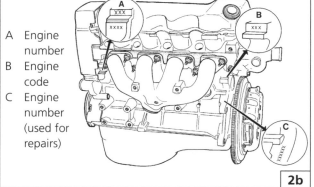

A   Engine number
B   Engine code
C   Engine number (used for repairs)

2b

Please read the whole of the Introduction to this Chapter before carrying out any work on your car.

SERVICING YOUR CAR

CHAPTER 3 - SERVICING YOUR CAR

Everyone wants to own a car that starts first time, runs reliably and lasts longer than the average. And there's no magic about how to put your car into that category, it's all a question of thorough maintenance! If you follow the Service Jobs listed here or even if you have a garage or mechanic do it for you - you can almost *guarantee* that your car will still be going strong when others have fallen by the wayside... or the hard shoulder.

If you want your car to be as well looked after as possible, you'll follow the Jobs shown here, but if you don't want to go all the way, you can pick and choose from the most essential items in the list. But do bear in mind that the Jobs we recommend are there for some very good reasons:

◆ **body maintenance** is rarely included in most service schedules. We believe it to be essential.

◆ **preventative maintenance** figures very high on our list of priorities. And that's why so many of our service jobs have the word "Check..." near the start!

making it easy! We think it's very important to keep things as straightforward as possible. And where you see this heading, you'll know there's an extra tip to help 'make it easy' for you!

The 'Catch-up' Service

When you first buy a used car, you never know for sure just how well it's been looked after. Even one with a full service history is unlikely to have been serviced as thoroughly as one with a Porter Manual Service History! So, if you want to catch-up on all the servicing that may have been neglected on your car, just work through the entire list of Service Jobs listed for the longest term servicing jobs listed in this Manual, and your car will be bang up to date and serviced as well as you could hope for. Do allow several days for all of this work, not least because it will almost certainly throw up a number of extra jobs - potential faults that have been lurking beneath the surface - all of which will need putting right before you can 'sign off' your car as being in tip-top condition.

The Service History

Those people fortunate enough to own a new car, or one that has been well maintained from new will have the opportunity to keep a 'Service History' of their car, usually filled in by a main dealer. Now you can keep your own complete record, using the tick list in the Appendix at the back of this book.

Your car's Service History will then be more complete and detailed than any manufacturer's service record, with the extra bonus that there is space for you to keep a record of all those extras: New tyres; replacement exhaust; extra accessories, so if your battery goes down only 11 months after buying it, you'll be able to look up where and when you bought it.

SAFETY FIRST!
SAFETY FIRST! information must always be read with care and always taken seriously. In addition, please read the whole of Chapter 1, Safety First! before carrying out any work on your car. There are many hazards associated with working on a car but all of them can be avoided by adhering strictly to the safety rules. Don't skimp on safety!

RAISING THE CAR

RAISING THE CAR

RAISING THE CAR

Raising The Car Before Working On It

RAISING A CAR - SAFELY!
You will often need to raise your car off the ground in order to carry out the Service Jobs shown here. To start off with, here's what you must never do: NEVER work beneath a car held only by a jack, not even a trolley jack. Quite a number of deaths have been caused by a car slipping off a jack while someone has been working underneath. The safest way is by raising the car on a proprietary brand of ramps. Sometimes, though, there is no alternative but to use axle stands. Please read the following information, and act on it!

When using car ramps:

(I) Make absolutely certain that the ramps are parallel to the wheels of the car and that the wheels are exactly central on each ramp.

Always have an assistant to watch both sides of the car as you drive up. Drive up to the end 'stops' on the ramps but never over them!

Apply the handbrake firmly, put the car in first or reverse gear or 'Park' in the case of an automatic.

(II) Chock both wheels remaining on the ground, both in front and behind, so that the car can't move in either direction. This also applies when the car is supported on axle stands.

INSIDE INFORMATION: Ramps tend to move as you drive on to them. To prevent this, wrap a strip of old carpet round each of the first 'rungs', double them back and drive over the doubled pieces of carpet as you approach the ramps. This will prevent them from skidding.

When using a jack:

On other occasions, you might need to work on the car while it is supported on an axle stand or pair of axle stands. These are inherently less stable than ramps, so you must take much greater care when working beneath them. In particular:

• ensure that the axle stand is on flat, stable ground, never on ground where any of the legs can sink in.

• ensure that the car is on level ground, that the handbrake is off and that the transmission is in neutral.

• raise the car with a trolley jack - invest in one if you don't already own one; the car's wheel changing jack is often too unstable. Place a piece of cloth over the head of the jack if your car is nicely finished on the underside. Ensure that the floor is sufficiently clear and smooth for the trolley jack wheels to roll as the car is raised and lowered, otherwise it could slip off the jack.

There are two jacking point layouts on the Fiesta. One applies to cars before the 1991 model year (which began in September 1990!) and the other applies to post-1991 model year cars.

PRE-1991 MODEL YEAR VEHICLES

(III) These are clearly identified by the fact that the jack has an arm which slots into a socket about half-way along the sill, on the outer edge of the floorpan.

On these earlier cars, the jack is stored under the spare wheel, in the luggage bay.

I

II

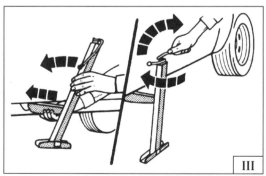

III

making it easy! On older Fiestas, you may be suspicious of your car's jacking point because of structural weakness and in some cases, the jacking point might even be missing! In such cases, you may want to try to get hold of a jack from a later Fiesta from your local breaker's yard and use it as described in XIII and XIV, on page 19 or buy a scissors jack from your local accessory shop.

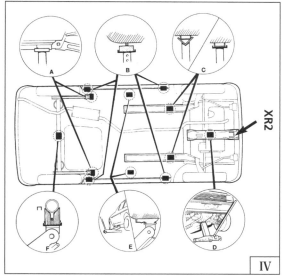

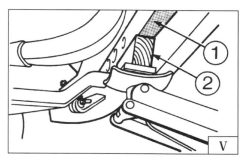

(IV) These are the recommended trolley jack jacking points with the exception of point D which is not to be used for XR2 models. Instead, Ford recommend that you raise the front of an XR2 in the position arrowed. Note that in several places, Ford recommend that a wooden block is used. It seems to us that to make a wooden block in the shape shown for point F is more trouble than it's worth for most people, and you might as well jack from the side, but of course, the choice is yours. Note also that points A, B and C are recommended as positions for locating axle stands, while D (except XR2), E and F are recommended trolley jack jacking points.

(V) This is the sort of shape and size of wooden block that you will need to raise the front of the XR2 at the jacking point indicated. The idea of the block of wood (2) is that it spreads the load on the front body cross-member (1) and allows the trolley jack to avoid the front body panel.

VANS ONLY

Do not use the rear suspension cross-tube to jack these vehicles when they are laden because there is a strong risk of causing damage or distortion.

1991 MODEL YEAR-ON VEHICLES

(VI) These vehicles have a different type of jacking system. The jack head hinges and has a groove in it which slots over the 'knife' edge on the bottom of the sill. See *Raising the Car in an Emergency* for details.

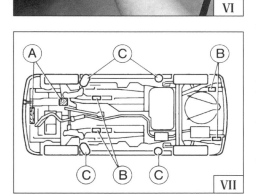

(VII) A - Jacking point for trolley jack. Always use a block of wood to protect the body. B - Axle stand positions. C - Jacking points for wheel change jack.

These are the jacking and axle stand positions for later Fiestas.

(VIII) We recommend jacking each corner of the car separately, using the area adjacent to the wheel change jacking point. Please see XIII for the correct jacking point position towards the rear of the sill.

(IX) The correct position for placing the axle stands (VII.B) is on the relevant box section, beneath the car, and has a double-skin. Just behind the pointing finger here, you can see the overlap in the steel work (arrowed). Place the axle stand just ahead of this overlap, where the pointing finger points! Look out for a similar overlap in the box section at the rear of the vehicle and place the jack or axle stand over the double skin section.

When, finally, your car or van is correctly raised and supported on axle stands apply the handbrake firmly, put the car in first or reverse gear (or 'Park' in the case of an automatic) and chock both wheels remaining on the ground, both in front and behind.

Be especially careful when applying force to a spanner or when pulling hard on anything when the car is supported off the ground. It is all too easy to move the car so far that it topples off the axle stand or stands. And remember that if a car falls on you, YOU

making it easy! You may not wish to jack up on the sill for one of two reasons. Either because you do not have the Ford car jack or, with an older car, because you suspect that the sill may not be as strong as it was when the car was new. You may also find that, when using the car's jack, it will not lift the car high enough to place your axle stand in the correct position.

If so, you can use your trolley jack to lift the whole side of the car. Make sure that **both** wheels on the side not being lifted are chocked, then put the trolley jack in a similar position for raising the front of the car but slightly further back along the 'chassis' box section with a piece of wood to spread the load. Be careful not to put it so far back that there is any danger of the head slipping where the section tapers off towards the floor. When the side is high enough at the back, place the axle stand as in picture IX. Take great care when lowering the car on to the axle stand as it will settle on the axle stand first and then 'rock' forwards as the front wheel comes down to the ground. Release the jack **very** slowly.

COULD BE KILLED!

INSIDE INFORMATION: When you have to pull hard on a spanner or socket bar, pull with one hand and use the other to push against the car as a reaction point. That way you are less likely to move the car than when just pulling.

Whenever working beneath a car on your own, have someone primed to keep an eye on you! If someone pops out to see how you are getting on every quarter of an hour or so, it could be enough to save your life! Do remember that, in general, a car will be more stable when only one wheel is removed and one axle stand used than if two wheels are removed in conjunction with two axle stands. You are strongly advised not to work on the car with all four wheels off the ground, on four axle stands. The car could be very unstable and dangerous to work beneath.

When lowering the car to the ground, remember to remove the chocks, release the handbrake and place the transmission in neutral.

IMPORTANT NOTE: Up to the 1988 model year, Ford Fiesta wheels were held in place with bolts but from then-on they changed to the much easier-to-use wheel nut mountings.

> **SAFETY FIRST!**
> **Wheel changing jacks can be dreadfully unstable! Take great care not to get any part of your body under the car when supported by one of these jacks.**

Raising the Car in an Emergency

It happens too often - a roadside puncture, probably in the dark, probably in the rain, the spare is flat, you don't know where the car jack is, or the wheel brace, and even if you did you don't know where the jack should go, and the wheel nuts/bolts are far too tight to be shifted by that bit of bent rod they call a wheel brace! If you've never done it before, changing a wheel is a daunting prospect, so practise the wheel-change routine at home, before the worst happens to you.

On early cars, the spare wheel is under a cover in the luggage bay and the jack is beneath the spare wheel.

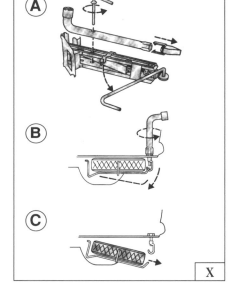

X

(X) From 1990-on, the spare wheel lives beneath the rear floor. Remove the jack and wheel brace from under the engine bay (don't lose the special screw!). Take off the plastic tip from the wheel brace, where fitted. See diagram A. Use the end of the wheel brace to unscrew the spare wheel retaining bolt from inside the luggage bay (diagram B). Then, from underneath the car, push up on the spare wheel carrier, unhook, then lower it slowly and slide out the spare wheel (diagram C).

(XI) Put the plastic tip back on the wheel brace and use it to lever off the wheel trim.

XI

XII

making it easy! **(XII)** *You'll find it far easier to undo the wheel nuts if you use an accessory wheel brace rather than the one supplied with the vehicle. Loosen but don't remove the nuts or bolts while the vehicle is still on the ground and with the handbrake on and the car in gear.*

(XIII) On post-1990 cars, the jack position is indicated - although not all that clearly! - on the edge of the sill. The saddle of the jack head has to fit

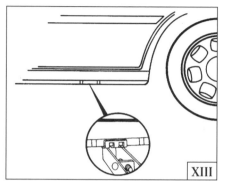
XIII

making it easy! **(XIV)** *Remember to carry a piece of timber in the boot so that it can be placed beneath the jack to spread the load and prevent it from sinking into soft ground. Once the car is raised, have the handbrake on. There are purpose-made chocks you can wedge each side of the wheel opposite to the one you are changing, to guard against the car rolling. In an emergency, use any old pieces of wood or bricks that you can find. Wind the jack handle until the required wheel is clear of the ground, remembering that if the tyre is flat, you need enough clearance for a wheel with a fully pumped up tyre. Do not put any part of your body beneath a car which is supported only on a jack.*

making it easy! *Once the required wheel is clear of the ground, fully undo the nuts or bolts, leaving one 'at the top' until last. Otherwise, the wheel tips forwards, making it harder to remove the remaining nuts/bolts.*

snuggly over the sill edge. See picture VI which shows how the jack head can be swivelled so that it fits the bottom edge of the sill properly.

Nip the nuts/bolts up finger-tight, then lower the wheel to the ground for final tightening, working diagonally, a little at a time, on each nut/bolt: do them up as tight as you can, using all your strength if it's the car-kit wheel brace, slightly less than full strength if it's the extended wrench. Note that the nuts' domed ends fit against the wheel.

Fitting the replacement wheel is easier where studs and nuts are used, because the studs give the wheel a positive location, but where bolts are used, it can be a bit of a struggle to try to locate the wheel on the projection on the hub/drum face. At

SAFETY FIRST! and INSIDE INFORMATION: *Always place the spare wheel, or the wheel you've just removed, under the car: partly for safety to help guard against being crushed; partly so that if the car topples off the wheel-change jack (and they DO, especially on soft ground) you'll be able to reposition the jack and start again.*

making it easy! **i)** *If your car's wheels are held on with bolts, have your local garage supply you with two pieces of threaded rod bolts with heads cut off would be ideal. You can screw them into two of the holes in the hub, 'hang' the wheel on them while you put in the 'proper' wheel bolts to the other holes, then unscrew them with your fingers and fit the two remaining wheel retaining bolts. Remember to carry them with you!* **ii)** *You can also try levering the wheel up into place with a shovel, a length of wood or anything else you can lay your hands on, by the roadside.*

XIV

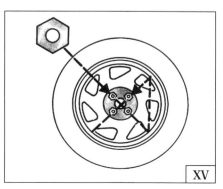
XV

the same time, you have to attempt to align the bolt holes and insert at least one bolt with one hand while steadying the wheel with the other!

(XV) Before retightening the wheel nuts or bolts, ensure that the handbrake is on. Carry out the final tightening in a diagonal

ENGINE BAY LAYOUTS

FACT FILE: ENGINE TYPES & ENGINE BAY LAYOUTS

ENGINE TYPES: Ford have used four main petrol engine types on the Fiesta.

i) OHV (Overhead Valve) describes the 950cc (1978-89); 1100cc (1978-89); 1300cc (1978-83) and 1600cc (XR2 1981-83) range of engines.

ii) HCS (High Compression Swirl) describes the OHV 1000cc and 1100cc engines from 1989.

iii) CVH (Compound Valve angle, Hemispherical chamber) describes the 1300cc (1983-86), 1400cc from 1986; and 1600cc from 1983 engines.

iv) DOHC (Double Overhead Camshaft). (Not covered by this book). Also sometimes called 'Z-tec', refers to the 1600cc and 1800cc fuel-injection engines from 1993.

v) There is also, the diesel engine, with its quite different layout.

The various types can be recognised by referring to the engine bay illustrations shown below. There are more types of Fiesta engine bay layouts than you can shake a stick at. Those shown below cover just about every eventuality, however.

ii) HCS (HIGH COMPRESSION SWIRL)

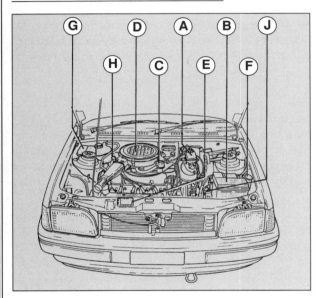

iii) CVH (COMPOUND VALVE ANGLE, HEMISPHERICAL CHAMBER) (Overhead camshaft engines)

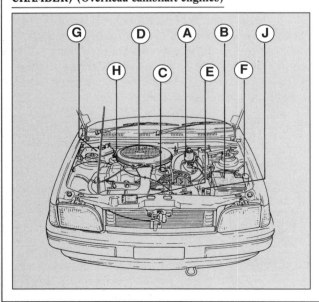

i) OHV (OVERHEAD VALVE)

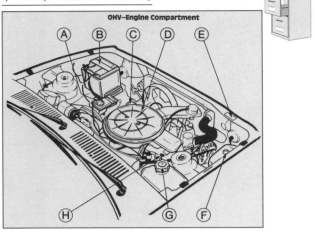

OHV–Engine Compartment

iv) DOHC (DOUBLE OVERHEAD CAMSHAFT)

v) DIESEL

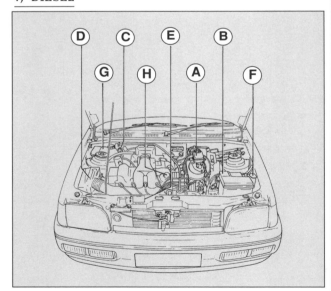

Key:
A. Brake fluid reservoir
B. Battery
C. Engine oil filler cap
D. Air cleaner
E. Vehicle Identification plate
F. Windscreen washer reservoir
G. Engine coolant reservoir
H. Engine oil dipstick
J. Automatic transmission fluid dipstick

Every 500 Miles, Weekly or Before Long Journeys

These are the regular checks that you need to carry out to keep your car safe and reliable. They don't include the major Service Jobs but they should be carried out as part of every 'proper' service.

SPECIAL NOTE: Up to 1989 all Fiestas have a front-hinged bonnet, i.e. one of which lifted up from its rear, or windscreen end. This means access to the engine bay has to be made from the sides of the car, over the front wings on these cars. To help with identification and location of components in this guide, references to the right and left side of the car will assume the reader is looking from the rear of the car forwards, so that on right-hand drive cars the right-hand wing will be that on the driver's side of the car.

1A

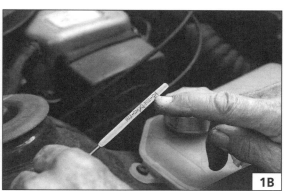

1B

Every 500 Miles - The Engine Bay

☐ Job 1. Engine oil level.

Although some engines barely need their sump oil topping-up between major services, even healthy ones sometimes have an unusual appetite for it while worn ones will certainly burn it. Even the best maintained engine can develop an oil leak and an engine low on oil runs the risk of internal damage, overheating and possible seizure - all of them ruining the engine.

Before you check the oil level, the engine should be switched off and left standing for a while to ensure that all oil has returned to the sump - probably the best time to do this is first thing in the morning after the car has been standing overnight.

INSIDE INFORMATION: Never overfill the engine with oil as any excess could find its way past an overloaded oil seal, or lead to over-heating and other problems.

If you're not sure where the dipstick on your engine is located, refer to *Fact File: Engine Bay Layouts on page 20.*

1A. Make sure the car is on level ground when you check the dipstick, which on nearly all Fiestas is coloured yellow. Carefully lift the dipstick out.

1B. Wipe the measuring end clean with a piece of cloth or tissue, put it back in and lift out again. The oil level should be clearly visible on the lower part of the dipstick but if not, wipe clean and try again, turning the stick so that it goes into the tube at a different angle.

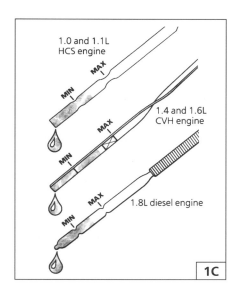

1.0 and 1.1L HCS engine

1.4 and 1.6L CVH engine

1.8L diesel engine

1C

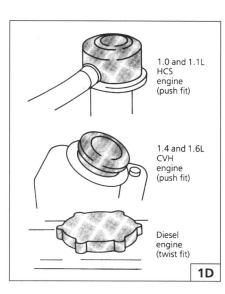

1.0 and 1.1L HCS engine (push fit)

1.4 and 1.6L CVH engine (push fit)

Diesel engine (twist fit)

1D

1C. The dipstick design may differ slightly between models, but will resemble one of those shown. The oil level must be maintained above the 'MIN' mark on the dipstick. Approximately one pint, or half a litre, will raise the level from the 'MIN' to the 'MAX' mark. (Illustration, courtesy Ford Motor Company Ltd)

1D. If topping-up is required, first remove the oil filler cap on the top of the rocker cover or cam cover. You may find that it is either a push-in fit, a bayonet fit (ie. one you twist anticlockwise and lift out), or a screw-on fit, similar to one of those shown here. (Illustration, courtesy Ford Motor Company Ltd)

1E. Add the oil a little at a time and allow a minute or so for the fresh oil to drain down into the sump before you check the level, not forgetting to start with a clean dipstick again.

On all models, check the ground over which the car has been parked for evidence of oil or other fluid leaks. If any leaks are found, do not drive the car without first establishing where the leaks have come from - they could have come from a major failure in the braking system which will probably call for **SPECIALIST SERVICE** attention.

1E

Job 2. Check coolant level.

It is important that all engines have the correct proportion of antifreeze in the coolant. This not only helps prevent freezing in the winter, but also overheating in summer temperatures. In addition, it also helps to prevent internal engine corrosion.

ALL MODELS UP TO 1983

2A. Early models use an 'expansion-tank' located on the front panel beside the radiator; in this arrangement the tank is non-pressurised and merely serves to collect, and feed back, excess coolant to and from the radiator. The level in the tank should be about one third its capacity when the engine is cold. IMPORTANT NOTE: The actual level of coolant in the system is checked by removing the radiator cap itself - coolant level should be up to the neck of the cap seat or housing. (Illustration, courtesy Ford Motor Company Ltd)

making it easy! For topping-up when only small quantities of oil are required, a small measuring jug, plastic bottle or funnel-measure like that shown, is useful to pour the oil with. Spills are less likely and you can also keep a check on oil consumption between service intervals.

SAFETY FIRST!
i) The coolant level should only be checked WHEN THE SYSTEM IS COLD. If you remove the pressure cap when the engine is hot, the release of pressure can cause the water in the system to boil and spurt into the air with the risk of severe scalding. ii) Take precautions to prevent antifreeze coming into contact with the skin or eyes. If this should happen, rinse immediately with plenty of water.

MODELS FROM 1983

2B. The coolant system (pressurised) expansion tank is found in the rear right-hand corner of the engine bay. HIGH and LOW level-marks are embossed on the side of the translucent tank, allowing the liquid level to be checked without removing the cap.

If topping-up is required, turn the cap a quarter-turn anticlockwise to release any slight pressure in the system, then turn fully and remove. NEVER ATTEMPT TO REMOVE THE FILLER CAP WHEN THE ENGINE IS HOT. If, in an emergency, the cap needs to be removed before the engine has completely cooled, wrap a rag around both the cap and your hands and open the cap in two stages, the first quarter turn to release any remaining internal pressure.

With the cap removed, add coolant from a measuring jug or bottle. If only a small quantity is required it is quite permissible to use neat antifreeze straight from the bottle as here, which saves the trouble of mixing it with water. There is no danger of increasing the concentration of antifreeze - water is added merely for reasons of economy, provided that you don't go over about 60% antifreeze to water.

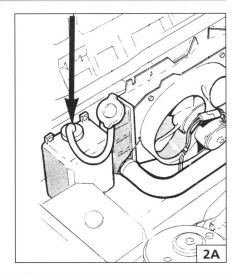

2A

making it easy! The coolant header tank on all models is made from semi-transparent material in order for the coolant level to be readily seen without needing to remove the cap. However, the inner surface of the tank often becomes discoloured making this impossible, but it is easily cured by cleaning the inner surface with a long-handled brush, such as those used in the kitchen for washing dishes.

2B

3A

3B

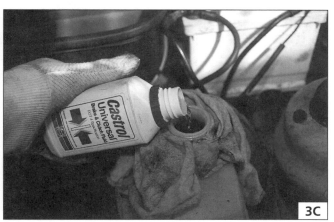

3C

☐ Job 3. Brake fluid level.

3A. The transparent brake fluid reservoir is on the top of the master cylinder in front of the servo. Wipe the top clean before removing the cap and be careful not to damage the wiring to the low-level warning switch. If necessary, top up the level to the 'MAX' mark on the side of the reservoir.

making it easy! Should the push-on connectors become disturbed, they can be replaced on the two terminals either way round. Also, before lifting the cap clear of the reservoir, allow the fluid in the tube on the underside of the cap to drain back into the reservoir rather than around your engine bay!

3B. Check the brake fluid level warning light. With the handbrake off - chock the wheels first and place the gearbox in first gear (or 'P' in the case of an automatic) - and, with the ignition switched on, lift the reservoir cap and its float clear of the fluid. The warning light on the dash should light up. If it does not, and the fluid level is satisfactory, have the circuit checked by a specialist without delay.

3C. Top-up using new, fresh fluid; place a rag around the filler to catch any spills, and allow space for the level float when the cap is re-fitted.

INSIDE INFORMATION: i) Check the ground on which the car has been parked, especially beneath the engine bay and each road wheel, for evidence of oil, clutch or brake fluid leaks. If any are found, investigate further before driving the car. ii) Brake fluid will damage painted surfaces if allowed to come into contact. Take care not to spill any but, if there is an accident, re-fit the master cylinder reservoir cap and wash off any accidental spillage immediately with hot soapy water.

☐ Job 4. Check windscreen wash level.

4A. On early cars, the windscreen washer reservoir is in the engine compartment alongside the right-hand suspension tower (arrowed). (Illustration, courtesy Ford Motor Company Ltd)

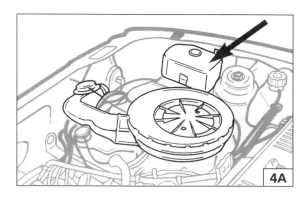

4A

4B. On later cars, as shown here, it is hidden behind the front inner wing on the right as you stand in front of the car. Only the neck, with a yellow filler cap, is visible. The cap is a simple push fit on the neck. If necessary, top up the reservoir with a mixture of water and screen wash fluid. Remember that in cold weather a stronger concentration of washer fluid will help to prevent the washer system from freezing up. Check the recommended dilution on the screenwash container.

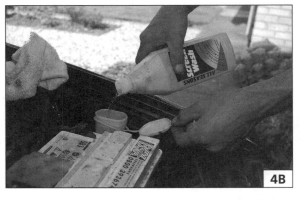

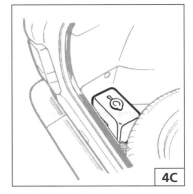

MODELS UP TO 1983

4C. Early models had a separate reservoir for the rear screen washers, located in the spare wheel compartment beneath the boot floor covering. (Illustration, courtesy Ford Motor Company Ltd)

☐ Job 5. Check battery electrolyte level.

5A. The battery is mounted by the bulkhead on the left of the engine bay. Remove the battery caps or covers and check the level of the electrolyte - the fluid inside each battery cell. The plates inside the battery should just be covered with electrolyte. If the level has fallen, top up with distilled water. NEVER use tap water, as it can destroy your battery. After replacing the covers, dry off the top of the battery.

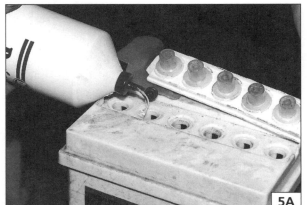

SAFETY FIRST!
i) The gas given off by a battery is highly explosive. Never smoke, use a naked flame or allow a spark to occur in the battery compartment. Never disconnect the battery (it can cause sparking) with the battery caps removed. ii) Batteries contain sulphuric acid. If the acid comes into contact with the skin or eyes, wash immediately with copious amounts of cold water and seek medical advice. iii) Do not check the battery levels within half an hour of the battery being charged with a separate battery charger because the addition of fresh water could then cause the highly acid and corrosive electrolyte to flood out of the battery. Many vehicles were fitted by the manufacturer with a 'sealed for life' battery, but it is possible that yours may have a 'normal' item, fitted by a subsequent owner. If yours is the former type, then no maintenance is required. This section relates to the common type of replacement battery.

FACT FILE: DISCONNECTING THE BATTERY

Many vehicles depend on a constant power supply from the battery and you can find yourself in all sorts of trouble if you simply disconnect the battery on those vehicles. You might find that the car alarm will go off, you could find that the engine management system forgets all it ever 'learned' and the car will feel very strange to drive until it has re-programmed itself, and you could find that your radio refuses to operate again unless you key in the correct code. And if you've bought the car second-hand and don't know the code, you would have to send the set back to the manufacturer for re-programming. So, on later cars with engine management systems you must ensure that the vehicle has a constant power supply even though the battery is removed. To do so, you will need a separate 12 volt battery supply. You could put a self tapping screw into the positive lead near the battery terminal before disconnecting it, and put a positive connection to your other battery via this screw. But you would have to be EXTREMELY CAREFUL to wrap insulation tape around the connection so that no short is caused. The negative terminal on the other battery would also have to be connected to the car's bodywork.

A better way is to use something like the Sykes-Pickavant Computer Saver shown here. Clip the cables to your spare battery and plug into your cigarette lighter. (You may have to turn the ignition switch to the 'Auxiliary' setting to allow the

cigarette lighter to function).

You have to hold in the red button on the Computer Saver while inserting it into the cigarette lighter, and if two green lights still show after the button is released, you have a good connection and your battery can now be disconnected and removed.

Be sure not to turn on any of the car's equipment while the auxiliary battery is connected.

5B. Check security of battery clamp at the base of the battery. If the terminals are furry with crystals, or corroded, clean them by pouring boiling water over them. Dry the battery top and coat the terminals with Vaseline (petroleum jelly).

INSIDE INFORMATION: i) Once water is mixed with acid inside the battery it won't freeze. So, in extremely cold weather, run the car (out of doors) so that you put a charge into the battery and this will mix the fresh water with the electrolyte, cutting out the risk of freezing and a cracked battery case. ii) If your battery persistently goes flat it may indicate a fault in the charging circuit, but it may be that the battery is nearing the end of its useful life. You can check the battery by checking the specific gravity of the electrolyte - see Job 56.

Every 500 Miles - Around the Car

☐ Job 6. Check tyre pressures.

6. Use a reliable pressure gauge to check the pressure in each tyre, including the spare. Always check pressures with the tyres cold, never just after using the car which warms up the tyres and increases their pressures.

Check the spare tyre too - in early cars (up to 1983) it will be found beneath the boot floor covering, while on later cars it is retained by a 'cage' beneath the floor.

☐ Job 7. Check front lights.

Check the operation of the sidelights and headlights, on both full and dipped beam. If one sidelight, or one headlight beam fails to work on either side, the bulb has probably failed.

SAFETY FIRST!
i) It is important, for reasons both of safety and legality, that your car's lights work correctly and that the reflectors and lenses are in good condition. Replace faulty bulbs as soon as possible and get any damaged lens renewed. ii) If removing a headlight bulb, be aware that these items get extremely hot in use and are capable of burning fingers for some minutes after switching off; allow at least five minutes for the bulbs, and their holders, to cool before attempting to remove them. NEVER hold a headlight bulb while it is switched on - it will burn you before you can let it go!

making it easy! When checking the rear lights it helps to have an assistant stand at the rear of the car to confirm each light is working, but the job can be done alone if the car is reversed close to a garage door or wall so that the reflections of the lights can be seen from the driver's seat. Also, test the stop-lights with the sidelights already switched on, then the indicators with the stoplights held on; this test causes maximum current to flow through the earth circuit of the rear-light clusters, which occasionally suffer from poor earth connections.

HEADLIGHTS

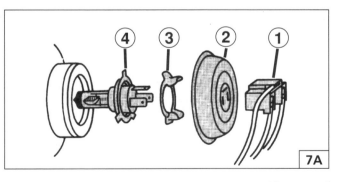

7A. The bulbs are removed from inside the engine bay; pull off the terminal connector (1). This is a three-prong terminal and the connector cannot be replaced the wrong way round. (Illustration, courtesy Ford Motor Company Ltd)

After removing the rubber cover (2), free the spring clip (3) which holds the bulb (4) in position. Note, if the bulb feels loose, gently bend the clip slightly when refitting, to give it more grip. Lift out the bulb to examine the filaments.

7B. INSIDE INFORMATION: Hold the bulb only by the metal part as shown. See MAKING IT EASY! box.

FRONT INDICATORS

7C. On early models, the connections are reached from inside the engine bay, alongside the headlights. Turn the bulb socket (A) anticlockwise and pull out. Remove the bulb (B) by pressing in, twisting and pulling out, in the normal way. (Illustration, courtesy Ford Motor Company Ltd)

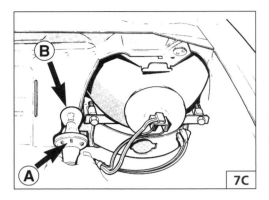

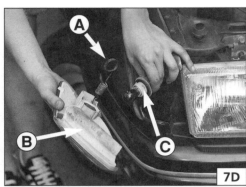

making it easy! If you touch a halogen headlight or driving light with bare fingers, the microscopic transfer of grease will shorten its life. Handle with a piece of tissue paper if the original wrapping is no longer there. If the bulb is touched - no worries! Just wipe carefully clean with methylated spirit on a fresh, clean tissue or cloth.

7D. On later vehicles, release the spring retainer (A) from inside the engine bay, remove the light unit (B) from outside the car, and disconnect the bulb holder (C) and bulb.

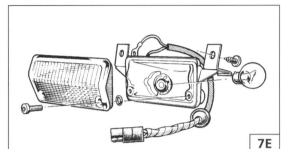

7E. XR2 models have separate indicator lights fitted to the bumper. Remove the lens unit by undoing the two screws securing it. (Illustration, courtesy Ford Motor Company Ltd)

SIDELIGHTS

7F. All cars have the sidelights integral with the headlights. To check the bulb, turn the bulbholder (A) anticlockwise and pull it out from the headlight back (B), from inside the engine bay. (Illustration, courtesy Ford Motor Company Ltd)

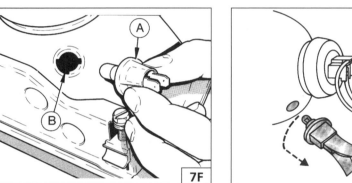

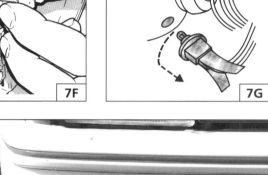

7G. Later cars have tabs attached to the bulbholder. To get to either bulb for checking, turn the bulbholder anticlockwise and lift it out with an anti-clockwise push and turn movement. (Illustrations, courtesy Ford Motor Company Ltd)

FRONT FOG LIGHT/AUXILIARY LIGHT

7H. Later XR2i cars have front fog lights mounted within the bumper.

7I. To replace the bulb, loosen the four screws behind the bumper, pull off the rubber cover to the relevant reflector and disconnect the bulb plug. Release the spring clip to remove the bulb.

7J. Where separate Ford driving lights are fitted, you loosen the screw to remove the lens reflector unit (don't let it drop!), then unplug the wiring connector. Release both sides of the spring clip to release the bulb. IMPORTANT NOTE: Do not touch the halogen bulb with your fingers! (Illustrations, courtesy Ford Motor Company Ltd)

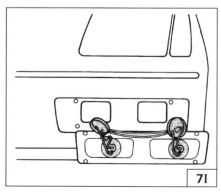

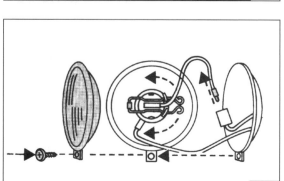

500 MILE/WEEKLY SERVICE

Job 8. Check side repeater indicators (if fitted).

8A. Two types of fixing are used for the side repeater indicator lights. On later types shown here, all you do is twist the bulbholder clockwise and pull it out. Then turn the bulbholder anticlockwise to get at the bulb.

8B. On the second type, you have to turn the complete assembly to the right-hand or left-hand side and pull it out. You may have to reach behind the wing and squeeze the tabs (A) to release the bulbholder. Disconnect the bulbholder (B). (Illustration, courtesy Ford Motor Company Ltd)

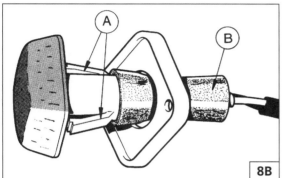

making it easy! On all types of side indicator, it helps to clean the mud from behind the wing (taking care not to damage the wiring) and ease it free with a hand each side of the wing, depressing the catch/catches if necessary.

Job 9. Check rear lights.

9A. On some early models, after removing the trim side panel, you can pull each bulb holder out individually to replace the bulb.

9B. To get to the bulbs on some models, first remove a fibreboard cover by undoing a screw (A) with a broad bladed screwdriver. A coin can be used if a suitable screwdriver is not available. The bulb holder, complete with all the bulbs, lifts out after releasing a plastic tab (B). In our drawing, 1 is the stop/tail light, 2 is the reversing light and 3 is the indicator light. To replace the bulb holder, feed the bulbs into their apertures and push the bulb holder firmly home. (Illustrations, courtesy Ford Motor Company Ltd)

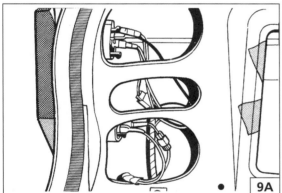

9C. On later models, the bulb holder unit is removed from inside the luggage compartment by pressing together two plastic tabs.

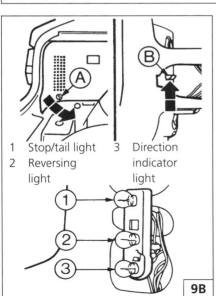

1 Stop/tail light
2 Reversing light
3 Direction indicator light

500 MILE/WEEKLY SERVICE

9D. After lifting the bulb holder out, bulbs can be changed individually.

COURIER VANS ONLY

On Courier vans, the complete light unit lifts out from outside the vehicle after undoing two plastic screws inside the load compartment. Then the backplate can be separated from the lens and individual bulbs changed as necessary.

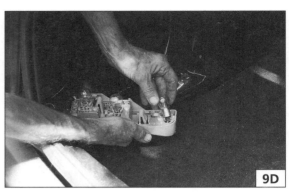

9D

REAR FOG LIGHTS

9E. Access to rear fog lights on all vehicles, where fitted, is by undoing two nuts inside the luggage compartment and lifting the light away from under the rear bumper. The reflector and bulb holder lift out after depressing two tabs, arrowed in our drawing. (Illustration, courtesy Ford Motor Company Ltd)

☐ Job 10. Check number plate light.

10. On all car models the number plate light is a push fit in the rear bumper. You may have to use a screwdriver to prise it out. After lifting out the number plate light you get to the bulb by releasing two catches (pushing them outwards), one catch each side of the light.

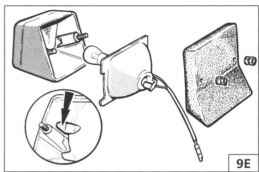

9E

☐ Job 11. Check interior lights.

All the interior lights, courtesy, footwell and reading lights, if fitted, are a push fit in the trim which holds them. Before removing a courtesy light, check that the switch is in the central, OFF, position to avoid any chance of a short circuit.

10

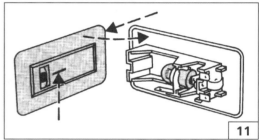

11

11. On all models, the interior light is prised out with a screwdriver. Take care not to damage trim with the screwdriver! The festoon bulb is 10 Watt. (Illustration, courtesy Ford Motor Company Ltd)

FACT FILE: FUSES

*INSIDE INFORMATION: If a complete 'set' of bulbs fails to operate (and especially if other electrical components fail at the same time) check the fuses before suspecting any other fault. If a replacement fuse blows, you probably have a circuit fault. **Seek specialist advice immediately.** If the fuse protecting the circuit has not blown, it may be that a relay has failed. In this case, seek SPECIALIST SERVICE.*

> *SAFETY FIRST!*
> *Make sure that all the electrical circuits, including the ignition, are switched OFF before removing or replacing a fuse. NEVER try to 'cure' a fault by fitting a fuse with a higher amperage rating than the one specified.*

The fuses are colour coded, red for 10 amp, blue for 15 amp, yellow for 20 amp, neutral or clear for 25 amp and green for 30 amp. A blown fuse is clearly identified by a break in the wire.

The fuses are numbered and the circuits protected by each fuse are indicated by international symbols on the fuse box cover and are also given in the owner's handbook. IMPORTANT NOTE: The numbers allocated by Ford to each circuit may differ from model to model and they also change with the age of the car. Make sure you identify the correct fuse for the circuit which has failed. Some circuits, such as the radio, may have a separate line fuse in the wiring to them. Refer to the owner's handbook or your Ford Dealer to check.

On later models there are extra fuses, usually for the rear fog lights, tailgate remote release and heated windscreen, together with most of the relays, in the main fuse/relay box behind the main fuse panel. To get to this, remove the two screws at the top of the main fuse panel, depress the two catches, one each side, and lift the whole panel into the car. Depending on the model, there may be extra relays either inside the steering column shroud or under the bonnet. Refer to your workshop manual to locate these.

There is also a fusible link in the main component feed cable from the battery. Should all the electrics fail, and the battery connections are good, it may be that this link has blown. However, it very rarely fails unless there is a serious short circuit. We advise that you seek SPECIALIST SERVICE if this does happen.

☐ Job 12. Check horn.

12. Operate the horn push to check that the horn sounds. If it does not, and the fuse has not blown, check the connections to the horn itself, which is mounted low down on the inner wing on the right hand side as you face the front of the car. If the connections are poor, remake them, but remember that with some circuits, one of the wires to the horn is live whenever the ignition is on. To be completely safe, disconnect the battery before removing either cable from the horn, or seek **SPECIALIST SERVICE**.

☐ Job 13. Windscreen wipers.

13A. Lift the wiper blade away from the screen and examine the edge for damage or waviness which indicates that it is worn out. Give each blade a wipe with clean methylated spirit or replace, as necessary.

13B. If the blade needs renewing it comes free of the wiper arm when you depress a small catch on the blade holder.

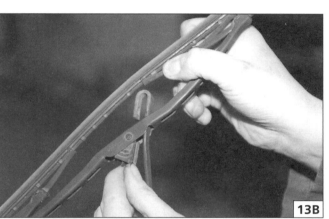

☐ Job 14. Check screen washers.

14. If the screen washer jets are not properly aimed, they can be adjusted with a pin. If one of the jets is blocked, it can usually be freed with a piece of thin wire (untwist the end of a length of multi-strand electric cable).

INSIDE INFORMATION: If the washer motor works, but the washers don't, suspect a break in the plastic supply pipe. It becomes brittle with age and is particularly prone to breaking at the top of the tailgate on Hatchbacks - look inside the black convoluted covering.

If, however, the washers do not work at all, you cannot hear the motor working and the fuse has not blown, the motor itself may have failed. The motor is incorporated in the washer reservoir, and getting to it on models where the reservoir is behind the inner wing is somewhat fiddling, involving undoing nuts both inside and underneath the wing. If underwing protectors are fitted, these may have to be removed as well, to make access easier. Once the reservoir is removed, the motor can be eased out of its socket, but you may prefer to seek **SPECIALIST SERVICE**. On early models with a rear wash-wipe system, there is a separate reservoir and pump inside the spare wheel carrier.

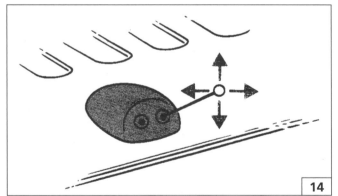

☐ Job 15. Check heater blower/demist.

15. Switch the heater blower motor on and check that, when you move the relevant controls, the air is directed either downwards or upwards to the screen. Check the motor on all its speed settings. If the motor does not work, it may be that a fuse has blown but, if the fuse controlling it is OK, either there is a fault in the wiring or the motor has failed. The blower motor is not easy to get at on a Fiesta, so consult your workshop manual or seek **SPECIALIST SERVICE**.

Every 1,500 Miles - or Every Month, whichever comes first

Every 1,500 Miles - Around the Car

First carry out the relevant jobs from the 500 Miles service interval.

☐ **Job 16. Check tyres.**

See also *Chapter 7, Getting Through the MoT* for a more detailed explanation of tyre wear and problems likely to be encountered.

16A. Check the tyres for sufficient tread depth using a special depth gauge and note that, in the UK, the minimum legal tread depth is 1.6mm. However, tyres are not at their safest at that level, particularly in the wet, and you might want to replace them earlier. Measure the tread across the width of the tyre, at three or four places around the circumference. This will give early warning of any uneven wear pattern, perhaps caused by a steering or suspension fault, or a defect in the tyre itself.

16B. Check the inner and outer sidewalls for bulges and splits, also the wheel rims if kerbstones etc. have been driven over (accidentally, of course!). Raise each wheel off the ground, supporting the car on an axle stand, otherwise you won't be able to examine the inside wall of the tyre properly, nor will you be able to check that part of the tyre in contact with the ground. If you find any splits or other damage, the tyre(s) should be inspected immediately by a tyre specialist who will advise whether repair is possible or replacement is required.

> **SAFETY FIRST!**
> *Tyres which show uneven wear tell their own story, if only you know how to speak the language! If any tyre is worn more on one side than another, consult your main dealer or a tyre specialist. It probably means that your suspension or steering is out of adjustment - probably a simple tracking job but conceivably symptomatic of suspension damage, so have it checked. If a tyre is worn more in the centre or on the edges, it could mean that your tyre pressures are wrong but, once again, have the car checked. Incorrectly inflated tyres wear rapidly, can cause the car's handling to become dangerous and can even cause the car to consume noticeably more fuel. When checking your tyres, don't forget to include the spare.*

16A

16B

making it easy! While you're checking the tread depth, dig out any small stones that have found their way into the tread. Most of those which are just caught in the tread will fling themselves out but any which have cut into the rubber might work their way further in. Attention to this now could well save you a puncture later.

☐ **Job 17. Check spare tyre.**

On earlier Fiestas the spare wheel is carried under the floor of the luggage compartment. On later models the spare wheel is in a carrier under the car at the back. See *RAISING THE CAR* at the start of this chapter.

Now check the tyre pressure. When allocating the wheel as a spare you should have checked that the tread depth was legal, as shown in *Job 16*.

making it easy! You should inflate the spare tyre to the maximum pressure recommended for high speed or load running. Then, if you have a puncture while on a journey, you'll be okay. It's always easier to carry a tyre pressure gauge with you and let some air out than to put some in.

☐ Job 18. Wash bodywork.

INSIDE INFORMATION: Many people choose to wash their cars weekly, which is commendable, while others never seem to wash them at all! But there's no denying that regularly washed-and-waxed bodywork lasts longer and helps maintain a car's value. Getting into a regular car washing routine has the advantage that minor damage to the paintwork does not go unnoticed and can be quickly treated before serious corrosion gets a hold.

Wash the paintwork and glass with water and a suitable car detergent taking care not to get 'wax-wash' on the glass. Finish by washing the wheels and tyre walls. Leather the paintwork dry and then polish. Use a separate leather on the glass to avoid transferring polish from the paintwork.

☐ Job 19. Touch-up paintwork.

19. Treat small areas of damage, like the stonechip shown here, as soon as possible, otherwise corrosion of the exposed metal will soon get a hold and prove difficult (and expensive) to repair. 'Touch-Up' type products are available from car accessory shops and garages in the form of paint 'pens' and even colour-matched film that is simply 'stuck' over the damaged area. These products may not give an invisible repair, but they do offer protection from road salt and water.

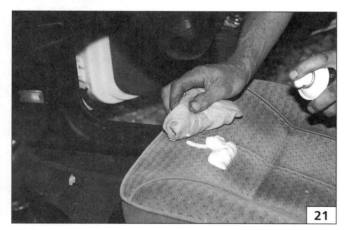

☐ Job 20. Lubricate aerial.

20. Clean each section of an extending aerial with a spray-on lubricant such as Castrol Easing Fluid and work the aerial up and down a few times. Do not leave excess lubricating oil on the aerial sections as this will simply encourage the adherence of grit and dirt.

INSIDE INFORMATION: With electrically-operated aerials it is especially important to keep the sections clean, otherwise the operating motor and/or gears will be over-stressed and quickly fail.

☐ Job 21. Valet interior.

21. Regularly vacuuming the seats and carpets will not only make the car more pleasant to drive, but will also remove a surprising amount of abrasive grit and dust, the main cause of worn patches. For stains and grease marks, use one of the many domestic upholstery cleaning materials. Some stains may only be effectively removed by the use of white spirit or methylated spirits - test these on an unseen area first though, to check for colour-fastness of the upholstery.

☐ Job 22. Improve visibility.

22. Use a proprietary glass cleaner to clean all the windows on the inside as well as the outside. Tar spots and dead insects can be removed with special cleaners available from garages and car accessory shops. 'Traffic film' can build up unnoticed and is a mixture of oil and grime thrown from the wheels of other vehicles, resulting in dangerous smearing of the windscreen in the wet, and which ordinary washer additives cannot shift. A proper traffic film remover is instantly effective however, and lasts well.

☐ **Job 23. Clean mirrors.**

23. Use the glass cleaner on the external and interior mirrors too, to make your rearward vision easier, and safer! Check also that your interior mirror is well secured, otherwise the blurred image won't allow you to tell the difference between a long-haul truck and the boys in blue!

23

Every 1,500 Miles - Under the Car

First carry out the relevant jobs from the 500 Miles service interval.

☐ **Job 24. Clean mud traps.**

24. All except the earliest Fiestas are fitted with mud deflectors under the front wings, but there is an area in front of the mud deflectors where road dirt can collect behind the front skirt and another at the rear end of the sills just in front of the rear wheels. Use a strong water jet to clean underneath the wheel arches front and rear. If available, a high pressure washer is the most effective method but take care: on a powerful spray the pressure may blast away the underseal!

INSIDE INFORMATION: Even where the car is fitted with plastic 'inner' wheel arch linings, mud can build-up around the edges and will act like a sponge to salt-laden water thrown from the tyres. The result is bubbling and flaking of paint from around the edges of the wheel arches.

24

SAFETY FIRST!
You may find it easier to put the car up on axle stands to clean the mud traps. Read carefully the information at the start of this chapter on lifting and supporting the vehicle, and wear goggles while you are cleaning.

Every 3,000 Miles - or Every Three Months, whichever comes first

Every 3,000 Miles - The Engine Bay

First carry out the relevant jobs from the earlier service intervals.

☐ **Job 25. Check alternator drive belt.**

You will find one of two different alternator adjustment types on your Fiesta.

INSIDE INFORMATION: Ford recommend that V-belt tension is measured by using a Ford special tool, a deflection gauge. We recommend that you set the deflection manually, then have it checked by your local Ford main dealer. Note that this does not apply to flat belts - see below.

25A. Check the tension of the alternator drive belt by deflecting it with firm finger or thumb pressure about halfway along the longest 'run' of the belt.

25B. The total amount of movement should be no more than 10mm (0.4in.).

SAFETY FIRST!
Disconnect the battery before working on drive belts so that the engine cannot inadvertently be started or turned over, causing personal injury.

25A

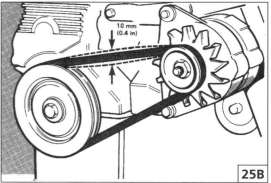

10 mm
(0.4 in)

25B

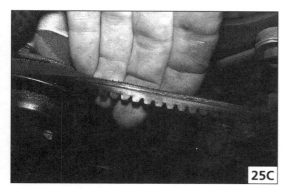

25C. Also check the general condition of the belt, looking for signs of cracking and frayed edges, and also for signs of 'polishing' of the belt's surface, which can indicate age and possibly imminent failure! Take out the spark plugs (on petrol engines) and turn the engine so that you can inspect every bit of the belt.

Tension the drivebelt (if necessary) by slackening the alternator bracket and adjuster bolts - loosen the adjuster bolt just sufficiently to allow movement of the alternator while maintaining a degree of 'grip'.

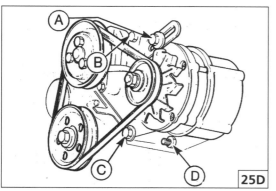

*25D. INSIDE INFORMATION: If you retighten the adjustment bolts in the wrong order, it is possible to break the aluminium alloy body of the alternator. Retighten in the order shown here, being **sure** to tighten bolt D last.*

1.6 LITRE DIESEL ENGINED MODELS (and some others)

25E. The drive belt on these models is located low down, below the fuel injector pump on diesel models and is therefore more difficult to see. It is easier to check the belt, and adjust it if necessary, with the front of the vehicle raised on stands. Refer to *RAISING THE CAR* at the beginning of this chapter for advice on how to do this safely. Checking and adjusting the

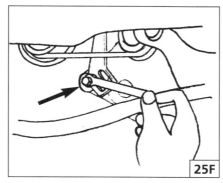

belt follows the procedure given above, although the position of the alternator and its clamp bolts are slightly different. Basically, the alternator 'hangs down' rather than being mounted high on the side of the engine. You have to remove the plastic shroud before you can see the belt or adjusters.

1.8 LITRE DIESEL MODELS

25F. These models also have the belt located low-down on the engine and it is easier to check the condition of the belt from underneath the car, as in *Job 25C* above. Tension of the belt is more critical as it also drives the power steering pump and a different tensioning mechanism to that previously described is used. Adjustment involves the use of special tools to apply and measure the tension of the belt, so we recommend this job is a **SPECIALIST SERVICE** for your local Ford agent - or at least, that you have the tension checked even if you carry out the work yourself. There are two hexagons on the adjuster (arrowed). The smaller one is a lock bolt; the larger operates the adjuster, moving the alternator in or out as you turn it. Tension the belt with great care, a little at a time! - by moving the alternator in or out, as necessary.

making it easy! 25G. Use a length of wood to apply sideways pressure to the alternator body - don't pull too hard! - (as near to the drive end bracket as possible) moving it away from the engine against belt tension. Provided the alternator bracket bolt hasn't been loosened too much, the alternator should 'stay-put' while the adjuster-stay nut and bolt are tightened. However, if you find this procedure difficult (it takes practice!) ask an assistant to hold the wooden lever while you tighten the bolt.

Job 26. Check oil filler cap.

OHV ENGINES ONLY

26. Check the oil filler cap for signs of blockage and physical damage to the casing. The oil filler cap plays an important part in re-circulating the fumes and gases from within the engine, while a filter screen inside the cap separates any oil and moisture from the fumes. Over a period of time the filter becomes choked either with a black sooty deposit or a wet, oily 'mayonnaise'-like substance that is actually emulsified oil and water. The oil filler cap has a wire gauze emission filter inside it. Remove the rubber emission control pipes from the cap and wash it out in paraffin. Shake it and wait for it to dry out before replacing it.

Job 27. Drain fuel filter.

DIESEL ENGINES ONLY

Drain the diesel fuel filter to remove any water residue.

INSIDE INFORMATION: The fuel filter on diesel engines is designed so that any water which passes through it will collect at the bottom of the filter housing, immediately above the drain plug. This means that any water present will be drained first and the drain plug closed as soon as fuel begins to flow. Under normal conditions, the amount of water likely to be present is usually very small. However, the careful diesel owner may wish to check the filter every 3,000 miles.

SAFETY FIRST!
Whenever you are dealing with diesel fuel, it's essential to protect your hands by wearing plastic gloves.

27A. On most models, the filter is located on the right-hand side of the engine block, immediately above the clutch housing. Place a small container or wad of thick rags beneath the filter, to catch the fuel and any water contained in it when the valve is opened and fit a short length of rubber tube to the bottom drain valve outlet, with the other end placed in the container. Drain the filter by unscrewing the drain plug fitted to the base of the filter unit by two or three turns.

INSIDE INFORMATION: Note that diesel fuel is damaging to the engine's rubber hoses, belts and mountings. Keep it off them!

Note that with the type of filter not provided with an air bleed valve, considerable cranking may be necessary before the engine starts, due to air in the fuel injector lines.

27B. On 1.8 and post-1987 1.6 litre models a slightly different pattern of filter housing is used.

27C. It may be necessary to open the bleed valve (1) a turn or two to allow the fuel to flow through the drain valve. On this type it is necessary to purge any air in the filter by opening the bleed valve and operating the hand-pump plunger (2) until bubble-free fuel escapes from the bleed valve outlet. (Illustration, courtesy Ford Motor Company Ltd)

SAFETY FIRST!
Before attempting to start the engine, make sure all drain or purge valves are closed and that any container or fuel-soaked rag is removed from the engine bay.

Job 28. Check brake and fuel lines.

28. Make a physical check of all the pipework and connections in the engine bay. Bend the flexible fuel lines, where fitted to non-fuel injected cars in order to expose hairline cracks or deterioration which may not be immediately obvious. Look for signs of rust or tell-tale fluid

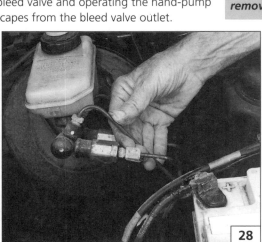

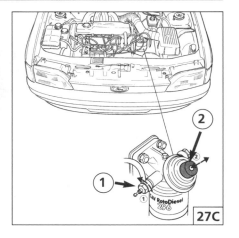

marks on brake pipes and unions. Start the engine and check that there are no fuel leaks.

Every 3,000 Miles - Around the Car

First carry out the relevant jobs from the earlier service intervals.

☐ Job 29. Check wheel nuts/bolts.

Early Fiestas were fitted with wheel bolts while later ones switched to wheel nuts. See *RAISING THE CAR* at the start of this chapter.

29

29. Check the tightness of all wheel nuts or bolts. The wheel brace supplied with the car is only intended for use in an emergency and we strongly recommend the use of a torque wrench for this job. This will avoid over-tightening the nuts or bolts and avoids the danger of stripped threads or over-stressed studs.

To 'torque' the wheel nuts/bolts correctly, first slacken each nut or bolt and check that the threads aren't stiff or corroded, then tighten with the wrench to a torque of 9 kg m (65 lb.ft).

☐ Job 30. Check handbrake adjustment.

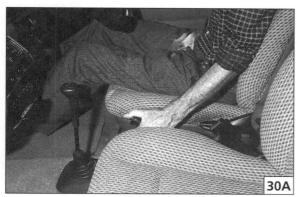

30A

30A. Apply the handbrake, without pressing the release knob at the end of the lever, and count the number of 'clicks' the lever goes through before the brake is firmly applied: the brake should lock at between 2 and 4 clicks. If more or less than these figures, the cable can be adjusted as follows:

Raise the rear of the vehicle sufficiently to allow the rear wheels to turn and to provide sufficient working clearance, and support the body on axle stands. Fully release the handbrake and apply the footbrake firmly several times to ensure the automatic adjusters on each wheel are correctly 'set'.

30B. The handbrake cable adjuster is located beneath the rear passenger-side floor and consists of two plastic 'handwheel' type nuts (A) and (B) threaded onto the outer casing of the cable. These screw up tight against a fixed bracket. Slacken locknut (B) and turn nut (A) to adjust the cable travel. Tightening (A) against the bracket reduces handbrake lever travel, while loosening (A) increases the travel. Retighten the locknut after carrying out the adjustment.

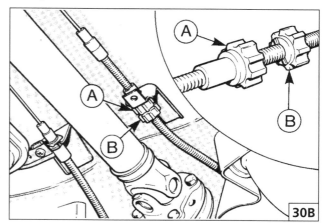

30B

30C. Later models have a plastic 'pin' (arrowed) projecting from the bracket parallel with the nuts, whose purpose is to prevent both nuts turning together. The pin can be pushed slightly to one side to allow the adjusters to turn.

Adjustment is correct when, with the handbrake lever raised one or two 'clicks', the rear wheels are only just free to turn under firm hand pressure.

30D. On models fitted with drum brakes, confirm correct adjustment by pushing in the plungers (A) on each brake backplate. The amount of movement should be 0.5 to 1.0mm. with the handbrake lever fully released.

On all models, apply the handbrake lever firmly several times to 'settle' the brake mechanisms and equalise the cables. Also, ensure the rear wheels are free to turn when the lever is fully released; a slight 'rubbing' sound from the brakes as the wheels are spun is permissible, provided there is no appreciable 'drag' affecting the wheels' freedom to turn.

When adjustment is correct, tighten the locking-nut (B) up to and against nut (A) ensuring the latter isn't disturbed, or turned in the process.

IMPORTANT NOTE: After carrying out the work, have the handbrake checked on an MoT garage's 'rolling road' - the only way of being certain of correct adjustment.

*INSIDE INFORMATION: If, during or after adjustment, braking effort on each side of the car seems unequal for a given number of 'clicks', or one side fails to work at all, there is a problem either with the cable to the wheel concerned (internal corrosion is the most common cause) or a fault with the handbrake mechanism contained within the drum. Refer to **Job 76** for details of the rear brake internal mechanisms, or seek professional advice.*

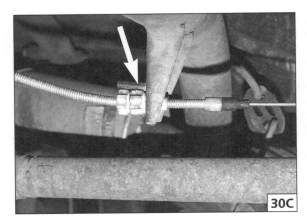

30C

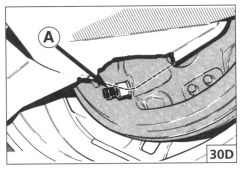

30D

☐ Job 31. Check door and tailgate seals.

To preserve the weather protection efficiency of door and tailgate (or bootlid) seals. They should be regularly cleaned and periodically treated with a proprietary 'conditioning' product. Also, if a sunroof is fitted to your car, treat the sunroof seal similarly.

☐ Job 32. Check rear view mirrors.

Check the security and condition of the glass on the interior and exterior mirrors. If a glass is cracked it should be renewed. If the mirror is loose it will vibrate on the road and be useless for viewing traffic approaching from behind.

☐ Job 33. Check windscreen.

33A. Check the windscreen for chips and scratches which are a potential MoT failure point depending on their location and size. See *Chapter 7, Getting Through the MoT*, for what is and is not acceptable according to UK regulations.

33A

33B. Most small chips less than 10mm wide can be repaired by specialists, while light scoring can often be polished out by the same people. Your local auto. accessory shop should also stock a DIY repair kit for use on smaller chips.

FACT FILE: DOOR MIRROR REPLACEMENT

Door mirrors are easily repaired using one of the glass replacements available from most good accessory shops. These are simply a new mirror glass, pre-shaped to fit individual models, with a self-adhesive layer on the rear surface. The new glass is positioned over the old, broken, glass (provided it is flat) and pressed into place.

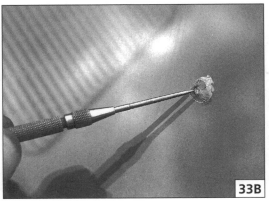

33B

Every 3,000 Miles - Under the Car

First carry out the relevant jobs from the earlier service intervals.

☐ **Job 34. Check exhaust system and mountings.**

34A. Examine the silencers (as far as safe access will allow) for signs of corrosion, especially along seams and at the ends where the pipes are welded. Check the system joints where the pipe sections are joined together for tell-tale 'soot' marks indicating a leak.

34B. If exhaust system mountings break, perish or come loose, the extra stresses on the exhaust system could cause the pipes or silencers to fracture. Always replace worn or damaged mountings before they break - it can save much hassle and expense later on. As well as a visual test, check the mountings by grasping the (cold) exhaust tailpipe with a piece of rag and 'shaking' it, listening for any rattles or bumps that indicate it is contacting the underside of the car - usually the result of weak or damaged mountings.

making it easy! If you suspect a leak but it's location isn't obvious, start the engine and try pressurising the system by holding a piece of board or something similar so that it blocks off the tailpipe. Under pressure, the leak should be more noisy, enabling you to track down its position. Get an assistant to help you if you can, but remember that an exhaust system can get very hot and touching the pipework can cause nasty burns.

☐ **Job 35. Check brake and fuel lines.**

35. Carefully examine all the pipes under the car for signs of rust or weeping unions. Deep pitting indicates severe rusting and this, or even the slightest of leaks can render the car dangerous to drive. It must not be driven until the problem has been rectified. Also check the pipes are held securely in their clips, and that there is no physical damage to the pipes.

Bend all flexible hoses to show up signs of cracking rubber - if any are found, the hose should be replaced as soon as possible. The hoses should also be free from bulges or chafing marks.

INSIDE INFORMATION: Bend the hoses double, and check visually near the union ends for any signs of wear or damage. Also, have an assistant press hard on the brake pedal while you check each hose for bulging. Any hose not in perfect condition should be replaced as soon as possible.

☐ **Job 36. Check fuel tank for leaks.**

36. Check around the fuel tank flanged joints for leaks (indicated by a damp 'stain' smelling of fuel) and also the flexible connectors between filler pipe and tank inlet and the smaller vent pipe. Test the worm-drive clips on the filler and vent pipes with a screwdriver, making sure they are tight.

☐ **Job 37. Check steering rack gaiters.**

SAFETY FIRST!
*This check requires the steering to be moved from lock-to-lock so the use of axle stands is essential. Refer to **RAISING THE CAR SAFELY**, at the beginning of this chapter for details of how to use them.*

The steering rack gaiters - also sometimes called 'boots' - are made of convoluted rubber, their purpose being to prevent dirt and grit getting inside the steering rack mechanism while keeping the lubricant inside it, and at the same time allowing the 'push-pull' motion of the steering arms as the steering wheel is turned.

After a few years of continual movement plus attack from stones, grit and other road dirt, the gaiter can split leading to dirt and water entering after which the rack will wear out in no time at all.

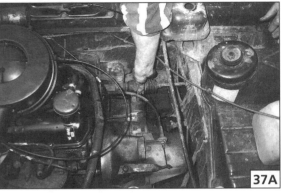

37A. With the steering turned on full lock (turned fully to the left or right) check the gaiter that is fully extended, (inside the engine bay) looking for splits, chafing, perishing etc. Normally a split gaiter will allow oil to leak out, indicated by a tell-tale mark.

Now turn the steering fully in the opposite direction and check the other gaiter in the same way, from beneath the car, where necessary.

37B. Make sure the gaiter securing clips are firm and doing their job. Clips can be metal bands either sprung or twisted into position, or plastic bands commonly known as 'cable-ties'.

Replacement of the gaiters involves removal of the track rod ends, a job beyond the scope of this book and is a **SPECIALIST SERVICE** item. Driving with a split gaiter will very quickly ruin an expensive steering rack, so the most economical course of action is to get it renewed as soon as possible.

☐ **Job 38. Check drive shaft gaiters.**

38A. Check the 'inner' drive shaft gaiters (those positioned each side of the gearbox - that shown is the right hand inner driveshaft gaiter). Check for condition of the rubber and for security of the fastenings at each end. Make sure there are no splits, pin-holes or signs of chafing. Any trace of grease leaking from the gaiter requires further investigation and probably replacement.

38B. Check the outer gaiters (arrowed) similarly, but note that because the outer joint has a greater range of movement than the inner gaiter, wear is more common here. Put the steering on full lock first in one direction, then the other while each gaiter is checked, so that the rubber is 'stretched' and any weakness or leak will be easier to spot.

FACT FILE:
EMERGENCY GAITER REPAIR

38C. Drive shafts are expensive items and their life expectancy will be close to nil if the gaiter splits and the universal joint inside runs dry. If you want to avoid the expense of a professionally fitted gaiter, you could try a DIY repair - but be warned that split gaiters can do just that - you can't expect them to be as robust as the proper job! There are a number of 'easy-fit' gaiter replacement kits on the market, their

main purpose being to enable the gaiter to be renewed without special tools or any dismantling.

38D. These gaiters are split longitudinally, which allows them to be simply placed over the joint, and then joined and sealed with a special cyanoacrylate glue. Fitting this type of gaiter successfully relies on absolute cleanliness as oil or grease will prevent the adhesive setting properly. Full instructions are supplied with each kit. (Illustration, courtesy Partco.)

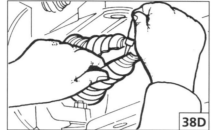

SPECIALIST SERVICE: If there is any doubt as to the condition of the gaiters, or if they are obviously in need of replacement, pay a visit to your Ford dealer, as a number of special tools and equipment are required to change them.

☐ Job 39. Check steering ball joints.

39. Steering joints, or 'track rod ends' provide the link between the steering arms and the roadwheels. A small rubber boot covers the steering joint and forms part of the assembly and is vital to the life of the joint - any splits or cracks will allow the grease to escape and dirt to enter and ruin the joint.

SPECIALIST SERVICE: Fitting a new ball joint/track rod end can be a difficult job for the inexperienced mechanic to carry out! A special ball joint separating tool will be needed and front wheel 'tracking' has to be professionally adjusted afterwards.

making it easy! It's easier to check joints and bushes if the front wheels are removed first. Refer to **RAISING THE CAR** at the beginning of this Chapter. Put the steering onto full lock so that each joint can be seen at the rear of the brake disc backplate. Check the condition and security of the protective boot on each track rod end. If split or damaged, the complete track rod end joint will have to be replaced. In theory you can fit a new boot, but it's false economy for the following reasons. i) Chances are that the old joint will be worn because the boot had a split in it and the resulting loss of lubricant, and ii), the joint will have to be removed from the steering arm in any case. This can be a difficult job so you might as well fit a relatively inexpensive new joint and have the wheel alignment checked at the same time.

☐ Job 40. Check suspension joints and bushes.

The suspension ball joints provide the link between the roadwheel/hub assembly and the lower track control arm. The ball joint allows the suspension to move up and down and the hub to swivel under the influence of the steering. The ball joint itself is protected by a small rubber boot similar to the steering joint, and its condition is vital to the joint it protects.

40A. Ideally, the road wheel should be removed to carry out the ball joint gaiter check so that the joint can be thoroughly examined for splits and/or cracking. If grease is evident on the outer surface of the rubber then the chances are there is a leak somewhere, but as the boot is in a somewhat 'squashed' and restricted position such a leak may not be readily obvious.

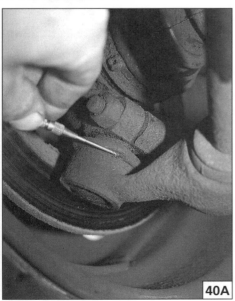

MODELS UP TO 1989 ONLY

40B. Test the inner suspension arm bushes (arrowed) by levering with a pry-bar or large screwdriver, trying to move them 'outwards'. There should only be just a perceptible amount of movement in the bushes. If there is more than this, the bushes need to be replaced.

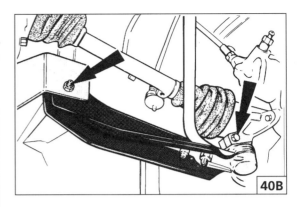

40B

> *making it easy!* When you are replacing the anti-roll bar bushes, leave all the nuts slightly loose, lower the car onto its wheels and bounce the front a few times to settle the bushes. This will prevent any of them being under torsion in use which can shorten their life. Then jack up again and use axle stands to let both front wheels hang free while tightening the nuts.

SPECIALIST SERVICE: Replacing the joint or arm is within the capabilities of an experienced home mechanic, but not a job for beginners! If in doubt about the condition of any of these components, seek professional advice.

40C. Check the rubber bushes (D) at the forward-end of the tie-bars (C), checking for distortion, splits or perishing. Replacement is a straight forward matter of removing the tie bar from the lower arm (see **40B**) and removing the nut (B). (Illustrations, courtesy Ford Motor Company Ltd)

INSIDE INFORMATION: You'll need to soak all the threads overnight with releasing fluid if you're to get them undone without shearing a bolt or two.

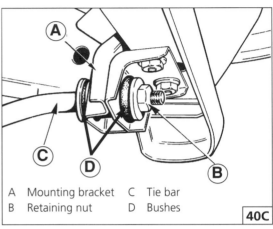

A	Mounting bracket	C	Tie bar
B	Retaining nut	D	Bushes

40C

☐ Job 41. Check underside for leaks.

Check along the car for any signs of fluid or oil leaks. Oil leaks are likely to come from the engine area and are probably a matter of gaskets or oil seals needing renewing. They should be cured because, apart from costing you a lot of money in oil, they make a mess on your garage floor and, if they are allowed to develop, could cause low engine oil level. Some leaks are simple to cure, others not so simple. Decide, with the help of a workshop manual, if you feel competent to tackle any leaks you find. If not, seek early **SPECIALIST SERVICE**.

> *making it easy!* Sometimes, because the oil from a leak tends to spread, it is difficult to spot exactly where the leak is coming from. One way of finding it is to clean everything off with paraffin or white spirit, dry it, and then dust along the gasket joints with talcum powder. When you run the engine, an oil leak will show up very quickly as a local stain on the talc.

☐ Job 42. Check ABS braking (where fitted).

Two types of ABS anti-lock braking have been offered as optional on Fiestas. Neither type of anti-lock system can be DIY serviced, however. Setting up and adjusting an anti-lock braking system is very much a **SPECIALIST SERVICE** job.

42. On both types there is a warning light on the dash panel (arrowed) which comes on if the system is not working and, in the case of the earlier type, a sensor switch is used to detect belt breakage by illuminating a warning light on the dash. The car will probably still be safe to drive but, should the light come on, seek **SPECIALIST SERVICE** as soon as possible.

BULB FAILURE: The anti-lock warning light comes on for about 60 seconds when you turn the ignition on. If it doesn't, have the bulb replaced.

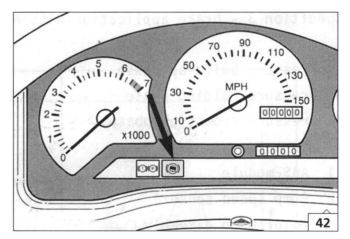

42

Every 3,000 Miles - Road Test

45A

45B

☐ Job 43. Clean controls.

The door handles, steering wheel, switches and gear lever knob may well have become greasy from handling while you were carrying out the service. Clean them with detergent.

☐ Job 44. Check instruments and controls.

Switch on the ignition while sitting in the driving seat and check that all the warning lights which should come on, do come on. Warning lights which do not work are useless as warnings! Non-functioning may be just a case of a blown bulb, but it may be a symptom of deeper electrical trouble. If changing a bulb does not cure the problem, or if the warning lights fail to go out when they should, seek **SPECIALIST SERVICE** from an auto electrician. Check that all the switches are secure and working.

☐ Job 45. Check throttle and choke action.

Operate the throttle pedal several times to check that it is smooth over its complete travel. A throttle pedal which is stiff or, worse still, which sticks, can be dangerous as well as making driving a misery.

45A. If your car has a manual choke control check the smoothness of operation of the choke knob.

45B. INSIDE INFORMATION: If either throttle or choke aren't as smooth as they should be, check the route of the cables to make sure there are no sharp bends or kinks and check that the inner cable isn't fraying where it comes out of the outer casing. Later throttle cables with a nylon inner sleeve are much smoother in operation than the older steel sleeve sort. Replacement cables are easily available. If the fault for a jerky or stiff throttle pedal or choke knob is not the cable, check the linkage at the carburettor for stiffness and lubricate if necessary.

☐ Job 46. Check clutch action.

46A. Operate the clutch pedal several times with the engine switched off. The action of the pedal should be smooth, once the initial take-up of the clutch mechanism occurs - this can be felt as a resistance to the pedal after the first inch or so of movement. Repeat the test with the engine running and listen for any whine or 'scrubbing' noise from the gearbox area when depressing the pedal, which can indicate a worn clutch release bearing, or possible problem with the clutch plate itself both of which require **SPECIALIST SERVICE** attention. (Illustration, courtesy Ford Motor Company Ltd)

If the pedal action feels jerky, 'dry' or heavy, first try lubricating the pivots and self-adjusting mechanism located at the top of the pedal with releasing fluid.

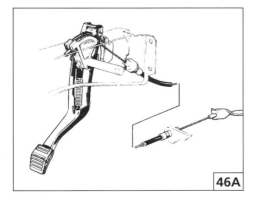
46A

46B

46B. After squirting releasing fluid into the clutch cable outer end, put on a good blob of grease, to discourage further water ingress. Work the clutch (cable) several times to encourage lubricant to travel along the cable.

If the fault persists then the clutch cable probably needs replacement - the usual cause is fraying of the inner 'stranded' cable causing it to bind in the outer sheath.

CHAPTER THREE

INSIDE INFORMATION: Replacing the clutch cable isn't a particularly difficult job in theory, but in practice the restricted working area in the upper reaches of the footwell, coupled with the need to use two hands (preferably three!) to manipulate the cable and automatic adjusting mechanism makes this an awkward and often frustrating job for the inexperienced! Don't forget - if you start the job but can't finish it, the car will be undriveable and could involve a costly tow-in charge to the nearest garage. Unless you are experienced or live next door to an understanding mechanic, seek SPECIALIST SERVICE for this item.

☐ Job 47. Road test of brakes and steering.

Only a proper brake tester at an MoT testing station can check the operation of the brakes accurately enough for the MoT test, but you can rule out some of the most obvious braking problems on a short road test in the following way. Always check the brakes at low speed first, before attempting to brake from higher speeds. Drive at about 20 mph, dip the clutch and, with your hands only lightly gripping the wheel, try braking first gently, then harder, though there is no need to do an 'emergency' stop. Ideally, the car should pull up in a perfectly straight line. If the steering wheel kicks in your fingers, if there are any 'clonks' or other noises from underneath, if the car drifts heavily to one side as you brake, or if the brake pedal does not feel firm in operation, drive home very slowly and carefully to investigate further.

If all seems well, repeat the braking tests from a higher speed, say about 40 mph. Again, the car should, ideally, pull up in a straight line. If it drifts just gently to the left when you are on the nearside of the road, this may be due to road camber. Try to repeat the test on a non-cambered stretch of road or find a one-way street where you can try on the other side of the road to see if opposite camber has the same effect.

Check that the steering feels positive, does not kick back unduly over rough surfaces and that the car runs in a straight line when you are holding the steering wheel only lightly. Again, slight drifting may be due to road camber, but more persistent drifting needs investigating. Check that the steering self-centres when accelerating out of both left and right hand turns and, if you can find a suitably deserted stretch of road, pull the car from side to side to see that it straightens itself up. This check can be carried out at quite low speed, 15 to 20 mph is sufficient to show up any faults.

Braking and steering are a vital part of a car's safety. If you find any faults, or even if you are uneasy about anything, seek **SPECIALIST SERVICE** before you carry on using the car.

Every 6,000 Miles or Every Six Months - whichever comes first

Every 6,000 Miles - The Engine Bay

First carry out the relevant jobs from the earlier service intervals.

☐ Job 48. Change engine oil.

48A. Probably the one service operation on which most DIY motorists will 'cut their teeth' is an engine oil change - and no matter how technically complex the engine, an oil change still remains basically a simple operation requiring a minimal amount of expertise and tools.

48A

making it easy! Apart from small differences in location of the oil filter and the sump drain plug, the procedure is the same for all models. Before draining the sump, run the engine (if cold) for around five minutes to warm the oil slightly, so that it will drain more freely - but not so hot that it will scald. Use an oil drainage container to catch the oil as it drains from the sump - note that the oil will fall in an arc away from the drain hole, so position the container to allow for this. Spread newspaper on the floor beneath the engine bay to protect it from oil spills and drips. An old 5-litre plastic oil container with the side cut out makes an ideal container in which to catch the oil.

48B. This is the location of the oil drain plug on the great majority of Fiesta engines, viewed from under the car. As we stated previously, the plug will often be tight and require some force to move initially, when it may suddenly 'give' and offer little or no resistance - be careful not to rap your knuckles! Rubber or plastic gloves can compromise your grip on the spanner, so it may be wise to leave them off for the initial 'tug', but remember to don them immediately the plug has been slackened and before removing the plug completely, as some oil will inevitably spill onto your hands.

48C. Once the plug has started to move in its thread it can be undone with the (gloved) fingers; remember to hold onto the plug when fully unscrewed. Be ready to reposition your bowl - the angle of 'spurt' changes as the oil flows out of the sump!

48D. Remember to replace the drain plug once the oil has FULLY drained, and use a new copper or nylon washer which you can buy from the accessory shop or garage where you bought your oil. Buy it at the same time, then you won't forget it.

If you also intend changing the oil filter at this stage, see *Job 49*.

48B

making it easy! It isn't necessary to use excessive force when re-fitting the sump plug. Simply grip the spanner so that the thumb rests on the spanner head, thereby limiting the amount of leverage that can be applied; use 'firm' pressure only. Before re-fitting the plug, wipe around the drain hole with a piece of clean cloth to remove any dirt, and check that the (new) sealing washer is fitted. Check for leaks after running the engine.

SAFETY FIRST!
DON'T pour the old oil down the drain - it's both illegal and irresponsible. Your local council waste disposal site will have special facilities for disposing of it safely. Moreover, don't mix anything else with it, as this will prevent it from being recycled.

OIL CARE FOLLOW THE CODE

Also, see page 4.

48C

☐ Job 49. Change oil filter.

49A. The oil filter is the familiar screw-on, throw-away thin metal cartridge type and is more easy to reach from underneath the car especially on later cars, whose engine bays are fuller - although you can do it from above, as shown here. The easiest way to remove this type of filter is with a strap or chain wrench similar to that shown, which you can buy from any accessory shop.

48D

49A

49B. One full turn of the filter using the wrench is usually enough to get it started, after which it can be unscrewed by hand. Note that some oil loss will occur, so position an oil tray or container under the engine to catch it. It's also a good idea to place a cloth round the filter when unscrewing it to prevent the oil dribbling over your (gloved!) hand and down your arm! Clean the filter sealing face on the engine with a clean rag. This shot is from beneath where access is definitely better for gripping the thing!

49C. Make sure the rubber sealing ring is properly fitted to the new filter, then apply a smear of clean engine oil to the ring to prevent it buckling as the filter is screwed home.

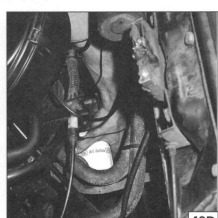

49D. Top-side again, on this older car, you can screw the new filter onto the threaded stub, taking care to avoid cross-threading. As you can see, access is easier from beneath. Essentially all filters are fitted by screwing on by hand only. When the sealing ring contacts the face on the engine, tighten it a further three-quarters of a turn and leave it - there's no need to tighten it any further as this will only distort the sealing ring and make it difficult to remove the filter next time.

49E. Lower the car to the ground and pour in fresh oil gradually so you do not get a sudden air lock in the valve cover which can make the oil spurt out over the top. Dip the level occasionally, allowing time for the oil to drain down into the sump. After filling, run the engine for a few minutes to allow the oil to circulate and to fill the filter. Switch off and dip the level again, finally topping up if necessary. Check underneath the car, especially in the areas of the sump plug and filter, making sure that there are no oil leaks.

☐ Job 50. Clean and check spark plugs.

PETROL ENGINES ONLY.

50A. Numbered spark plug leads (traditionally called 'HT' or 'High Tension' leads) are fitted from new on Fiestas, the numbers being printed into the leads themselves. Note that the numbering starts from the drive-belt end of the engine, or the right-hand side as you look from the rear of the car.

50B. INSIDE INFORMATION: If the lead numbers are illegible or non-original leads fitted, mark them with a spot of paint - typists' correction fluid is used by many mechanics as it is easy to apply and dries very quickly. Mark them from the radiator end of the engine in the sequence one, two, three and four 'dots'. (Correct identification of the plug leads is important because if incorrectly replaced, the engine will not run!).

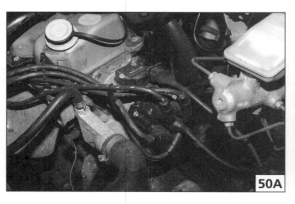

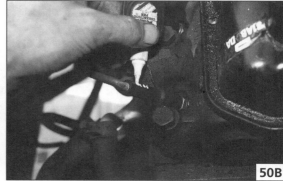

50C

50C. When this is done the plug caps can be pulled off. Be careful not to tug on the lead itself as you may pull it from the cap, which will remain on the plug!

50D. Using a suitable spark plug spanner or socket extension, unscrew the spark plugs. You'll need the extension with CVH engines, because they're more recessed. See *50E*. Each plug may be 'tight' to begin with so take care to keep the plug spanner or socket in line with the plug body, otherwise the porcelain insulator of the plug can break.

INSIDE INFORMATION: If you are trying to remove a plug which gets ever tighter as you turn it, there's every possibility that it is cross threaded. Once out, it probably won't go back in again. Tighten it up again and take the car to a Ford Dealer or specialist who may be able to clean up the threads with a purpose-made tool. If this can't be done, he will have to add a thread insert to your cylinder head. It pays to take great care when removing and fitting spark plugs, especially when dealing with aluminium cylinder heads as used on CVH engines!

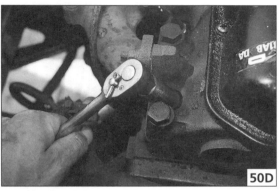

50D

50E. Clean the plug electrodes by vigorous use of a wire brush to remove any carbon deposits. If the electrodes of the plug look 'rounded' and worn (compare them to a new plug) they should be replaced.

50F. If using a flat feeler gauge select the 'blade' of the correct thickness (see *Chapter 8, Facts and Figures*) and slide it between the electrodes as shown. The gap between the two electrodes should provide a sliding fit, with no 'slack'. If necessary, adjust the gap using a pair of snipe-nosed (thin, pointed jaws) pliers, carefully bending the curved side-electrode towards or away from the tip of the centre electrode, until the feeler gauge fits the gap as described. Special gapping tools are available from accessory shops which make this easy and their use carries little risk of damaging the plug, which can occur if the electrode is clumsily moved by use of a screwdriver or pliers.

making it easy! Leave the spark plug in the socket spanner while using the wire brush - this is kinder on the fingers and lessens the risk of dropping the plug and breaking it.

Replace the plugs when the gaps are correct, adding just a slight smear of grease to the threads to make future removal easier. There is no need to screw the plugs down with great force - just tighten them firmly.

Before replacing the plug leads, clean them by use of a maintenance spray and a piece of rag or tissue. Also clean the exterior of the distributor cap (into which the plug leads fit) using the same method.

making it easy! 50G. To reduce the risk of putting in a plug cross-threaded - more likely and especially bad news on aluminium cylinder head CVH engines - screw each one in a few turns by hand. If the threads in the head seem 'sticky', have you local Ford Dealer clean them out with a spark plug thread chaser, or buy your own from your local accessory shop **use with care!**

50E

50F

50G

☐ **Job 51. Clean and check ignition components.**

INSIDE INFORMATION: From 1989 all petrol engined Fiestas have used a distributor-less ignition system (DIS) which combines the distributor and coil in one unit, positioned where the conventional distributor was formerly found.

Maintenance of these units is restricted to cleaning around the HT connectors and the HT leads themselves. DO NOT attempt to dismantle these systems.

OHV ENGINES ONLY

51A. On OHV engines, the Bosch distributor (Motorcraft up to 1983) is at the back of the engine and the cap lifts off after undoing the two spring clips - engine COLD! However, access can be difficult and prevent sufficient leverage to spring the clips off with your fingers, so you from gaining carefully use a broad-bladed screwdriver.

CVH (overhead camshaft) ENGINES WITHOUT COMBINED DISTRIBUTOR/COIL ONLY

51B. On CVH (overhead cam) engines the distributor is much more accessible, at the end of the camshaft housing. Before you can take the cap off you have to lift off this sprung-on metal cover.

51C. Then undo two spring clips or undo the screws and lift the distributor cap away. Clean the HT leads and check for signs of surface cracking, and loose connections where the lead fits on to the plug connector and into the distributor cap.

51D. Clean the distributor cap inside and out and check for any signs of 'tracking' - burnt lines where carbon has lodged in a faint crack to provide a short circuit for the HT current. Any signs of tracking means that the cap could let you down with poor starting and bad running as well as increasing your fuel consumption. Check also that the centre carbon brush (see pointer) still has plenty of length and that it is springy enough to bear on the centre of the

making it easy! If you have forgotten, until it is too late, to mark the HT leads and you have lost their order, don't despair. There's an easy way of finding it again. First put the rotor arm back on the distributor, but not the cap. Then get a helper to turn the engine over, clockwise looking at the pulley end, with a spanner on the pulley bolt while you put your thumb over the plug hole of No. 1 cylinder - the one nearest the pulley end of the engine. When you feel air pressure under your thumb indicating that the cylinder is on compression, stop and then ease the pulley nut round until the timing notch on the pulley is opposite the 0 (zero) mark on the timing cover. This is Top Dead Centre, very close to the firing point for No. 1 cylinder, and the rotor arm will be pointing to the stud in the distributor cap which takes the HT lead for No. 1 plug. Notice while the engine was being turned over that the rotor arm was going round anticlockwise. So, having found No. 1 HT lead you can find the others by going round the cap anticlockwise looking at the top, marking the leads in their firing order. REMEMBER that the firing order is NOT the same for OHV engines and overhead cam CVH engines. For OHV engines it is 1, 2, 4, 3. For CVH engines it is 1, 3, 4, 2.

rotor arm. Check the studs in the distributor cap for burning. Light burning can be cleaned up with fine glasspaper - better than emery paper because it does not leave any conducting dust behind.

51E. Check it out by pulling the pipe off the inlet manifold end - engine NOT running - and sucking quite hard on the pipe. As you let go, you should hear the base plate inside the distributor return back to its original position with a click. (It's spring loaded.) If you can suck freely with no resistance, or you don't hear a click

from the base plate, then either the diaphragm has failed completely or the mechanism inside the distributor has seized solid. A second-hand replacement can be a cheaper solution, but check the replacement carefully before buying it.

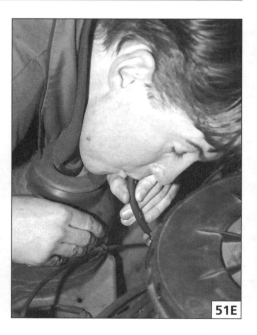

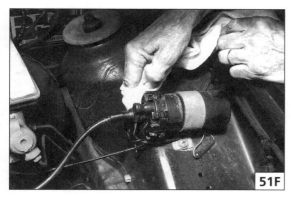

51F

Be warned that you can end up with a mouth full of petrol carrying out this check! Use a bicycle pump with the valve inside turned round so that it 'sucks' - but be careful not to pull too hard and cause damage.

51F. Clean the top of the coil tower and check for any signs of HT current tracking. Check that the HT lead, and the two low tension leads, are firm and secure. This is the position of the coil on cars with electronic ignition. For cars with contact breaker points, coil position is shown in *Job 51A(B)*.

OHV ENGINES WITH CONTACT BREAKERS ONLY

51G. Check that the rotor arm (shown here on the right) fits firmly and not loosely on the centre cam of the distributor and check the end of it for burning. Again, light burning can be cleaned up but severe burning of either the distributor cap studs or the rotor arm means renewal - not too expensive at all.

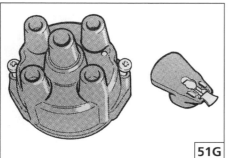

51G

51H. The inside of an electronic ignition distributor requires no adjustment, only a careful wipe over. Here, for reference, is the early Lucas electronic distributor. Lubricate as *52E* but *keep oil off all electrical components.*

INSIDE INFORMATION: If you have to renew either the HT leads or the distributor cap, renew the leads one at a time so you don't get them out of order. With a new cap, compare the position of the connection for number 1 cylinder with the old cap, using the depression where it locates on the body of the distributor as a reference point.

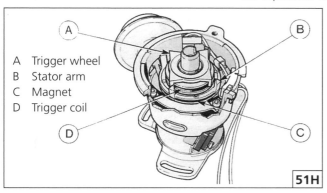

A   Trigger wheel
B   Stator arm
C   Magnet
D   Trigger coil

51H

CVH ENGINES, COMBINED DISTRIBUTOR/COIL

No servicing possible on these distributors.

☐ Job 52. Check/set CB points/dwell angle.

OHV ENGINES ONLY

52A. The distributor on OHV Fiestas is tucked away down the back of the engine where it is rather difficult to get at, but you can check the points gap and condition without removing it. See *Job 51* for details of location and removal of the distributor cap and rotor arm. A is the Motorcraft distributor with a black cap; B is the Bosch unit with a red cap. Either one may be fitted. (Illustration, courtesy Ford Motor Company Ltd)

IMPORTANT NOTE: Be sure to switch the ignition off before carrying out the following checks and adjustments.

52B. To check the points gap (A), turn the engine (via the road-wheel) until the heel of the moving point (B) is on one of the lobes of the centre cam (C). Insert a feeler gauge of the appropriate thickness between the points (see *Chapter 8, Facts and Figures*).

If you find it difficult to slide the feeler gauge between the points, because they appear burnt or pitted, the points require replacement as it will be difficult to obtain a satisfactory gap if their condition is poor: see *Job 53* for points renewal.

making it easy! *Checking and adjusting the points requires the engine to be turned slowly by hand - not a particularly easy proposition given the close proximity of the crankshaft pulley to the inner wing panel, which makes use of a spanner on the pulley bolt awkward. A far easier method is to apply the handbrake firmly, select second gear and support the right-hand (driver's side) wheel off the ground on an axle stand. Remove the spark plugs. Now, when the road wheel is turned by hand, the engine will also turn, because of the car's being in gear.*

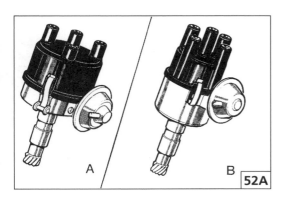

A   B   52A

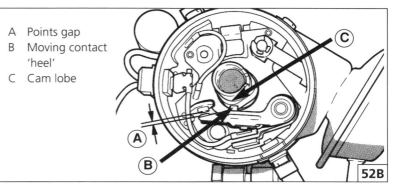

A   Points gap
B   Moving contact 'heel'
C   Cam lobe

52B

6,000 MILE SERVICE

52C. If the points are clean but need adjusting, first slacken the screw (B) holding the fixed point to the baseplate. A notch (C) is provided in the baseplate against which a screwdriver blade can be inserted and turned to increase or decrease the points gap. Adjust the fixed

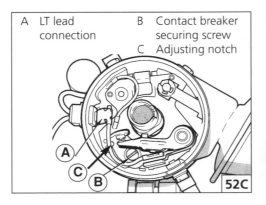

A   LT lead connection
B   Contact breaker securing screw
C   Adjusting notch

52C

52D

point and tighten the screw when the appropriate feeler gauge is a sliding fit between the points.

52D. The method as described will give you a points gap which is accurate enough for starting the engine but, to get the gap absolutely accurate, you need to use a dwell meter. This is a job that your dealer will do for you, or you can buy a dwell meter - DIY versions are not expensive - and learn to use it by following the instructions. They are reasonably simple to use.

52E. Before you replace the distributor cap, dribble a few drops of oil down the side of the baseplate to lubricate the mechanical advance and control mechanism. On engines which have been neglected, it does no harm to give a brief squirt of releasing fluid behind the baseplate first in case the advance and retard weights have become partially seized.

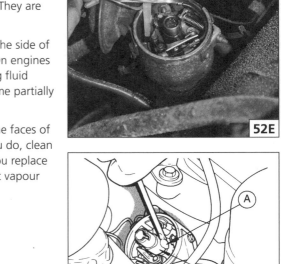

52E

52F. Finally, put just the smallest smear of high melting point grease (A) on the faces of the cam (B). Take care not get any oil or grease on the points faces but, if you do, clean it off with methylated spirit. Make sure all the spirit has evaporated before you replace the distributor cap. Even points in good condition spark slightly and any spirit vapour left in an enclosed space is a potential fire bomb.

☐ Job 53. Contact breaker points renewal.

NON-ELECTRONIC IGNITION ONLY

BOSCH DISTRIBUTORS (OHV ENGINES ONLY)

53. With the distributor cap and rotor arm removed (*Job 51*) pull the LT (low tension) lead connector (A) from its terminal, then undo and remove the points securing screw (B) and lift out the old points. Position the new set of points on the baseplate and replace the screw but do not tighten it fully; push the LT wire connector onto its terminal. Now refer to *Job 52* for details on setting the correct points gap.

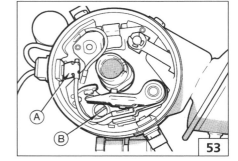

52F

INSIDE INFORMATION: On OHV engines be extra careful not to allow the screw to fall down into the distributor body, otherwise the distributor will have to be removed to retrieve it.

With both types of distributor, position a slip of paper moistened with methylated spirits between the closed points and work it to-and-fro a couple of times to remove any oil or other anti-corrosion substance placed there by the manufacturer.

53

☐ Job 54. Check ignition timing.

PETROL ENGINED MODELS UP TO 1988 ONLY

SAFETY FIRST!
THE ELECTRONIC IGNITION SYSTEM INVOLVES VERY HIGH VOLTAGES! All manufacturers recommend that only trained personnel should go near the high-tension circuit (coil, distributor and HT wiring) and it is ESSENTIAL that anyone wearing a medical pacemaker device does not go near the ignition system. Also, stroboscopic timing requires the engine to be running - take great care that parts of the timing lights or parts of you don't get caught up in the moving parts! Don't wear loose clothing or hair.

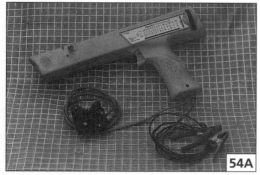

54A. INSIDE INFORMATION: To check or adjust the ignition timing with the required degree of accuracy calls for the use of a stroboscopic timing light, such as the Gunson's model shown here. Although a 'static' timing figure may be given in some workshop manuals, this is only a guide, mostly used to get an engine started after the distributor has been disturbed and the previous settings lost.

making it easy! 54B. After removing the spark plugs - ignition turned off - turn the engine by hand so that the timing mark or 'notch' on the rim of the crankshaft pulley can be seen. Highlight it, and the timing marks (B) on the timing cover, with a dab of white paint or typists' correction fluid. This ensures that the marks will be clearly visible when illuminated by the timing light.

INSIDE INFORMATION: Timing checks and adjustments are made with the vacuum pipe (the one that connects between the inlet manifold and distributor) disconnected at the distributor end and plugged with something suitable, such as a small Phillips-type screwdriver, or wooden 'bung'.

54C. These are the timing marks as found on the OHV engine. Note the notches on the fixed pointer are numbered 12, 8, 4, 0; these numbers relate to degrees of 'advance', that is, the point at which the spark occurs before the '0' mark - otherwise known as Top Dead Centre or TDC. Therefore, if the timing for a particular model were specified as 10 degrees before TDC (BTDC) then the pulley notch should appear between the 12 and 8 marks when illuminated by the brief flashes of the timing light.

54D. On CVH engines there are no numbers to distinguish the timing marks, but the '0' or TDC mark is made larger than the others, which in turn are arranged in 4 degree steps. (Illustrations, courtesy Ford Motor Company Ltd)

A. Timing notch on front pulley   B. Timing marks on front cover

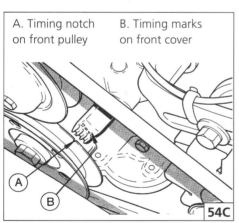

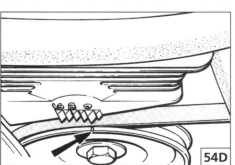

54E. Connect the timing light according to the maker's instructions, start the engine and let it tick-over at the correct idle speed (see **Chapter, 8 Facts & Figures**) and point the flashing beam of the light at the timing marks. The strobe effect of the flashing beam 'freezes' the moving mark on the pulley and should appear stationary, adjacent to the static mark on the engine if the timing is set correctly. If the mark appears at the wrong place, the distributor will have to be slackened and turned to bring the marks into alignment, as follows:

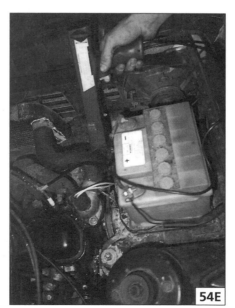

OHV ENGINES ONLY

54F. The distributor clamp bolt on OHV engines can be difficult to see, being located on the bottom of the distributor at the back of the engine. However, in all cases the bolt-head will be found pointing towards the engine oil dipstick tube - locate it by touch if necessary. Slacken the bolt just sufficiently to allow the distributor body to be turned by hand, but not loose enough as to be disturbed when the bolt is tightened. Turn the distributor clockwise to increase the amount of 'advance', or anticlockwise to retard it. Tighten the clamp bolt when the desired setting is reached. (Illustration, courtesy Ford Motor Company Ltd)

CVH ENGINES ONLY

54G. The distributor is retained by three bolts arranged at the base of the body - arrowed in the illustration. Slacken all three bolts but leave one with enough 'grip' to hold the distributor in position but enable it to move under firm pressure. Turning the distributor clockwise increases the amount of 'advance', while anticlockwise decreases it. Tighten the clamp bolts when the correct setting is achieved.

making it easy! (Or at least, a little easier!) Switch off the engine and slacken the distributor clamp bolt as shown in **54F** and **54G**, just enough to enable the distributor to move under firm pressure. Turn the distributor clockwise to 'retard' the timing, or anticlockwise to 'advance' it. For example, if the specified timing for your model is given as 10 degrees B.T.D.C but the timing light shows the 4 degree mark next to the pointer, the distributor will need to be rotated anticlockwise, to advance the timing by 6 degrees and bring the 10 deg. mark to align with the pointer. Note that only half the required movement (in degrees) is required at the distributor body, due to the gearing of its drive-chain.

DO NOT try to adjust the distributor with the engine running; make an adjustment, start the engine and check with the timing light if further movement is necessary. If so, stop the engine, adjust, and start it again. When the timing is correct, stop the engine and tighten the distributor clamp bolt, taking care not to alter the position of the distributor while doing so. Make a final check on the timing before disconnecting the timing light.

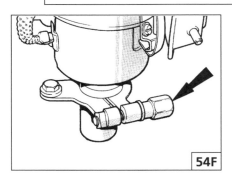

54F

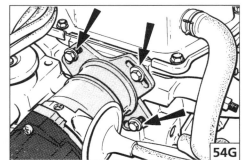

54G

In all cases, double-check the setting is correct after the clamp bolts have been tightened. If correct, disconnect the timing light, unplug and reconnect the vacuum tube to the distributor.

☐ Job 55. Check/lubricate wiper mechanism.

55. Wiper motors 'migrate' around the back of the engine bay on different models. This is the position on a later car. Lubricate each of the swivel joints - feel for them on both sides - with a blob of grease on each, or Releasing Fluid if they're stiff or noisy. On earlier cars, take off the bonnet lock plate (6 bolts).

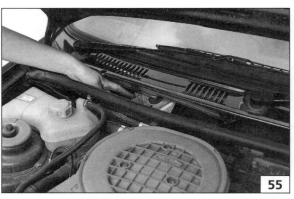

55

INSIDE INFORMATION: If the wipers don't make a full sweep, check that the motor mounting bolts are tight. If they are not tight, you will 'lose' some wiper movement.

☐ Job 56. Check battery electrolyte.

56A. The strength, or specific gravity, of a battery's electrolyte is the best indication of its state of charge. This is checked using a hydrometer, a simple instrument which you can buy cheaply at most accessory shops. Place the end of the hydrometer into each cell of the battery in turn, squeeze and release the rubber bulb so that a little of the acid is drawn up into the transparent tube. The float, or floats, inside the tube (small coloured beads are sometimes used) give the specific gravity and indicate the state of charge.

56A

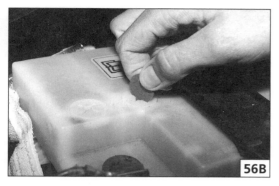

making it easy! 56B. Use a coin to undo cell caps, rather than a screwdriver. The slots are very wide, made of soft plastic and just chew up if you try to use an ordinary screwdriver.

56B

INSIDE INFORMATION: If a battery is flat because the car has been left standing for too long, use a small battery charger to recharge the battery, following the maker's instructions and disconnecting the battery on the car first. A battery that goes flat too rapidly in use may have one or more cells which are failing. The hydrometer will indicate this by giving a lower reading on the faulty cells after charging. If the hydrometer indicates that all the cells are in good condition, suspect a wiring fault allowing the current to drain away but do be aware that some car alarms will drain a battery in around a week. They are designed primarily for cars that are used almost every day, rather than those that may not be used so often.

making it easy! As the radiator picks up most of its debris from the air flowing in from the front, the best way to clear any which is inside the fins is to blow it out from the back. We don't recommend blasting the core with high pressure compressed air as this could damage it. However, if you have the type of vacuum cleaner that will blow as well as suck, put it on 'blow', fit the nozzle with the attachment having the smallest opening to give the fastest air flow and pass it over the back of the radiator. Don't actually touch the radiator with the nozzle as the fins are easily bent, just keep it an inch or so away. It's sometimes surprising how much muck this will blow out.

☐ Job 57. Clean radiator.

A radiator on which the airflow is partly blocked by dead flies and other rubbish cannot work efficiently. Almost all this rubbish collects on the front face of the radiator and it can be cleaned off using either a small paint brush or flushed through with a hose, but use a spray rather than a solid jet, as the fins of the radiator core are delicate and can be damaged by excessive pressure.

☐ Job 58. Check water pump.

OHV ENGINES ONLY

58A

58A. Some people will tell you that a water pump either works or it leaks, which is a generally accurate statement. However, leaks usually start in a small way and, if you spot one in time, it could well save you being stranded on the road with, at worst, a ruined, overheated engine. The water pump on Fiesta engines is rather tucked away, to the left of the alternator belt on OHV engines - but it pays to check it thoroughly for any signs of leaking. If you find signs of wetness, and you're sure it isn't dripping down from the top hose coupling, the water pump needs changing. It's **SPECIALIST SERVICE** time.

CVH ENGINES

58B

58B. The water pump is not visible on these engines without taking off the cam belt cover which is a relatively large amount of work for a simple check. However, why not combine it with *Job 59* and kill two birds with one stone. If you see a water leak, check the hoses first!

☐ Job 59. Check CVH camshaft belt.

59

59. Although it involves removing the cover (one-piece or two-piece, depending on model: remove the screws on both types), it's well worth going to the trouble of checking the timing belt for damage, cracking or fraying. A belt which breaks can cause terminal damage to your engine, so don't just ignore it! If the belt needs replacement, it's a **SPECIALIST SERVICE** job, if you're not an accomplished mechanic.

☐ Job 60. Check manual gearbox oil.

INSIDE INFORMATION: This check requires the car to be on level ground, otherwise the oil level will be inaccurate. As the level is more easily checked from beneath the car it will be necessary to raise both the front and rear of the vehicle on axle stands - see RAISING THE CAR at the beginning of this chapter for details of how to do this safely.

60A

60A. The gearbox combined level/filler plug is located on the forward-facing side of the gearbox. It can be reached from the engine bay, but it is generally easier to check the level and top up if necessary from underneath.

60B. The plug may either have a hexagon recess to take an Allen key, or be in the form of a bolt-head. Either type is usually very tight and you may need an Allen key adaptor and bit for your socket set for the former. If oil dribbles from the level/filler hole when the plug is removed, the level can be taken as being correct and the plug replaced.

60C. If necessary, top up the gearbox with oil of the appropriate grade, see *Chapter 8, Facts & Figures*. Gearbox oil can be bought in squeezable plastic container with a plastic spout which makes topping up relatively easy. The correct level is when oil just starts to run out of the filling hole. Remember to clean, replace and tighten the plug.

60B

☐ Job 61. Check automatic transmission fluid.

Two types of automatic transmission have been fitted to the Fiesta. The earlier 3-speed type is known as the ATX transmission and the later continuously variable transmission is the CTX type. Don't Ford just love those initials!

making it easy! On later cars, the automatic transmission dipstick handle is coloured BLACK to distinguish it from the engine oil dipstick, which is coloured YELLOW. See *FACT FILE: ENGINE BAY LAYOUTS* at the start of this chapter.

60C

ATX TYPE

Check the oil level only after a run when the gear oil has reached its normal operating temperature. With the engine still running, park the vehicle on level ground, apply the handbrake and the footbrake. Now move the gear selector lever through all its positions three times. Now move the selector lever to the Park ('P') position and wait for at least one minute.

61A. You can now get out of the car and, with the engine still running, pull out the dipstick, using a clean rag so that you don't get burnt. Wipe the dipstick clean, re-insert it and withdraw it again. The level must lie between the MIN and MAX marks.

INSIDE INFORMATION: If the gear oil is dark brown or black, this indicates a worn transmission unit. Seek SPECIALIST SERVICE advice.

CTX TYPE

61B. The process to be followed is exactly the same as that for the ATX type of transmission although the dipstick markings appear different, as shown.

SAFETY FIRST!
Auto. transmission fluid levels have to be checked with the engine hot and running. The car must be out of doors because of dangerous exhaust fumes. Make sure that hair, jewellery and loose clothing cannot become caught by moving parts, do not touch any part of the electrical system and take care not to be burnt by the hot engine.

☐ Job 62. Check steering column couplings.

The couplings in the Fiesta's steering column are not easy to check visually, but you can check them by trying the free play at the steering wheel. There will be a very small amount of free play because of backlash in the steering rack but, if you feel any real free

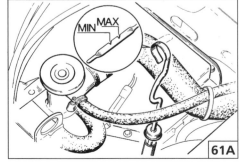
61A

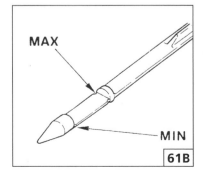
61B

63A

play with the steering wheel easy to joggle a few degrees either way, suspect that the couplings are worn. Have them checked by **SPECIALIST SERVICE**.

Job 63. Check/adjust valve clearances.

OHV PETROL ENGINES ONLY

This job does not apply to CVH engines because the overhead camshaft valve clearance are hydraulically operated and adjust automatically.

63A. Remove the air filter housing (undo the retaining screws and disconnect the breather hose clip). Then, remove the rocker cover (four screws around its periphery) and remove the spark plugs to make it easier to turn the engine.

Ford numbers the cylinders and valves from the crankshaft pulley end of the engine, that is the left hand end as you stand facing the front of the car.

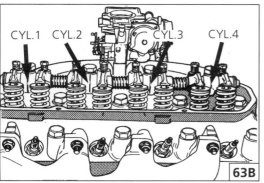

CYL.1 CYL.2 CYL.3 CYL.4

63B

NON-HCS OHV ENGINES UP TO 1989 ONLY

63B. The valves run alternately: exhaust, then inlet; so that valves numbers 1 and 2 are the exhaust and inlet respectively of cylinder No. 1; valves 3 and 4 are the exhaust and inlet of cylinder 2; valves 5 and 6 are the exhaust and inlet of cylinder 3 and valves 7 and 8 are the exhaust and inlet of cylinder 4. The exhaust and inlet valves have different clearances see *Chapter 8, Facts & Figures*. (Illustration, courtesy Ford Motor Company Ltd)

1.0 & 1.1 HCS OHV ENGINES FROM 1989 ONLY

The valves on these engines are arranged in a different order to the earlier OHV engine as follows: Starting from No 1 cylinder: Exhaust, inlet; exhaust, inlet; inlet, exhaust; inlet, exhaust. The rest of the procedure is the same as for the non-HCS (high-compression swirl) OHV engine shown below.

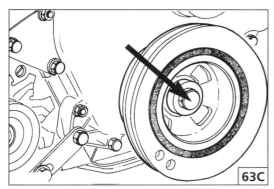

63C

63C. Adjusting the valve clearances is carried out with the engine cold. The valves are set in the sequence given below. But first, use a spanner on the crankshaft pulley bolt (arrowed) to turn the engine...

63D. ...until the notch on the pulley is opposite the 0 (zero) mark on the timing cover.

63E. At this point, the valves of No. 4 cylinder will be in the 'rocking' position. By this it is meant that the slightest rotation of the crankshaft pulley in either direction will start the rockers moving in opposite directions, one up and the other down, as indicated in our drawing. If the valves of No. 4 cylinder are not rocking with the timing notch opposite the 0 mark, turn the engine one full turn clockwise and check again. (Illustrations, courtesy Ford Motor Company Ltd)

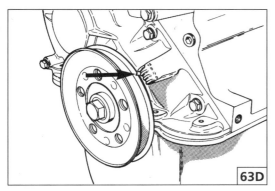

63D

63F. With the valves of No. 4 cylinder rocking, check and set the clearances on the valves of No. 1 cylinder. Then turn the crankshaft pulley half a turn clockwise to bring the valves of No. 3 cylinder rocking and adjust the clearances on the valves of No. 2 cylinder. Carry on in the following order, turning the pulley half a turn each time, until all the clearances have been checked and adjusted if necessary.

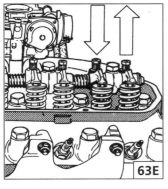

63E

63F

Cylinder No. 4 rocking - check clearances on cylinder No. 1
Cylinder No. 3 rocking - check clearances on cylinder No. 2
Cylinder No. 1 rocking - check clearances on cylinder No. 4
Cylinder No. 2 rocking - check clearances on cylinder No. 3

There are no lock nuts on the rocker adjusters. The adjusting screws are known as 'stiff thread' screws with the thread of the screw cut at a slightly different pitch from the thread in the rocker. Insert the appropriate feeler gauge between the end of the rocker and the top of the valve and turn the adjusting screw with a ring spanner until the feeler is a stiff sliding fit.

Replace the spark plugs, rocker cover and air cleaner housing. IMPORTANT NOTE: always fit a new gasket to the rocker cover, if it's of the paper type. Black neoprene ones re-seal perfectly well, provided that they're not damaged.

64A

☐ Job 64. Lubricate carburettor linkages.

NON-FUEL INJECTED ENGINES ONLY

64A. Dribble a few drops of oil on the external linkages of the carburettor throttle and choke and operate the linkages several times to let it work in.

ALL TYPES

64B. On both carburettor and fuel injection engines, lubricate the end of the throttle cable and the linkage and operate the throttle a few times to let it work in.

64B

64C. Grease cable ends where you can get at them...

64D. ... and any springs and cams within reach.

☐ Job 65. Adjust carburettor.

NOT FUEL INJECTION ENGINES

One of three carburettors may be fitted to the Fiesta engine, Ford's VV carburettor, the Weber/Ford 1V or the twin-choke Weber 2V.

64C

> **SAFETY FIRST!**
> *Carburettor adjustment has to be carried out with a warm, running engine. Therefore: i) Watch out for rotating cooling fan and belt and do not wear loose clothing or jewellery and tie back long hair. ii) Take care that you do not burn yourself on the hot engine parts and/or exhaust manifolds. iii) Always work out of doors. DO NOT perform this check in your garage or any confined space - exhaust gases are highly poisonous and can kill within minutes! iv) Apply a strict No Smoking! rule whenever you are servicing your fuel system. Remember, it's not just the petrol that's flammable, it's the fumes as well. Overall, if you're not (justifiably) confident, give the job to someone who is fully competent. Some manufacturers recommend that only trained mechanics should carry out work on a vehicle's fuel system. Read Chapter 1, Safety First!.*

64D

65A. With the Ford VV carburettor, the adjustments are on the side of the carb as you stand over the right-hand side wing. The idle speed adjustment is the long sloping rod (1 in our photo) and the mixture adjusting screw (2) is just below it, and should be covered by a 'tamperproof' plug - lever it out. The engine must be at normal operating temperature and the air filter must be in position, though it is removed in our drawing for clarity.

65B. Adjust the idle screw until the engine is running at its idle speed see *Chapter 8, Facts & Figures*. Setting this accurately requires an rpm meter but, if you do not have one, set the engine to run at the slowest speed at which it is comfortable without stalling. Rev the engine to approximately 3,000 rpm for half a minute to clear and stabilise the carburettor and check the idle speed again. The mixture should not need adjusting at this service but, if you cannot

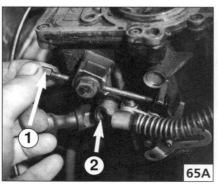
65A

65B

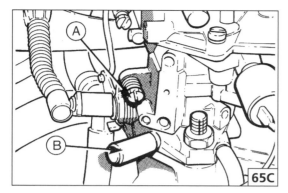

65C

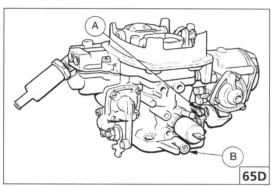

65D

67

68

get the engine to idle smoothly, the mixture may be inaccurate. See *Job 68*.

65C. On the Weber/Ford 1V carburettor, the idle speed screw (A in our drawing) and mixture screw (B in our drawing) are at the back of the carburettor, but face the right-hand side of the car. Follow the same procedure as with the Ford VV carburettor.

65D. On the twin-choke Weber 2V the adjusting screws for idle speed and mixture face the rear of the car. Follow the procedure as with the Ford VV carburettor. (Illustrations, courtesy Ford Motor Company Ltd)

☐ Job 66. Check petrol injection idle speed.

MODELS WITH FUEL INJECTION ONLY

INSIDE INFORMATION: It is seldom necessary to adjust the idle speed on fuel injection systems and on models from 1989 no adjustment is provided for. 'Tinkering' with the idle setting will also affect the mixture and it is very easy for the inexperienced to quickly put a car 'out of tune' simply by altering the idle speed setting. If the idle speed appears too high or low, have the car checked as a SPECIALIST SERVICE job.

☐ Job 67. Check diesel idle speed.

DIESEL ENGINES ONLY

67. On diesel engines, the idle adjustment is on the fuel injection pump at the front of the engine, labelled A in our photograph. IMPORTANT NOTE: The screw labelled B is the maximum engine speed governor and MUST NOT BE ALTERED. Loosen the lock nut and turn the screw until the correct idle speed is obtained see *Chapter 8, Facts & Figures*. Tighten the lock nut without disturbing the position of the screw.

> **SAFETY FIRST!**
> **Carbon monoxide is extremely poisonous and can kill within minutes - even when a catalytic converter is fitted. ALWAYS carry out emission testing in the open - NEVER in your garage or other confined space.**

☐ Job 68. Check exhaust emission.

68. Since the introduction of relatively inexpensive test meters for exhaust emissions, such as the Gunson one shown here, mixture testing and adjustment has become feasible for home mechanics. Follow the instructions with the meter, remembering to rev the engine between each adjustment of the mixture screw to stabilise the carburettor. IMPORTANT NOTE: On the Bosch K-Jetronic fuel injection system used on Fiestas, the mixture adjustment screw is an Allen-headed screw under a tamper-proof plug on the right hand side of the fuel distribution unit. However, as it is very easy to damage the fuel distribution unit by heavy-handed adjustment of this screw, we recommend that you check the exhaust emission and, if the mixture needs adjusting, leave it to **SPECIALIST SERVICE**.

These home meters are NOT suitable for checking diesel exhaust emissions. With a diesel, allow the engine to idle for a few moments and then rev it and hold it at moderately high revs. There may be a puff of black smoke as you first raise the revs but this should clear. If black smoke persists, the injectors may need cleaning. Seek **SPECIALIST SERVICE**.

making it easy! Generally, the newer the car the more accurately this can be set, but with older cars it may be necessary to allow an increase in the CO setting to ensure the engine runs smoothly in use. Some trial and error may be necessary to balance the lowest desirable CO content with smooth running. See **Chapter 7, Getting Through the MoT**, for the maximum allowable CO readings.

Every 6,000 Miles - Around the Car

First carry out the relevant jobs from the earlier service intervals.

☐ Job 69. Check seat belts and mountings.

69. Examine the seat belts for chafing and tug hard at them to check their fixings to the body. With inertia reel seat belts, check the inertia lock by giving the belt a sharp tug. Fit each seat belt catch into its socket and check that it holds properly and frees easily when the catch is pressed. NEVER try to repair a seat belt or its catch, and do not mix catches and sockets from different belts. If you find anything faulty, replace the whole belt and socket.

☐ Job 70. Check fuel filler seal.

70. Check the sealing rubber on the fuel filler cap to make sure it is not damaged or badly worn. A worn seal here is an MoT failure.

☐ Job 71. Lubricate locks, check straps and hinges.

NOT HIGH SECURITY LOCKS

71A. Apply grease or an aerosol spray lubricant to the jaws of the lock catches in the edges of the doors, and open and close the doors a few times to distribute it. Wipe off the surplus to avoid soiling your clothes.

71B. Oil the hinges of the check straps at each door.

Also, apply a few drops of oil to the hinge pins of the doors and tailgate or boot lid as appropriate.

71C. Apply a small amount of oil to the keyholes of the door and tailgate locks unless they are high security locks. THESE SHOULD NOT BE OILED.

☐ Job 72. Lubricate bonnet release.

72A. Apply grease liberally to the jaws of the bonnet release and open and close the bonnet a few times to distribute it. Wipe off the surplus - especially important on front-opening bonnets, where you will lean against it.

72B. This is where the bonnet release is situated on rear-opening Fiesta bonnets. On all models, you should also lubricate the

release cable, putting a blob of grease over the end of the cable where the 'inner' enters the 'outer' to discourage water ingress.

74

☐ Job 73. Check seat mountings.

Check the seats for security by trying to rock them and check the seat adjustment mechanism. Grease the runners lightly and wipe off any surplus to avoid soiling clothes. Check, if applicable, that the folding seat backs lock securely in the upright position and that the release catches work smoothly.

☐ Job 74. Check shock absorber action.

74. Press down on each corner of the car in turn and release your weight. The suspension should 'bounce' back once or twice at the most. If it is easy to compress the springs, and the car 'bounces' several times when you release your weight, the shock absorbers may need renewing. Seek SPECIALIST SERVICE advice.

☐ Job 75. Check/renew front brake pads.

75A

SAFETY FIRST!
i) Raise the front of the car off the ground once again, after reading carefully the information at the start of this chapter on lifting and supporting the car. ii) Obviously, your car's brakes are among its most important safety related items. Do NOT dismantle or attempt to perform any work on the braking system unless you are fully competent to do so. If you have not been trained in this work, but wish to carry it out, we strongly recommend that you have a garage or qualified mechanic check your work before using the car on the road. See also the section on BRAKES AND ASBESTOS in Chapter 1, Safety First! for further information. iii) Always start by washing the brakes with a proprietary brand of brake cleaner - brake drums removed where appropriate - never use compressed air to clean off brake dust. iv) Always replace the brake pads and/or shoes in sets of four never replace the pads/shoes on one wheel only. v) After fitting new brake shoes or pads, avoid heavy braking - except in an emergency - for the first 150 to 200 miles (250 to 300 km).

75A. You can check the pad thickness without removing the caliper. The maker's recommended minimum thickness for the friction material is 1.5mm (0.06in) but you may want to renew earlier than this because you won't be looking at the pads again for another 6,000 miles. It is normal for one pad to wear slightly more than the other but, if it appears that only one pad is doing the work and the other has hardly worn at all, it is a sign that the caliper is sticking. This means **SPECIALIST SERVICE**. Have the calipers checked by a garage. Here, a brand new pad is held alongside, so you can see what the thickness of an unworn pad looks like.

REPLACING FRONT DISC PADS

ALL MODELS UP TO 1989, EXCEPT XR2.

75B. This is an exploded view of the caliper type fitted to Fiestas up to 1989.

75C. After removing the road wheel, pull out the key-retaining split-pins (P) from each of the two keys (O); apply inwards pressure to the caliper and slide out the keys, as in the drawing.

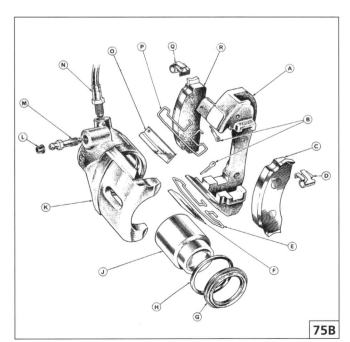

75B

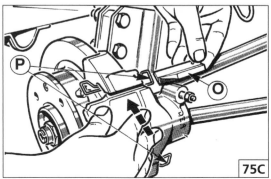

75C

75D. The caliper can now be lifted away from the pad housing (75B.A), leaving the pads behind - gently lever sideways to free them, taking care not to lose the anti-rattle springs (75B.Q) & (75B.D) from the top and bottom edges of the pads as they will be needed for the new pads.

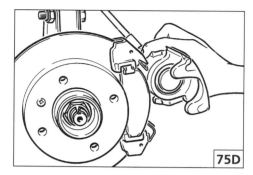

75D

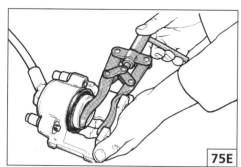

75E

75E. The piston has to be retracted into its housing so that it will pass over the increased width of the new pads; a special Ford tool is specified for this job (see drawing) but the job can be done using a woodworkers G-cramp, or a large pair of grips. IMPORTANT NOTE: See **75W** before doing so.

75F. Note how the anti-rattle clips fit onto the old pads, then transfer them to the new ones - our sketch will help you position them.

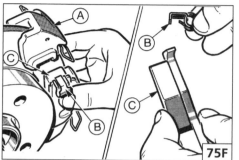

75F

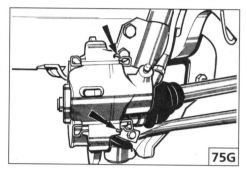

75G

75G. Fit the new pads into the housing, followed by the caliper. Replace the keys (75B.O) and fit new retaining pins (75B.B).

IMPORTANT NOTE: Remember to work the brake pedal several times, after the car has been lowered to the ground, to force the pistons to take up the space between themselves and the pads.

'TEVES' CALIPER - FROM 1989 AND ALL XR2 MODELS

75H. This exploded diagram shows the layout of the 'Teves'-type caliper. Note, on some late models the flat spring (C) has been replaced by a round-wire version. (Illustrations, courtesy Ford Motor Company Ltd)

75I. INSIDE INFORMATION: *You will need some form of 'tool' to retract the caliper piston into its bore. The latter can be improvised using a woodworking G-cramp or valve spring compressor tool and one of the old brake pads.*

ALWAYS replace disc pads in sets of four across the car: that is, both front wheels or both rear wheels at the same time. Failure to do this may well result in unequal and dangerous braking.

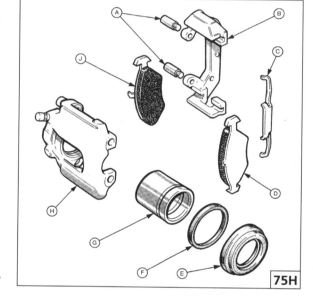

75H

75J. First disconnect the brake wear indicator wiring, if fitted to your car, by pulling the connector (A) apart. The caliper is retained by two hollow bolts (B) for which an Allen key is required, either of the socket-adapter type shown at (C) or...

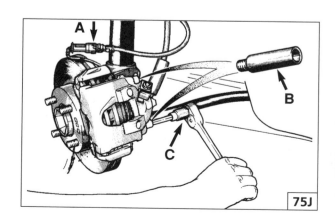

75J

75I

75K. ...you could use the type referred to earlier, as shown here and available from your local accessory shop. IMPORTANT NOTE: later models have plastic caps fitted to the bolt dust-excluding tubes which surround the bolts - remove them first. The bolts themselves are likely to be very stiff to turn initially, but take care as they often release quite suddenly, 'skinning' the knuckles of the unwary!

75L. Remove both bolts completely, but don't remove the caliper until...

75M. ...the caliper assembly has been doused with brake cleaner to prevent brake dust being disturbed into the atmosphere - or your lungs!

75N. If a wear-ridge is present on the outer edge of the disc you may find it necessary to lever the caliper carefully against the disc to retract the piston slightly; use a screwdriver as shown, or refer to *75S* if a large pair of grips are available. Note that you must never lever vigorously against the disk because of the risk of damaging it.

75O. The caliper assembly can now be pulled forwards over the disc. Note that the outer pad may remain with the carrier bracket and require a sharp tap or two from a hammer to free it.

75P. The inner pad has a three-legged spring retaining it to the hollow piston - the pad usually comes away easily, but might need a tap from a hammer to free it if corroded.

75Q. Spray brake cleaner over the carrier bracket, paying particular attention to the pad seatings and those areas not accessible when the pads are fitted.

75R. Wire brush the pad seatings on the bracket, removing any hard scale or rust by scraping with an old screwdriver or chisel.

75S. Retracting the piston is necessary before fitting new pads; this can be done earlier in the sequence when the caliper is still attached to the carrier as shown here, or at this stage, before cleaning. See *MAKING IT EASY!* panel on page 61, *Job 75W*, regarding fluid level in the master cylinder reservoir.

SAFETY FIRST!
75T. NEVER allow the caliper to hang by the flexible brake hose: Unseen damage can occur to the hose that may not materialise until later, possibly when the brakes are needed in an emergency. Improvise a simple 'hook' from stout wire and suspend the caliper from the shock absorber/spring seat.

75U. Check the piston dust-excluder seal for splits, chafing or perishing. If any sign of brake fluid is present a leak is indicated, and you should have the affected caliper inspected by a qualified specialist or Ford dealer, or fit an exchange overhauled replacement, from your local auto. parts store.

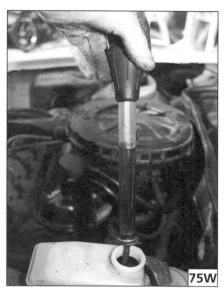

75V. Re-assemble the new pads to their seats, fit the caliper and bolts, replace the pad retaining spring (if fitted) and reconnect the wear indicator wiring. Do not over-tighten the caliper bolts - firm hand pressure is sufficient.

*INSIDE INFORMATION: Put a **very thin** smear of special brake grease (NOT ordinary grease) on the steel backs of the brake pads to reduce the risk of noisy brakes. KEEP GREASE OFF ALL FRICTION SURFACES!*

IMPORTANT NOTE: See the relevant sections above for details of cleaning and lubrication.

---

making it easy! *75W. As the piston is forced into its bore, the brake fluid it displaces will cause the master cylinder reservoir level to rise, possibly to the point of overflowing. Raise the bonnet so that the master cylinder can be observed as the piston is pushed home - it may be necessary to syphon a small quantity of fluid from the reservoir, for which purpose an old battery hydrometer is particularly useful to 'suck' fluid from the reservoir.*

SAFETY FIRST!
If you are in any doubt as to the condition of the disc or discs, seek professional advice. Corroded or pitted areas of the disc's working surface indicates a possible problem with the caliper, which may be partially seized. Additionally, deep scoring causes the pad friction material to contact only onto the 'peaks' of the ridges, thereby drastically reducing the area of contact and subsequent braking efficiency. New discs are not too expensive - shop around!

ALL MODELS

SPECIALIST SERVICE: Consult your Ford dealer and have them examine the disc and measure it with a micrometer if deep scoring is evident. Badly scored or ridged discs will seriously reduce braking efficiency even with fully bedded-in pads. New pads would take forever to bed-in on them and meanwhile braking efficiency could be virtually nil!

After you have replaced the caliper with its new pads, pump the brake pedal several times to centralise the caliper and check that the pedal feels firm. If it does not, you may have introduced air into the system, so seek **SPECIALIST SERVICE** before using the car on the road.

SAFETY FIRST!
*i) Raise the front of the car off the ground once again, after reading carefully the information at the start of this chapter on lifting and supporting the car. ii) Obviously, your car's brakes are among its most important safety related items. Do NOT dismantle or attempt to perform any work on the braking system unless you are fully competent to do so. If you have not been trained in this work, but wish to carry it out, we strongly recommend that you have a garage or qualified mechanic check your work before using the car on the road. See also the section on BRAKES AND ASBESTOS in **Chapter 1, Safety First!** for further information. iii) Always start by washing the brakes with a proprietary brand of brake cleaner - brake drums removed where appropriate - never use compressed air to clean off brake dust. iv) Always replace the brake pads and/or shoes in sets of four never replace the pads/shoes on one wheel only. v) After fitting new brake shoes or pads, avoid heavy braking - except in an emergency - for the first 150 to 200 miles (250 to 300 km).*

☐ Job 76. Check/renew rear brake shoes.

The design of Fiesta rear brakes has differed little over the period of production, other than moving the wheel cylinder from the bottom of the backplate to the top for models from 1983, and other minor changes in 1989 which necessitated a different method of drum/hub removal. This latter procedure isn't recommended to inexperienced mechanics and to those and we recommend it be regarded as a **SPECIALIST SERVICE**.

76A. This is an exploded view of the rear drum/hub assembly.

In preparing to remove the drum, just slightly slacken the roadwheel bolts and release the handbrake fully. Lever off the outer grease-cup (L) with a screwdriver, working around the cap and gradually easing it from its seat.

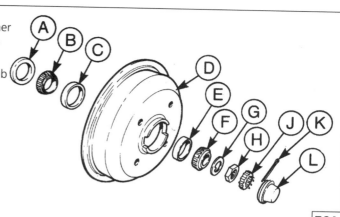

A. Grease retainer
B. Bearing cone
C. Inner cup
D. Drum and hub
E. Outer cup
F. Bearing cone
G. Tab washer
H. Locknut
J. Nut retainer
K. Split pin
L. Grease cup

76A

76B. Take out the split pin (*76A.K*) holding the hub nut locking plate, remove the plate (*76A.J*) and undo the nut, removing the washer with internal splines (*76A.G*). Fish out the outer bearing (*76A.F*) with a small screwdriver. Pull the hub away by pulling on the road wheel.

If the drum refuses to come off over the linings, you may have to slacken the handbrake adjustment fully off to free it (see *Job 30*). If, even after slackening the handbrake cable, the drum still catches on the linings, it is probably because the inside of the drum has worn and this, together with a coating of rust, has left a lip on the edge. Rock it free.

IMPORTANT NOTE: If, when you remove the outer bearing, you find it is a nylon caged one, TAKE GREAT CARE. The cages are very easily damaged, particularly if you have to rock the hub over the linings. Examine the bearing before pulling the hub. If it's a nylon caged bearing, replace the bearing, washer and nut temporarily, and remove the wheel so that you are only pulling on the hub itself.

76B

making it easy! If the bearing has a metal cage around the taper rollers, it is safe to replace the wheel and use it to help lift the drum over the linings. If the linings catch the drum, try rocking the wheel from top to bottom (where there are no linings on the shoes) rather than from side to side where the linings are catching the drum edge. However, towards the end of 1994, Ford changed from metal-caged taper roller bearings to nylon-caged bearings.

76C. INSIDE INFORMATION: For later cars, Ford changed the design of the integral rear hubs and drums, and recommend that the hub bearings are not disturbed. Instead, they suggest you undo four bolts at the rear of the brake backplate (see illustration) and lift off the drum and hub complete with the stub axle. However, many fitters in Ford dealerships find difficulty in lining up the bolt holes when they come to replace the stub axle, the only way to do it being to feed the stub axle over long guide rods pushed through the holes in the backplate. For this reason, many find it easier to remove the hub and leave the stub axle attached, as with earlier cars. (Illustration, courtesy Ford Motor Company Ltd)

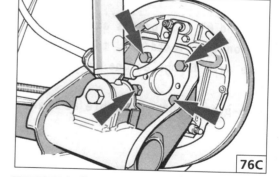

76C

CHECK LINING THICKNESS

76D. With the drum off, inspect the linings for wear. The leading shoe lining will be more worn than on the trailing shoe, but never replace just one shoe nor, indeed, the shoes on only one side of the car. Always renew the shoes both sides as a set of four. The minimum thickness given by Ford is 1mm (0.04in) but you may want to renew the shoes before this limit. Remember that you will not be inspecting them again for another 6,000 miles.

76D

76E. Ease back the rubber boots at the ends of the wheel cylinder to check for fluid leaks. It is not unusual to find very slight moistness but, if the boot has fluid in it, or fluid is leaking from it, the wheel cylinder needs replacing. You can do this yourself, bleeding the brakes with the help of a workshop manual, but you may prefer to seek **SPECIALIST SERVICE**. If you decide to go ahead yourself, note that there were three sizes of wheel cylinder fitted to Fiestas. These are identified by letters T, L or H stamped on the rear face. IT IS VITAL TO REPLACE A WHEEL CYLINDER WITH ONE HAVING THE SAME LETTER STAMPED ON IT.

76F. INSIDE INFORMATION: If the linings are fit for further use, and there are no leaks, lever the shoes from side to side to check that both pistons in the wheel cylinder are free. If the shoes do not move, jerk, or feel very tight, the pistons in the wheel cylinder may be seized or partly seized and the cylinder should be replaced.

76G. Lever the handbrake cable upwards with a screwdriver to check that the handbrake lever is free to pivot. It pivots about the rivet indicated. If it is seized, the shoe will have to be removed to free it.

making it easy! Before dismantling brake shoes, but after the drum has been removed, make a careful record of where everything goes, especially brake shoe return springs. Make a careful sketch, take a couple of photographs (a Polaroid would be ideal) or 'video' the assembly - it could turn out to be a life saver - literally! Also, only work on one side at a time, so that you've always got the other one to refer to. If applicable, refer to the illustrations here.

BRAKE SHOE REMOVAL - ALL TYPES

76H. To remove the shoes, first undo the 'hold-down' retaining washers and springs (arrowed).

76I. These washers are a bayonet fit over pins coming from the backplate. Push and turn them with a pair of pliers to remove them. Be careful not to lose the springs and the pins, which are loose in the backplate.

76J. Pull the shoe without the handbrake lever away from the wheel cylinder and unhook the pull-off springs. Then remove the shoe with the handbrake lever, lift it away from the backplate and unfasten the handbrake cable. IMPORTANT NOTE: Twist a piece of soft wire round the ends of the wheel cylinder, or use a stout rubber band, to make sure that the pistons do not fall out while the shoes are off. If they do, you may have to bleed the brakes, possibly a **SPECIALIST SERVICE** job, or follow your workshop manual.

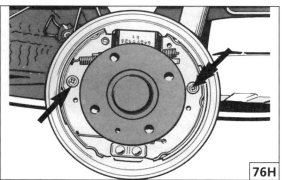

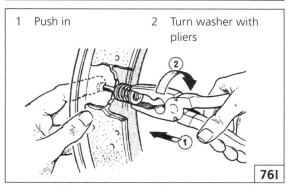

1   Push in   2   Turn washer with pliers

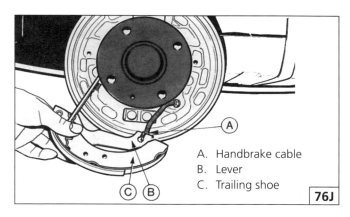

A. Handbrake cable
B. Lever
C. Trailing shoe

76K. There is a strut between the shoes at the top which carries the automatic shoe adjuster - remove it by twisting sideways towards the spring.

76L. Make sure the snail cam (arrowed) is not seized. If it is, free it with easing fluid before replacing the strut.

When buying new shoes, take the old ones with you, or quote the car's VIN number, to make certain you get the right type. If any of the pull-off springs are stretched, renew them at the same time.

Fit the new shoes in the reverse order of taking off the old ones, and centralise them before you re-fit the drum.

Replace the washer and do the nut up tight while you turn the hub to settle the bearings. Then back the nut off until you can just rock the washer slightly with a screwdriver. This gives the taper roller bearings their necessary clearance. Fit the locking washer and fit a new split pin.

If you had to slacken the handbrake cable to get the hubs off, remember to re-adjust it, see *Job 30*).

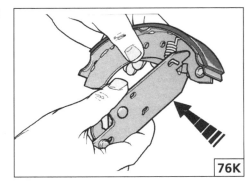

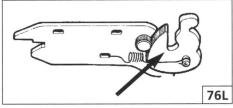

BRAKE PROPORTIONING VALVE
All models have a brake proportioning valve, adjusting brake balance front-to-rear to compensate for loads. On Vans in particular, it is essential that this valve is set correctly, - a **SPECIALIST SERVICE** job.

Every 12,000 Miles, or Every Twelve Months - whichever comes first

Every 12,000 Miles - The Engine Bay

First carry out the relevant jobs from the earlier service intervals.

☐ Job 77. Change air filter element.

77A. On carburettor engined cars, remove the top of the air filter housing, (two, three or five screws, depending on model) and unclip the upper 'lid'.

77B. Lift out the element and replace it with a new one.

77C. The illustration shows the three main types of filter housing.

77D. On fuel injected petrol and diesel engined cars the air filter element is larger and is inside a box at the end of the air inlet trunking.

☐ Job 78. Clean air filter housing.

When you lift out the old air filter element you may find dirt and dust inside the housing bowl. Wipe it clean before fitting the new element. It is normal to find a slight oil mist inside the bowl but, if there is a lot of oil, investigate the valves and filters in the breathing system, see Jobs *82* and *83*).

INSIDE INFORMATION: Fiesta engines with carburettors have a coarse plastic foam filter in the duct leading from the air cleaner housing to the crankcase. It doesn't usually get changed, even though it costs next to nothing! Prise it out with a screwdriver and renew it.

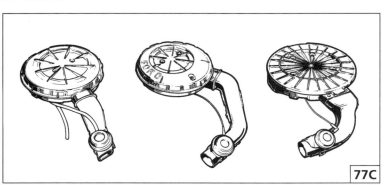

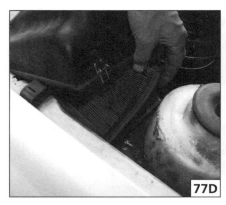

CHAPTER 5 - RUSTPROOFING

When mechanical components deteriorate, they can cost you a lot of money to replace. But when your car's bodywork deteriorates, it can cost you the car, if corrosion goes beyond the point where repairs are economical to carry out. Rust prevention should be regarded as a regular maintenance job, one which enables you to extend the life of your car by many years - and that will save you *real* money!

If you want to prolong its life, you'll have to inject rustproofing fluid into all the enclosed box sections and 'chassis' sections on your car. In many cases, you'll find holes already in place; in others, you'll be able to take off a cover, a piece or trim or a door lock in order to gain access. But in quite a few cases, you'll need to drill holes to gain an entry.

Don't be a drip!

*INSIDE INFORMATION: i) Place **lots** of newspaper beneath the car to catch the inevitable drips. ii) Some seat belts retract into a cavity that you will want to spray with fluid. Pull each belt out and hold it there until you have finished spraying the fluid. iii) All electric motors should be covered up with plastic bags so that none of the rustproofing fluid gets in and all windows should be fully wound up. iv) Ensure that all drain channels are clear so that any excess rustproofing fluid can drain out and also check once again that they are clear after you have finished carrying out the work to ensure that your application of the fluid has not caused them to be clogged up, otherwise water will become trapped, negating much of the good work you have carried out.*

making it easy! Decide on your drill size with reference to the size of the injector nozzle and the size of grommets that you can obtain for blanking the holes off again afterwards. You'll feel a bit foolish if you drill first, only to find that they don't make grommets to fit the holes you've drilled!

Choose Your Weapon

Those hand pump injectors that you can buy from DIY shops are often worse than useless. They don't usually make a proper spray, but simply squirt a jet of fluid that does nothing to give the all-over cover required. Make a dummy 'box section' out of a cardboard box - cut it and fold to make it about 10 or 15 cm square - and try a dummy run. Open up and see if it has worked. If you haven't obtained full misting of the fluid, you could be making the problem worse.

INSIDE INFORMATION: Rust strikes even harder in those areas that aren't properly covered!

Consider taking your car to a garage with suitable equipment and having them do the work for you. Full, professional injection equipment, as shown in the following picture sequence, will make the fluid reach much further and deeper than amateur equipment, and if you enlist the services of the best experts as featured here, you'll be able to benefit from their experience.

SAFETY FIRST!
*Before using rustproofer, read the manufacturer's safety notes. Keep rustproofing fluid off the exhaust or any other components where it could be ignited. Keep it away from brake components, covering them up with plastic bags before starting work. Follow **Chapter 1, Safety First!**, and advice at the start of **Chapter 3, Servicing Your Car** especially with regard to safe working beneath a car raised off the ground. Rustproofers all contain solvents. In a confined space, such as a garage, solvents can build up, creating both a health and a fire hazard. Wear an efficient face mask so that you don't inhale vapour and work out of doors, keeping out of confined spaces. Wear gloves and goggles, but if you do get any fluid in your eyes, wash out with copious amounts of water and immediately seek medical advice if necessary. If any welding has to be carried out on the vehicle within a few months of rustproofing being carried out, you must inform those who are carrying out the work because of the fire risk.*

Our thanks are due to Dinol Ltd. for carrying out the work shown here, using Dinitrol rustproofing fluid.

☐ Job 1. Clean underbody.

You will have to hose off the underside of the body, paying particular attention to the undersides of the wings and wheel arches, before you can start to apply new rustproofing. Scrape off any hard, thick deposits of mud, and any old flaking body sealant under the car. One of the quickest ways to do the job is to use a power washer with a long lance. Many garages have this equipment for customer use in a wash bay and this is a very efficient way of doing the job. You will, however, still have to go underneath with a scraper afterwards as even a power jet won't take off flaking body sealant. You will also have to wait up to a week for the underside of the car to dry thoroughly (in warm, dry weather) before applying new rustproofing.

☐ Job 2. Equipment.

2. Gather together all the materials you need to do the job before you start. You will also need lifting equipment and axle stands.

> *making it easy!* A compressor-driven gun of this type won't break the bank - try your local motor trade parts factors - but you'll need to buy or hire a compressor. Results will be perfect.

Bear in mind the safety equipment you will need - referred to in *Safety First!* - see *page 81*. You will need copious amounts of newspaper to spread on the floor because quite a lot of rustproofing fluid will run out of the box sections and other areas under the car and you may have to park your car over newspaper for a couple of days after carrying out this treatment. Remember that the vapour given off by the materials will continue for several days, so park your car in the open for a week or so if you can, rather than in an enclosed garage.

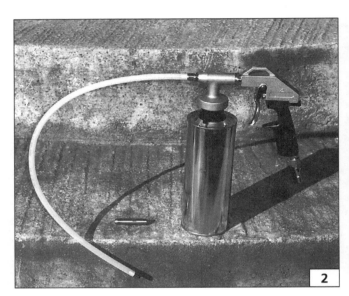

Around the Car

☐ Job 3. Chrome trim and seams.

Some rustproofing fluids in aerosol cans are thin enough for injecting behind chromium trim strips and badges but some people find that they are inclined to leave a stain on the paintwork around the trim. As an alternative to a rustproofing fluid, you could use a water dispersant or a thin oil.

☐ Job 4. Front suspension strut towers.

4. Spray rustproofing fluid from both above and below into this particularly vulnerable area.

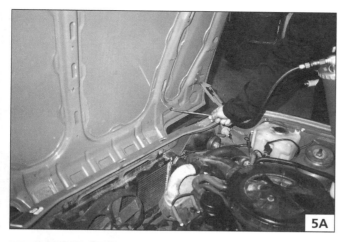

5A

☐ Job 5. Bonnet pressing.

5A. Apply rustproofing fluid generously inside the inner pressing which supports the bonnet hinge. In the case of the Fiesta, you will have excellent access, but the whole assembly must be treated meticulously including right into the vulnerable nose section.

5B. Also, inject fluid into the cross-section at the rear of the bonnet, making sure that you reach right out to the side edges. Don't forget to treat the front body panels, while you're in the area.

☐ Job 6. Inside doors and tailgate.

6A. Some rustproofing firms drill a hole in the end of the door, or use an existing drain hole, to inject rustproofing fluid. However, you will be able to make a better and more thorough job of it if you remove the interior trim so that you can see where the fluid is going.

5B

Unlike some cars, you don't have to drill holes inside a Fiesta's tailgate to get the fluid inside box sections and pressings. If you carefully remove the interior trim panel, you can get to all the nooks and crannies that are likely to attract corrosion.

6B. After removing the trim panel, carefully peel away the plastic membrane that covers the door inner cavity.

INSIDE INFORMATION: If you accidentally ruin it, make a new one out of plastic sheet (from a builders' merchant), gluing it in place.

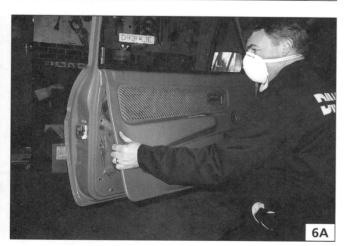

6A

6C. Make sure you get plenty of 'creeping' fluid into the steel joints, where water could collect and corrosion could occur. Naturally, the main problem is that moisture collects in the bottom of the doors and rots them out from the inside - use plenty of fluid here. If you don't want to remove the door trims, then fluid can be sprayed through the lower drain slots, but note that this will only provide protection for the lower surfaces and seams.

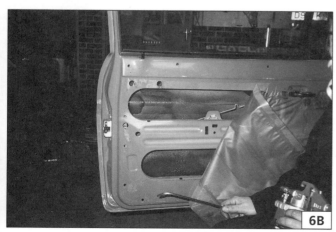

6B

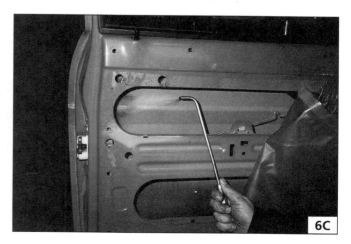

6C

☐ Job 7. Rear side inner wheel arch pressing.

7. Inside the rear compartment, there is a large hollow section above the wheel arch. Injecting fluid here will protect all around the joint between inner and outer wheelarch.

Also at the side, insert your nozzle or lance down behind the openings in the side panels to give a good coating of rust-proofing fluid deep into the well.

Inside the Car

☐ Job 8. Floor panels.

Because most rust proofing fluids never dry completely, most owners prefer not to coat over the inside of the floor panels. However, these are vulnerable because of condensation under the carpet, and from rain which can get in before you have had time to close the windows when a shower starts. As part of the rust-proofing process, you should take out the seat runners and carpets, wire brush any existing rust, coat it with a rust killing paint, and then you could paint the inside of the floor with an undersealing body compound. Allow this to dry out for a day or two and then cover it with a sheet of polythene before replacing the carpet.

☐ Job 9. Door pillars.

While you have the carpets out, lift the trim on the door hinge pillar and door shut pillar each side and inject rust proofing fluid into each pillar. The vulnerable area is at the base, so make sure the fluid coats this area thoroughly.

Beneath the Car

INSIDE INFORMATION: Think carefully before drilling holes to insert rustproofing fluid, especially in the 'chassis', where there are numerous holes already. If you do drill a hole in steel, make sure that you file off the rough burrs and then apply an anti-rusting agent, followed by a coating of paint followed by a layer of wax. Make sure the area you drill into is indeed hollow and not the inside of the car or luggage bay! Spend time looking out for wires or pipes. Disconnect the car's battery.

☐ Job 10. Sills.

10. Drill two holes in the sills to inject the fluid both fore and aft along the sills. Use a long pipe or lance, pushing this right in and then injecting as you withdraw it. Afterwards, it is advisable to use a short lance or the oil can to make sure that the rustproofing fluid has penetrated around the jacking point.

☐ Job 11. Front and rear wheel arches.

11. Make sure there is no mud trapped in the crevices underneath and spray fluid liberally round the inside of the wheel arch. Remember to wear goggles and a mask while you are spraying any part of the underside of the car.

Spray liberally round the inside of the front wheel arches with particular attention to the bottom part of the front wing where it curves underneath. These are notorious areas for rust to start. As you can see access is hopeless with the wheel still attached, and you won't be able to cover the brakes to keep fluid off them. If you can't be bothered to take off the wheels, you won't be able to do the job properly!

Job 12. Longitudinal box sections.

On the longitudinal sections at the sides, both front and back, there are access holes. Poke your lance or plastic pipe well into them along the section and inject fluid as you withdraw it.

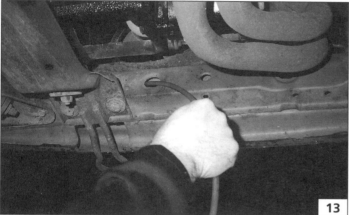

Job 13. Rear floor box sections.

There are plenty of round and oblong holes in the box sections all over the underside of the Fiesta. Use them to the maximum advantage and poke the lance or flexible pipe inside them where you can. You cannot over-protect your car!

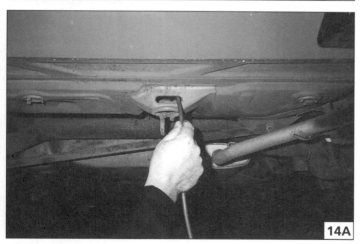

Job 14. Rear floor pressings.

14A. The pressings are full of curves and corners built in to strengthen the structure. The rust protection will help to preserve this strength for many years, provided it is in all the corners you can find.

14B. While the car is in the air, take your time to find every conceivable rust trap and make the job worthwhile. Mechanical parts may be relatively easy to replace, but bodywork problems can cause the premature death of a car.

☐ Job 15. Toe board cross-member.

15. The toe board cross-member, where it joins the bulkhead pressing, is prone to rusting at the outer bottom parts. If you look up, you will see an opening where you can inject the rustproofing fluid. Make sure the inside of this section is well coated.

☐ Job 16. Front box sections.

16. And there are yet more right at the front of the car, again with access holes already kindly provided by Mr. Ford.

☐ Job 17. Underside of floor panels.

17. *INSIDE INFORMATION: After making sure that there is no loose or flaking body sealing on the floor panels, spray the thinner, creeping type of rustproofer (Dinitrol make two types of rustproofer available) onto and into all of the seams and joints. Since road use would blast this away, spray the tougher, thicker, semi-setting type of rustproofer/underseal compound on top.*

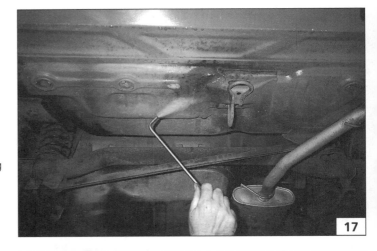

☐ Job 18. Fit grommets to holes.

18. Fit grommets to all of the holes you have drilled, dipping each one in rustproofing fluid first, so that the edges of the holes are protected.

making it easy! Tip from Dinol, the manufacturers of Dinitrol: *Except in a heat wave, it is essential to stand the container of rustproofer in a tub of hot water to keep it fluid. Top up the tub from time to time with more hot water while you are working. Not only will warm rustproofer penetrate seams better, it will flow through the applicator better and not clog so easily. Some people thin the rustproofer with white spirit, but warming it is better. Wash the gun and lances out with white spirit afterwards. If you let the rustproofer set, it is almost impossible to clean them.*

CHAPTER 6 - FAULT FINDING

This Chapter aims to help you to overcome the main faults that can affect the mobility or safety of your vehicle. It also helps you to overcome the problem that has affected most mechanics - amateur and professional - at one time or another... Blind Spot Syndrome!

It goes like this: the vehicle refuses to start one damp Sunday morning. You decide that there must be no fuel getting through. By the time you've stripped the fuel pump and fuel lines and "unblocked" the fuel tank, it's time for bed. And the next day, the local garage finds that your main HT lead has dropped out of the coil! Something like that has happened to most of us!

Don't jump to conclusions: if your engine won't start or runs badly, if electrical components fail, follow the logical sequence of checks listed here and detailed overleaf, eliminating each "check" (by testing, not by "hunch") before moving on to the next. And remember that the great majority of failures are caused by electrical or ignition faults: only a minor proportion of engine failures come from the fuel system. Follow the sequences shown here - and you'll have a better chance of success in finding that fault. Before carrying out any of the work described in this Chapter please read carefully *Chapter 1, Safety First!*

Engine won't start.

1. Starter motor doesn't turn.

2. Is battery okay?

3. Check battery connections for cleanliness/tightness.

4. Have battery 'drop' test carried out by specialist.

5. Test battery with voltmeter or, preferable, with a hydrometer.

6. Can engine be rotated by hand?

7. If engine cannot be rotated by hand, check for mechanical seizure of power unit, or pinion gear jammed in mesh with flywheel - 'rock' car backwards and forwards until free, or apply spanner to square drive at front end of starter motor.

8. If engine can be rotated by hand, check for loose electrical connections at starter, faulty solenoid, or defective starter motor.

9. Starter motor turns slowly.

10. Battery low on charge or defective - re-charge and have 'drop' test carried out by specialist.

11. Internal fault within starter motor - e.g. worn brushes.

12. Starter motor noisy or harsh.

13. Drive teeth on ring gear or starter pinion worn/broken.

14. Main drive spring broken.

15. Starter motor securing bolts loose.

16. Starter motor turns engine but car will not start. See 'Ignition System' box.

Ignition system.

> **SAFETY FIRST!**
> It is essential that you read **Chapter 1, Safety First!, The Ignition System** before carrying out work on this part of the car.

(Carry out the following checks as appropriate. For example, some vehicles have contact breaker ignition while the majority of modern cars have electronic ignition. Only Step 17 can be carried out on cars with electronic ignition. If any faults are found - **SPECIALIST SERVICE**.)

17. Check for spark at plug (remove plug and prop it with threads resting on bare metal of cylinder block). Do not touch plug or lead while operating starter.

MODELS WITHOUT ELECTRONIC IGNITION ONLY

18. If no spark present at plug, check for spark at contact breaker points when 'flicked' open (ignition 'on'). Double-check to ensure that points are clean and correctly gapped, and try again.

19. If spark present at contact breaker points, check for spark at central high tension lead from

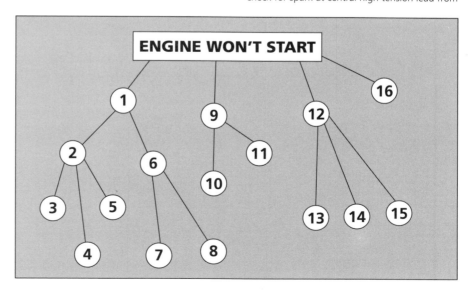

coil. NOTE: Don't carry out this check with electronic ignition systems. An uncontrolled spark can, in some cases, seriously damage the ECU (Electronic Control Unit).

20. If spark present at central high tension lead from coil, check distributor cap and rotor arm; replace if cracked or contacts badly worn.

21. If distributor cap and rotor arm are okay, check high tension leads and connections - replace leads if they are old, carbon core type suppressed variety.

22. If high tension leads are sound but dirty or damp, clean/dry them.

23. If high tension leads okay, check/clean/dry/re-gap sparking plugs.

24. Damp conditions? Apply water dispellant spray to ignition system.

25. If no spark present at contact breaker points (cars without electronic ignition only), examine connections of low tension leads between ignition switch and coil, and from coil to contact breaker (including short low-tension lead within distributor).

26. If low tension circuit connections okay, examine wiring.

27. If low tension wiring is sound, is capacitor okay? If in doubt, fit new capacitor.

28. If capacitor is okay, check for spark at central high tension lead from coil. NOTE: DON'T carry out this check with electronic ignition systems. An uncontrolled spark can, in some cases, seriously damage the ECU (Electronic Control Unit).

29. If no spark present at central high tension lead from coil, check for poor high tension lead connections.

30. If high tension lead connections okay, is coil okay? If in doubt, fit new coil.

31. If spark present at plug, is it powerful or weak? If weak, see '27' (non-electronic ignition models only).

32. If spark is healthy, check ignition timing.

33. If ignition timing is okay, see 'Fuel System' box.

Fuel system.

FUEL INJECTED ENGINES ONLY

34. Do not disconnect fuel pipes to check fuel flow, as system is pressurised; check fuel pump operation by listening for "buzz" when ignition is switched on - buzz should last no more than 1 or 2 seconds; if longer, suspect fuel pump. If no buzz, suspect fuel pump relay - seek professional help.

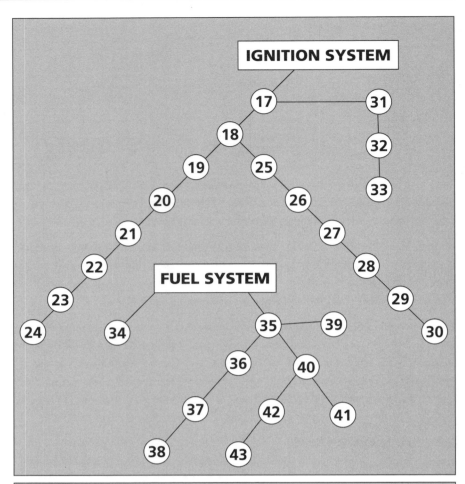

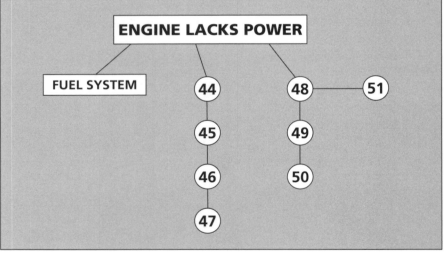

NON FUEL INJECTED ENGINES ONLY

35. Check briefly for fuel at feed pipe to carb. See 36. If no fuel present at feed pipe, is petrol tank empty? (Rock car and listen for 'sloshing' in tank, as well as looking at gauge).

36. Check for a defective fuel pump. With outlet pipe disconnected AND AIMED AWAY FROM HOT EXHAUST COMPONENTS, ETC. as well as your eyes and clothes, and into a suitable container, turn the engine over (manual

*SAFETY FIRST! Before working on the fuel system, read **Chapter 1, Safety First!** Take special care to 1) only work out of doors, 2) wear suitable gloves and goggles and keep fuel out of eyes and away from skin: 3) if fuel does come into contact with skin, wash off straight away, 4) if fuel gets into your eyes, wash out with copious amounts of clean, cold water. Seek medical advice if necessary, 5) when testing for fuel flow, pump into a sufficiently large container, minimising splashes, 6) don't smoke, work near flames or sparks or work when the engine or exhaust are hot.*

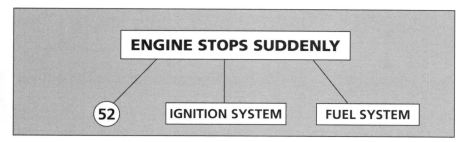

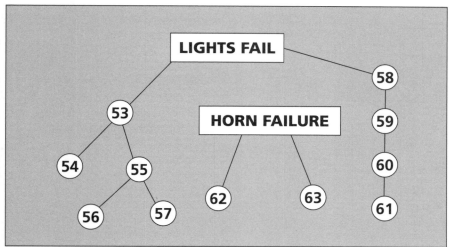

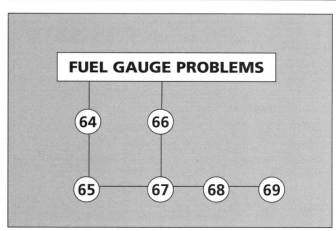

pump) or switch on ignition (electric pump) and fuel should issue from pump outlet.

37. If pump is okay, check for blocked fuel filter or pipe, or major leak in pipe between tank and pump, or between pump and carb.

38. If the filter is clean and the pump operates, suspect blocked carburettor jet(s) or damaged/sticking float, or incorrectly adjusted carburettor.

39. If there is petrol in the tank but none issues from the feed pipe from pump to carburettor, check that the small vent hole in the fuel filler cap is not blocked and causing a vacuum. NOTE: On some cars there is no vent hole in the filler cap. Other arrangements are made for venting the tank. There are many systems - **SPECIALIST SERVICE**.

40. If fuel is present at carburettor feed pipe, remove spark plugs and check whether wet with unburnt fuel.

41. If the spark plugs are fuel-soaked, check that the choke is operating as it should and is not jammed 'shut'. Other possibilities include float needle valve(s) sticking 'open' or leaking, float punctured, carburettor incorrectly adjusted or air filter totally blocked. Clean plugs before replacing.

42. If the spark plugs are dry, check whether the float needle valve is jammed 'shut'.

43. Check for severe air leak at inlet manifold gasket or carburettor gasket. Incorrectly set valve clearances.

Engine lacks power.

44. Engine overheating. Check oil temperature gauge (where fitted). Low oil pressure light may come on.

45. Air cleaner intake thermostat not opening/closing at the correct temperatures. Replace or free-off as necessary.

46. If thermostat okay, check oil level. BEWARE - DIPSTICK AND OIL MAY BE VERY HOT.

47. If oil level okay, check for slipping fan belt, cylinder head gasket 'blown', partial mechanical seizure of engine, blocked or damaged exhaust system.

48. If engine temperature is normal, check cylinder compressions.

49. If cylinder compression readings low, add a couple of teaspoons of engine oil to each cylinder in turn, and repeat test. If readings don't improve, suspect burnt valves/seats.

50. If compression readings improve after adding oil as described, suspect worn cylinder bores, pistons and rings.

51. If compression readings are normal, checkfor mechanical problems, for example, binding brakes, slipping clutch, partially seized transmission, etc.

Engine stops suddenly.

52. Check for sudden ingress of water/snow onto ignition components, in adverse weather conditions. Sudden failure is almost always because of an ignition fault. Check for simple wiring and connection breakdowns.

Lights fail.

53. Sudden failure - check fuses.

54. If all lamps affected, check switch and main wiring feeds.

55. If not all lamps are affected, check bulbs on lamps concerned.

56. If bulbs appear to be okay, check bulb holder(s), local wiring and connections.

57. If bulb(s) blown, replace!

58. Intermittent operation, flickering or poor light output.

59. Check earth (ground) connections(s).

60. If earth(s) okay, check switch.

61. If switch okay, check wiring and connections.

Horn failure.

62. If horn does not operate, check fuse, all connections (particularly earths/grounds) and cables. Remove horn connections and check/clean. Use 12v test lamp to ascertain power getting to horn.

63. If horn will not stop(!), disconnect the horn and check for earthing of cable between button and horn unit and the wiring and contacts in the horn switch housing. **SPECIALIST SERVICE**. Horn wiring and connections are more complex than they appear at first. If necessary, have them checked by a specialist.

Fuel gauge problems.

64. Gauge reads 'empty' - check for fuel in tank!

65. If fuel is present in tank, check for earthing of wiring from tank to gauge, and for wiring disconnections.

66. Gauge permanently reads 'full', regardless of tank contents. Check wiring and connections as in '65'.

67. If wiring and connections all okay, sender unit/fuel gauge defective.

68. With wiring disconnected, check for continuity between fuel gauge terminals. Do

NOT test gauge by short-circuiting to earth. Replace unit if faulty.

69. If gauge is okay, disconnect wiring from tank sender unit and check for continuity between terminal and case. Replace sender unit if faulty.

FACT FILE: EMERGENCY STARTING

Pushing or Towing

NOTE: This is not possible for vehicles with automatic transmission. Diesel engines: only attempt in warm weather or with a warm engine.

Turn off all unnecessary electrical load; switch on ignition and depress the clutch pedal. Select second or third gear; release the clutch when the car reaches a person's running speed.

Starting with Jump Leads

> **Safety First!**
> **This process can be dangerous and the following instructions must be followed to the letter. Also see Chapter One, Safety First! and the relevant part of Chapter 3 for information on safe handling of car batteries.**

Ensure that the battery providing the jump start has the same voltage (12 volt) as the battery fitted to your car.

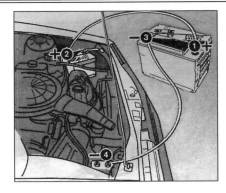

Do not lean over the battery during jump starting.

Switch off all unnecessary electrical loads and apply the hand brake. Auto. Transmission: Place gear selector in 'P'. Manual Transmission: Place gear shift lever in neutral.

Note that on some batteries and on battery connections, '+' (positive) terminals are coloured red and '-' (negative) terminals are coloured blue or black.

Run the engine of the vehicle providing the jump start (if battery fitted to vehicle).

(The following instruction numbers refer to the numbers on the drawing.)

1. Connect one end of the jump lead to the positive ('+') terminal of the battery providing the jump start.

2. Connect the other end of the same lead to the positive terminal on the car being started.

3. Connect one end of the other jump lead to the negative ('-') terminal on the 'slave' battery...

4. ...and the other end to the negative battery lead on the car, or to some bare metal in the car's engine bay.

Now try to start the car as quickly as is reasonably possible.

IT IS IMPORTANT that the leads are removed in the exact reverse sequence to that shown above. Keep hands, hair and loose clothing away from moving parts in both engine bays.

Supplementary information - diesel engines

The following fault finding chart covers only those parts of the system that can be checked at home. If a simple solution is not found, it will be necessary to call on the services of a main dealer or diesel injection specialist.

1. No fuel. *If the tank is allowed to run dry, the system will have to be bled.*

2. Fuel blockages from the tank to the pump can be checked at home. *However, see Safety First! below...*

> **SAFETY FIRST!**
> **It is most important that any checks on the fuel system from the pump to the engine are carried out by a specialist. The high pressure means that a blockage is unlikely but also means that there is a safety hazard involved in working on this part of the system. Very high pressure can remain in the system even when the engine is not running.**

3. Air in fuel system. *Bleed as described in Chapter 3, Servicing Your Car.*

4. Glow plugs (cold engine). These only fail after a very high mileage and usually one at a time. The usual symptom is an engine which starts, misfires and smokes badly until warmed up. *Proper checking is usually a SPECIALIST SERVICE job.*

5. Slow cranking speed. *Can be caused by bad electrical connections or a flat battery.*

6. Worn bores will affect a diesel engine more severely than a petrol engine. *A worn out engine is less likely to start or run properly.*

7. Stop control faulty. *Check that the solenoid in the stop control 'clicks' when the solenoid is switched on or off, in which case you can assume it is*

working. If a manually-controlled valve is fitted, check that the valve at the pump operates when the knob is moved. Otherwise this is also a SPECIALIST SERVICE job.

8. Injection pump faulty. *SPECIALIST SERVICE*

9. Injector faulty. *SPECIALIST SERVICE*

10. Injector feed pipe leaking. *SPECIALIST SERVICE*

See **PORTER MANUALS' DIESEL CAR ENGINES SERVICE GUIDE** for more detailed information

	1	2	3	4	5	6	7	8	9	10
Engine will not start	✓	✓	✓	✓	✓	✓	✓	✓		
Engine will not stop							✓			
Engine misfires	✓					✓		✓	✓	✓
Excessive (black) smoke from exhaust								✓	✓	

CHAPTER 7
GETTING THROUGH THE MOT

This Chapter is for owners in Britain whose vehicles need to pass the 'MoT' test. The Test was first established in 1961 by the then Ministry of Transport and it attempts to ensure that vehicles using British roads reach minimum standards of safety. Approximately 40 per cent of vehicles submitted for the test fail it, but many of these failures could be avoided by knowing what the vehicle might 'fall down on', and by taking appropriate remedial action before the test 'proper' is carried out.

It is true that the scope of the test has been considerably enlarged in the past few years, with the result that it is correspondingly more difficult to be sure that your vehicle will reach the required standards. In truth, however, a careful examination of the relevant areas, perhaps a month or so before the current certificate expires, will highlight components which require attention, and enable any obvious faults to be rectified before you take the vehicle for the test.

Getting Ahead

It is also worth noting that a vehicle can be submitted for a test up to a month before the current certificate expires - if the vehicle passes, the new certificate will be valid for one year from the day of expiry of the old one, provided that the old certificate is produced at the time of the test.

PART I: THE BACKGROUND

Keeping Up To Date

Alterations are being made to the Test on a regular basis - almost always making it tougher than it was before. It is MOST IMPORTANT that UK owners find out for themselves about any changes in the requirements that might have been made since this book was written. Your local MoT Testing Station should be able to help - if not, take your custom elsewhere! Also, non-UK owners should obtain information on the legal requirements in their own territory - and act accordingly.

Making A Good Impression

If your vehicle is muddy or particularly dirty (especially underneath) it would be worth giving it a thorough clean a day or two before carrying out the inspection so that it has ample time to dry. Do the same before the real MoT test. A clean vehicle makes a better impression on the examiner, who can refuse to test a vehicle which is particularly dirty underneath.

On the other hand, a clean vehicle makes a better impression and it will help the examiner to see what he is supposed to be examining. Generally, this will work in the owner's favour. For example, if a component or an area of underbody or chassis is particularly difficult to examine due to a build-up of oily dirt etc., and if the examiner is in doubt about its condition, he is entitled to fail that component because it was not possible for him to conclude that it reached the required standard. Had it been clean, it might well have been tested, and passed!

MoT testers do not dismantle assemblies during the test but you may wish to do so during your pretest check-up for a better view of certain wearing parts, such as the rear brake

SAFETY FIRST!
The MoT tester will follow a set procedure and we will cover the ground in a similar way, starting inside the vehicle, then continuing outside, under the bonnet, underneath the vehicle, etc. When preparing to go underneath the vehicle, do ensure that it is jacked on firm level ground and then supported on axle stands or ramps which are adequate for the task. Wheels which remain on the ground should have chocks in front of and behind them, and while the rear wheels remain on the ground, the hand brake should be firmly ON. For most repair and replacement jobs under your vehicle these normal precautions will suffice. However, the vehicle needs to be even more stable than usual when carrying out these checks. There must be no risk of it toppling off its stands while suspension and steering components are being pushed and pulled in order to test them. Read carefully **Chapter 1, Safety First!** *and the first part of* **Chapter 3, Servicing Your Car** *for further important information on raising and supporting a vehicle above the ground.*

shoes for example. See *Chapter 3, Servicing Your Car* for information on how to check the brakes.

Buying And Selling

This chapter provides a procedure for checking your vehicle's condition prior to its official MoT test. The same procedure could be equally useful to UK and non-UK owners alike when examining vehicles prior to purchase (or sale for that matter). However, it must be emphasised that the official MoT certificate should not be regarded as any guarantee of the condition of a vehicle. All it proves is that the vehicle reached the required standards, in the opinion of a particular examiner, at the time and date it was tested.

Pass The MoT!

The aim of this chapter is to explain what is actually tested on a vehicle and (if it is not obvious) how the test is done. This should enable you to identify and eliminate problems before they undermine the safety or diminish the performance of your vehicle and long before they cause the expense and inconvenience of a test failure.

Tool Box

Dismantling apart, few tools are needed for testing. A light hammer is useful for tapping panels underneath the vehicle when looking for rust. If this produces a bright metallic noise, then the area being tapped is solid metal. If the noise produced is dull, the area contains rust or filler. When tapping sills and box sections, listen also for the sound of debris (that is, rust flakes) on the inside of the panel. Use a screwdriver to prod weak parts of panels. This may produce holes of course, but if the panels have rusted to that extent, you really ought to know about it. A strong lever (such as a tyre lever) can be useful for applying the required force to suspension joints etc. when assessing whether there is any wear in them.

You will need an assistant to operate controls and perhaps to wobble the road wheels while you inspect components under the vehicle.

Age Related Checks

Two more brief explanations are required before you start your informal test. Firstly, the age of the vehicle determines exactly which lights, seat belts and other items it should have. Frequently in the next few pages you will come across the phrase "Cars first used ..." followed by a date. A vehicle's "first used" date is either its date of first registration, or the date six months after it was manufactured, whichever was earlier. Or, if the vehicle was originally used without being registered (such as a vehicle which has been imported to the U.K. or an ex-H.M. Forces model, etc.) the "first used" date is the date of manufacture.

Rust And Load Bearing Areas

Secondly, there must not be excessive rust, serious distortion or any fractures affecting certain prescribed areas of the bodywork. These prescribed areas are load-bearing parts of the bodywork within 30 cm (12 in.) of anchorages or mounting points associated with testable items such as seat belts, brake pedal assemblies, master cylinders, servos, suspension and

steering components and also body mountings. Keep this rule in mind while inspecting the vehicle, but remember also that even if such damage occurs outside a prescribed area, it can cause failure of the test. Failure will occur if the damage is judged to reduce the continuity or strength of a main load-bearing part of the bodywork sufficiently to have an adverse effect on the braking or steering.

The following notes are necessarily abbreviated, and are for assistance only. They are not a definitive guide to all the MoT regulations. It is also worth mentioning that the varying degrees of discretion of individual MoT testers can mean that there are variations between the standards as applied. However, the following points should help to make you aware of the aspects which will be examined. Now, if you have your clipboard, checklist and pencil handy, let's make a start...

The 'Easy' Bits

Checking these items is straightforward and should not take more than a few minutes - and could avoid an embarrassingly simple failure...

Lights

Within the scope of the test are headlights, side and tail lights, brake lights, direction indicators, and number plate lights (plus rear fog lights on all cars first used on or after 1 April, 1980, and any earlier cars subsequently so equipped, and also hazard warning lights on any vehicle so fitted). All must operate, must be clean and not significantly damaged; flickering is also not permitted. The switches should also all work properly. Pairs of lights should give approximately the same intensity of light output, and operation of one set of lights should not affect the working of another - such trouble is usually due to bad earthing.

Front fog and spot lights are not part of the MoT test (although their use is covered by *Construction and Use* regulations so that, for instance, spot lights should go out when headlights are turned off main beam) and won't be tested, provided they're not a physical hazard. Rear fog lights are part of the Test however. See later in this Chapter for details.

Indicators should flash at between 60 and 120 times per minute. 'Rev' the engine to encourage them, if a little slow (although the examiner might not let you get away with it!) Otherwise, renew the (inexpensive) flasher unit and check all wiring and earth connections.

Interior 'tell-tale' lights, such as for indicators, rear fog lights and hazard warning lights should all operate in unison with their respective exterior lights.

Headlight aim must be correct - in particular, the lights should not dazzle other road users. An approximate guide can be obtained by shining the lights against a vertical wall, but final adjustment may be necessary by reference to the beam checking machine at the MoT station. Most testers will be happy to make slight adjustments where necessary but only if the adjusters work. Make sure before you take the vehicle in that they are not seized solid!

Reflectors must be unbroken, clean, and not obscured - for example, by stickers.

Wheels And Tyres

Check the wheels for loose nuts, cracks, and damaged rims. Missing wheel nuts or studs are also failure points, naturally enough!

There is no excuse for running on illegal tyres. The legal requirement is that there must be at least 1.6 mm of tread depth remaining, over the 'central' three-quarters of the width of the tyre all the way around. From this it can be deduced that there is no legal requirement to have 1.6 mm (1/16 in.) of tread on the 'shoulders' of the tyre, but in practice, most MoT stations will be reluctant to pass a tyre in this condition. In any case, for optimum safety - especially 'wet grip' - you would be well advised to change tyres when they wear down to around 3 mm (1/8 in.) or so depth of remaining tread.

Visible 'tread wear indicator bars', found approximately every nine inches around the tread of the tyre, are highlighted when the tread reaches the critical 1.6 mm point.

Tyres should not show signs of cuts or bulges, rubbing on the bodywork or running gear, and the valves should be in sound condition, and correctly aligned.

Old-fashioned cross-ply and radial-ply tyre types must not be mixed on the same axle, and if pairs of cross-ply and radial-ply tyres are fitted, the radials must be on the rear axle.

Windscreen

The screen must not be damaged (by cracks, chips, etc.) or obscured so that the driver does not have a clear view of the road. Permissible size of damage points depends on where they occur. Within an area 290 mm (nearly 12 in.) wide, ahead of the driver, and up to the top of the wiper arc, any damage must be confined within a circle less than 10 mm (approx. 0.4 in.) in diameter. This is increased to 40 mm (just over 1.5 in.) for damage within the rest of the screen area swept by the wipers.

Washers And Wipers

The wipers must clear an area big enough to give the driver a clear view forwards and to the side of the vehicle. The wiper blades must be securely attached and sound, with no cracks or 'missing' sections. The wiper switch should also work properly. The screen washers must supply the screen with sufficient liquid to keep it clean, in conjunction with the use of the wipers.

Mirrors

Your vehicle must have at least two, one of which must be on the driver's side. The mirrors must be visible from the driver's seat, and not be damaged or obscured so that the view to the rear is affected. Therefore cracks, chips and discolouration can mean failure.

Horn

The horn must emit a uniform note which is loud enough to give adequate warning of approach, and the switch must operate correctly. Multi-tone horns playing 'in sequence' are not permitted, but two tones sounding together are fine.

Seat Security

The seats must be securely mounted, and the sub-frames should be sound.

Seat Belts

Seat belts must be in good condition (i.e. not frayed or otherwise damaged), and the buckles and catches should also operate correctly. Inertia reel types, where fitted, should retract properly.

Belt mountings must be secure, with no structural damage or corrosion within 30 cm (12 in.) of them.

Number (Registration) Plates

Both front and rear number plates must be present, and in good condition, with no breaks or missing numbers or letters. The plates must not be obscured, and the digits must not be repositioned (to form names, for instance).

Vehicle Identification Numbers (VIN)

Vehicles first used on or after 1 August, 1980 have to have a clearly displayed VIN - Vehicle Identification Number (or old-fashioned 'chassis numbers' for older cars) which is plainly legible. See *Chapter 2, Buying Guide* for the correct location on your vehicle.

Exhaust System

The entire system must be present, properly mounted, free of leaks and should not be noisy - which can happen when the internal baffles fail. 'Proper' repairs by welding, or exhaust cement, or bandage are acceptable, as long as no gas leaks are evident. Then again, common sense, if not the MoT, dictates that exhaust bandage should only be a very short-term emergency measure. For safety's sake, fit a new exhaust if yours is reduced to this!

PART II: THE CHECKLIST

You've checked the easy bits - now it's time for the detail! Some of the 'easy bits' referred to above are included here, but this is intended as a more complete check list to give your vehicle the best possible chance of gaining a First Class Honours, MoT Pass!

Inside The Vehicle

☐ 1. The steering wheel should be examined for cracks and for damage which might interfere with its use, or injure the driver's hands. It should also be pushed and pulled along the column axis, and also up and down, at 90 degrees to it. This will highlight any deficiencies in the wheel and upper column mounting/bearing, and also any excessive end float, and movement between the column shaft and the wheel. Look, too, for movement in the steering column couplings and fasteners (including the universal joint if applicable), and visually check their condition and security. They must be sound, and properly tightened.

In the case of cars (the majority) with steering racks, rotate the steering wheel in both directions to test for free play at the wheel rim - this shouldn't exceed approximately 13 mm. (0.5 in.), assuming a 380 mm. (15 in.) diameter steering wheel.

In the case of the smaller number of cars with steering boxes, free play at the wheel rim shouldn't exceed approximately 75 mm (3.0 in.), assuming a 380 mm (15 in.) diameter steering wheel.

In both cases where the steering wheel is larger or smaller the amount of permissible free play should be raised or lowered accordingly.

☐ 2. Check that the switches for headlights, sidelights, rear fog lights direction indicators, hazard warning lights, wipers, washers and horn, appear to be in good working order and check that the tell-tale lights or audible warnings are working where applicable.

☐ 3. Make sure that the windscreen wipers operate effectively with blades that are secure and in good condition. The windscreen washer should provide sufficient liquid to clear the screen in conjunction with the wipers.

☐ 4. Check for windscreen damage, especially in the area swept by the wipers. From the MoT tester's point of view, Zone A is part of this area, 290 mm (11.5 in.) wide and centred on the centre of the steering wheel. Damage to the screen within this area should be capable of fitting into a 10 mm (approx. 0.4 in.) diameter circle and the cumulative effect of more minor damage should not seriously restrict the driver's view. Windscreen stickers or other obstructions should not encroach more than 10 mm (approx 0.4 in.) into this area. In the remainder of the swept area the maximum diameter of damage or degree of encroachment by obstructions is 40 mm (approx. 1.6 in.) and there is no ruling regarding cumulative

multi-tone horns (which alternate between two or more notes) are not permitted at all. On cars first used after 1 August 1973, the horn should produce a constant, continuous or uniform note which is neither harsh nor grating.

☐ 6. There must be one exterior mirror on the driver's side of the vehicle and one other mirror - either an exterior mirror fitted to the passenger's side or an interior mirror. The required mirrors should be secure and in good condition.

☐ 7. Check that the hand brake operates effectively without coming to the end of its working travel. The lever and its mechanism must be complete, securely mounted, unobstructed in its travel and in a sufficiently good condition to remain firmly in the "On" position even when knocked from side to side. The 30 cm rule on bodywork corrosion applies in the vicinity of the hand brake lever mounting.

☐ 8. The foot brake pedal assembly should be complete, unobstructed, and in a good working condition, including the pedal rubber (which should not have been worn smooth). There should be no excessive movement of the pedal at right angles to its normal direction. When fully depressed, the pedal should not be at the end of its travel. The pedal should not feel spongy (indicating air in the hydraulic system), nor should it tend to creep downwards while held under pressure (which indicates an internal hydraulic leak).

☐ 9. Seats must be secure on their mountings and seat backs must be capable of being locked in the upright position.

☐ 10. The law requires all models to be fitted with seatbelts for the driver and front passenger. These have to be three-point lap and diagonal belts. Rear seat belts are a requirement for vehicles first used after 31 March 1987 with three anchorage points for the 'outer' passengers, and at least a lap belt only for the centre passenger position. Examine seat belt webbing and fittings to make sure that all are in good condition and that anchorages are firmly attached to the vehicle's structure. Locking mechanisms should be capable of remaining locked, and of being released if required, when under load. Flexible buckle stalks (if fitted) should be free of corrosion, broken cable strands or other weaknesses. Note that any belts fitted which are not part of a legal requirements may be examined by the tester but will not form part of the official test.

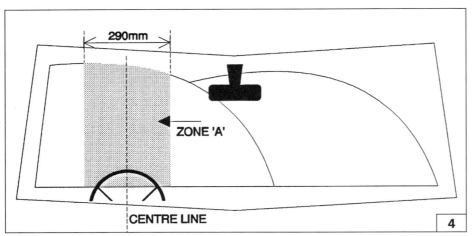

damage. Specialist windscreen companies can often repair a cracked screen for a lot less than the cost of replacement. Moreover, the cost of repair is often covered by comprehensive insurance policies. DIY repair kits are also available.

☐ 5. The horn control should be present, secure and readily accessible to the driver, and the horn should be loud enough to be heard by other road users. Gongs, bells and sirens are not permitted (except as part of an anti-theft device) and

☐ 11. On inertia reel belts, check that on retracting the belts, the webbing winds into the retracting unit automatically, albeit with some manual assistance to start with.

☐ 12. Note the point raised earlier regarding corrosion around seat belt anchorage points. The MoT tester will not carry out any dismantling here, but he will examine floor mounted anchorage points from underneath the vehicle if that is possible.

☐ 13. Before getting out of the vehicle, make sure that both doors can be opened from the inside.

Outside The Vehicle

☐ 14. Before closing the driver's door, check the condition of the inner sill. Usually the MoT tester will do this by applying finger or thumb pressure to various parts of the panel while the floor covering remains in place. For your own peace of mind, look beneath the sill covering, taking great care not to tear any covering. Then close the driver's door and make sure that it latches securely and repeat these checks on the nearside inner sill and door.

Now check all of the lights, front and rear, (and the number plate lights) while your assistant operates the light switches.

☐ 15. As we said earlier, you can carry out a rough and ready check on headlight alignment for yourself, although it will certainly not be as accurate as having it done for you at the MoT testing station. Drive your vehicle near to a wall, as shown. Check that your tyres are correctly inflated and the vehicle is on level ground.

Draw on the wall, with chalk:
• a horizontal line about 2 metres long, and at same height as centre of headlight lenses.
• two vertical lines about 1 metre long, each forming a cross with the horizontal line and the same distance apart as the headlight centres.
• another vertical line to form a cross on the horizontal line, midway between the others.

Now position your vehicle so that:
• it faces the wall squarely, and its centre line is in line with centre line marked on the wall.
• the steering is straight.
• headlight lenses are 5.0 metres (16 ft.) from the wall.

Switch on the headlights' 'main' and 'dipped' beams in turn and measure their centre points. You will be able to judge any major discrepancies in intensity and aim prior to having the beams properly set by a garage with beam measuring equipment.

Headlights should be complete, clean, securely mounted, in good working order and not adversely affected by the operation of another lamp, and these basic requirements affect all the lights listed below. Headlights must dip as a pair from a single switch. Their aim must be correctly adjusted and they should not be affected (even to the extent of flickering) when lightly tapped by hand. Each headlight should match its partner in terms of size, colour and intensity of light, and can be white or yellow.

☐ 16. Side lights should show white light to the front and red light to the rear. Lenses should not be broken, cracked or incomplete. Stop lights must be red, of course.

☐ 17. Check your indicators, doing what the MoT tester will do: turn on side lights and apply the brake lights while ensuring that the indicators still work properly, and that none of the lights interfere with each other, causing dimness or intermittent failure. Check side repeater lights, too.

☐ 18. Vehicles first used before 1 April 1986 do not have to have a hazard warning device, but if one is fitted, it must be tested, and it must operate with the ignition switch either on or off. The lights should flash 60-120 times per minute, and indicators must operate independently of any other lights.

☐ 19. There must be two red rear reflectors - always fitted by the manufacturers, of course! - which are clean and are securely and symmetrically fitted to the vehicle.

☐ 20. Your vehicle must have at least one rear fog light fitted to the centre or offside of the vehicle. If there are two, they must be spaced an equal distance from the centre. It must comply with the basic requirements (listed under headlights) and emit a steady red light. Its tell-tale light, inside the vehicle, must work to inform the driver that it is switched on.

☐ 21. There must be registration number plates at the front and rear of the vehicle and both must be clean, secure, complete and unobscured. Letters and figures must be correctly formed and correctly spaced and not likely to be misread due to an uncovered securing bolt or whatever. The year letter counts as a figure. The space between letters and figures must be at least twice that between adjacent letters or figures.

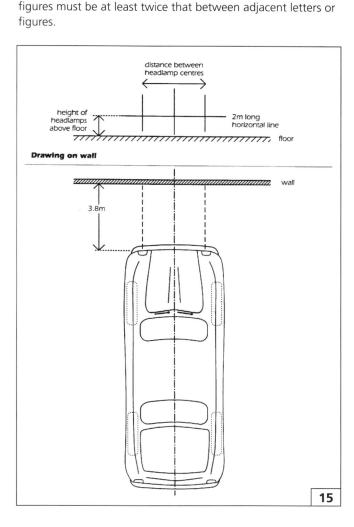

22. Number plate lights must be present, working, and must not flicker when tapped by hand, just as for other lights. Where more than one light or bulb was fitted as original equipment, all must be working.

Wheels And Tyres

The MoT tester will examine tyres and wheels while walking around the vehicle and again when he is underneath it.

23. Front tyres should match each other and rear tyres should match each other, both sets matching in terms of size, aspect ratio and type of structure. For example, you must never fit tyres of different sizes or types, such as cross-ply or radial, on the same 'axle' - both front wheels counting as 'on the same axle' in this context. If cross-ply or bias belted tyres are fitted to the rear of the car, you must not fit radial-ply tyres to the front. If cross-ply tyres are fitted to the rear, bias belted tyres should not be fitted to the front. (We recommend that you do not mix tyre types anywhere on the car.)

24. Failure of the test can be caused by a cut, lump, tear or bulge in a tyre, exposed ply or cord, a badly seated tyre, a re-cut tyre, a tyre fouling part of the vehicle, or a seriously damaged or misaligned valve stem which could cause sudden deflation of the tyre. To pass the test, the grooves of the tread pattern must be at least 1.6 mm deep throughout a continuous band comprising the central three-quarters of the breadth of tread, and round the entire outer circumference of the tyre.

We are grateful to Dunlop/SP Tyres for the photographs and information in this section.

24A. Modern tyres have tread wear indicators built into the tread groves (usually about eight of them spread equidistantly around the circumference). These appear as continuous bars running across the tread when the original pattern depth has worn down to 1.6 mm. There will be a distinct reduction in wet grip well before the tread wear indicators start to show, and you should replace tyres before they get to this stage, even though this is the legal minimum in the UK.

24B. Lumps and bulges in the tyre wall usually arise from accidental damage or even because of faults in the tyre construction. You should run your hand all the way around the side wall of the tyre, with the vehicle either jacked off the ground, or moving the vehicle half a wheels revolution, so that you can check the part of the tyre that was previously resting on the ground. Since you can't easily check the insides of the tyres in day-to-day use, it is even more important that you spend time carefully checking the inside of each tyre - the MoT tester will certainly do so! Tyres with bulges in them must be scrapped and replaced with new, since they can fail suddenly, causing your vehicle to lose control.

24B

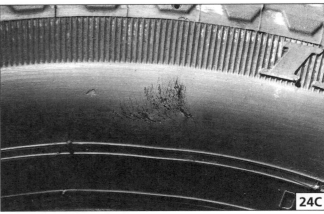

24C

24C. Abrasion of the tyre side wall can take place either in conjunction with bulging, or by itself, and this invariably results from an impact, such as the tyre striking the edge of a kerb or a pothole in the road. Once again, the tyre may be at imminent risk of failure and you should take advice from a tyre specialist on whether the abrasion is just superficial, or whether the tyre will need replacement.

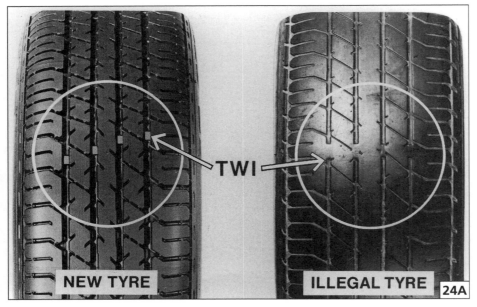

NEW TYRE   TWI   ILLEGAL TYRE   24A

☐ 24D. All tyres will suffer progressively from cracking, albeit in most cases superficially, due to the effects of sunlight. If old age has caused the tyres on your vehicle to degrade to this extent, replace them.

24D

☐ 24E. If the outer edges of the tread are worn noticeably more than the centre, the tyres have been run under inflated which not only ruins tyres, but causes worse fuel consumption, dangerous handling and is, of course, illegal.

Over-inflation causes the centre part of the tyre to wear more quickly than the outer edges. This is also illegal but in addition, it causes the steering and grip to suffer and the tyre becomes more susceptible to concussion damage.

24E

24F

☐ 24F. Incorrect wheel alignment causes one side of the tyre to wear more severely than the other. If your vehicle should hit a kerb or large pothole, it is worthwhile having the wheel alignment checked by a tyre specialist since this costs considerably less than new front tyres!

☐ 25. Road wheels must be secure and must not be badly damaged, distorted or cracked, or have badly distorted bead rims (perhaps due to "kerbing"), or loose or missing wheel nuts, studs or bolts.

☐ 26. Check the bodywork for any sharp edges or projections, caused by corrosion or damage, which could prove dangerous to other road users, including pedestrians.

☐ 27. Check that the fuel cap fastens securely and that its sealing washer is neither torn nor deteriorated, or its mounting flange damaged sufficiently to allow fuel to escape (for example, while the vehicle is cornering).

Under The Bonnet

☐ 28. The vehicle should have a Vehicle Identification Number fitted to the bodywork. This can be on a plate secured to the vehicle or, etched or stamped on the bodywork. See *Chapter 2, Buying Guide* for more information.

☐ 29. Check the steering rack or box for security by asking your assistant to turn the steering wheel from side to side (with the road wheels on the ground) while you watch what happens under the bonnet. Then, check for free play in the steering assembly as a whole. This is done by turning the steering wheel from side to side as far as possible without moving the road wheels - and measuring how far the steering wheel can be moved in this way. More than 75 mm (approx. 3 in.) of free play, on a steering box system, or 13 mm (approx. 0.5 in.), on a steering rack, at the perimeter of the steering wheel, due to wear in the steering components, is sufficient grounds for a test failure. Note that the free play is based on a steering wheel diameter of 380 mm (approx 15 in) and will be less for smaller steering wheels - which all of them virtually are! Also check for the presence and security of retaining and locking devices in the steering column assembly.

☐ 30. While peering under the bonnet, check that hydraulic master cylinders and reservoirs are securely mounted and not severely corroded or otherwise damaged. Ensure that the caps are present, that fluid levels are satisfactory and that there are no fluid leaks.

☐ 31. Also check that the brake servo is securely mounted and not damaged or corroded to an extent that would impair its operation. Vacuum pipes should be sound, that is, free from kinks, splits and excessive chafing and not collapsed internally.

☐ 32. Still under the bonnet have a thorough search for evidence of excessive corrosion, severe distortion or fracture in any load bearing panelling within 30 cm (12 in.) of important mounting points such as the master cylinder/servo mounting, front suspension mountings etc.

Under The Vehicle - Front End

☐ *33. SAFETY FIRST! On some occasions there is no alternative but for your assistant to sit in the vehicle whilst you go beneath. Therefore: 1) Place ramps as well as axle stands beneath the vehicle's structure so that it cannot fall. 2) Don't allow your assistant to move vigorously or get in or out of the vehicle while you are beneath it. If either of these are problematical, DON'T CARRY OUT CHECK 34 - leave it to your garage.*

☐ 34. Have an assistant turn the steering wheel from side to side while you watch for movement in the steering mechanism. Make sure that the rack or box mountings are secure, that the ball joints show no signs of wear and that the ball joint dust covers are in sound condition. Ensure that all split pins, locking nuts and so on are in place and correctly fastened, throughout the steering and suspension systems.

☐ 35. With each wheel raised in turn, spin the wheel listening for roughness in the bearings. There must be none.

☐ 36. Under the vehicle, check the condition of the front springs. Wearing goggles, use a stuff brush to clean off the mud and other debris so that you don't miss a hidden 'crack'. Make sure that all suspension mountings are sound.

☐ 37. Inspect the front shock absorbers. Their upper shrouds (outer casing) tend to rust. Any sign of leaks will cause failure of the test - look for weeping hydraulic fluid just below the lower edge of the upper shroud. Take a firm grip on the upper and lower shroud in turn with both hands and try to twist the damper to check for deterioration in the top and bottom mounting bushes.

☐ 38. With all four wheels on the ground, push down firmly a couple of times on each front wing of the vehicle, then let go at the bottom of the stroke. The vehicle should return to approximately its original level within two or three strokes. Continuing oscillations will earn your vehicle a 'failure' ticket for worn front shockers!

Under The Vehicle - Rear Suspension

☐ 39. Check the operation of the rear shock absorbers in the same way as the front (Check 38).

☐ 40. Check the rear wheel bearings as described in check 35.

☐ 41. Check the condition of the rear springs and suspension components as described in check 36.

☐ 42. Check the condition of the rear shock absorbers as described in check 37.

Braking System

☐ 43. The MoT brake test is carried out on a special 'rolling road' set-up, which measures the efficiency in terms of percentage. For the foot brake, the examiner is looking for 50 per cent; the hand brake must measure 25 per cent. Frankly, without a rolling road of your own, there is little that you can do to verify whether or not your vehicle will come up to the required figures. What you can do, though, is carry out an entire check of the brake system, which will also cover all other aspects the examiner will be checking, and be as sure as you can that the system is working efficiently.

IMPORTANT! See *Chapter 3, Servicing Your Car* for important information, including *SAFETY FIRST!* information before working on your vehicle's brakes.

☐ 44. The MoT examiner will not dismantle any part of the system, but you can do so. So, take off each front wheel in turn, and examine as follows:

Disc Brakes

Check the front brake discs themselves, looking for excessive grooving or crazing, the calliper pistons/dust seals (looking for signs of fluid leakage and deterioration of the seals), and the brake pads - ideally, replace them if less than approximately 3mm (1/8th in.) friction material remains on each pad - but check the recommendations in *Chapter 3*.

Drum Brakes

Remove each brake drum and check the condition of the linings (renew if worn down to anywhere near the rivet heads), the brake drum (watch for cracking, ovality and serious scoring, etc.) and the wheel cylinders. Check the cylinder's dust covers to see if they contain brake fluid. If so, or if it is obvious that the cylinder(s) have been leaking, replace them or - ONLY if the cylinder bore is in perfect condition - fit a new seal kit.

☐ 45. Ensure that the drum brake adjusters (where fitted) are free to rotate (i.e. not seized!). If they are stuck fast, apply a little penetrating oil (but if possible, only from behind the backplate; if you have to work inside the brake drum, take great care to avoid the risk of getting oil on the brake shoes), and gently work the adjuster backwards and forwards with a brake adjuster spanner. Eventually the adjusters should free and a little brake grease can be applied to the threads to keep them in this condition. Now rotate the adjuster until the brake shoes contact the drum (preventing the road wheel from turning), then reverse the adjustment just enough to allow the wheel to turn.

☐ 46. A similar procedure can be applied to the handbrake adjustment. Check that the handbrake applies the brakes fully, well before it reaches the end of its potential range of movement. Ensure that the handbrake lever remains locked in the 'on' position when fully applied, even if the lever is knocked sideways.

☐ 47. Closely check the state of ALL visible hydraulic pipework. If any section of the steel tubing shows signs of corrosion, replace it, for safety as well as to gain an MoT pass. Look too for leakage of fluid around pipe joints, and from the master cylinder. The fluid level in the master cylinder reservoir must also be at its correct level - if not, find out why and rectify the problem! At the front and rear of the vehicle, bend the flexible hydraulic pipes (by hand) near each end of each pipe, checking for signs of cracking. If any is evident, or if the pipes have been chafing on the tyres, wheels, steering or suspension components, replace them with new items, rerouting them to avoid future problems. Note also that where the manufacturers fitted a clip to secure a piece of pipe, then it must be present and the pipe must be secured by it.

☐ 48. Have an assistant press down hard on the brake pedal while you check all flexible pipes for bulges. As an additional check, firmly apply the foot brake and hold the pedal down for a few minutes. It should not slowly sink to the floor (if it does, you have a hydraulic system problem). Press and release the pedal a few times - it should not feel 'spongy' (due to the presence of air in the system). Now check the operation of the brake servo by starting the engine while the brake pedal is being held down. If all is well, as the vacuum servo starts to work, the pedal should move a short distance towards the floor. Check the condition of the servo unit and its hoses - all MUST be sound. If there is the risk of any problems with the braking system's hydraulics, have a qualified mechanic check it over before using the vehicle.

☐ 49. A test drive should reveal obvious faults (such as pulling to one side, due to a seized calliper piston, for example), but otherwise all will be revealed on the rollers at the MoT station...

Bodywork Structure

A structurally deficient vehicle is a dangerous vehicle, and rust can affect many important areas, including the sills, any 'outriggers' and the floorpan. Examine these areas carefully.

☐ 50. Essentially, fractures, cracks or serious corrosion in any load bearing panel or member (to the extent that the affected sections are weakened) need to be dealt with. In addition, failure will result from any deficiencies in the structural metalwork within 30 cm (12 in.) of the seat belt mountings, and also the steering and suspension component attachment points. Repairs made to any structural areas must be carried out by 'continuous' seam welding, and the repair should restore the affected section to at least its original strength.

☐ 51. The MoT examiner will be looking for metal which gives way under squeezing pressure between finger and thumb, and will use his wicked little 'Corrosion Assessment Tool' (i.e. a plastic-headed tool known as the 'toffee hammer'!), which in theory at least should be used for detecting rust by lightly tapping the surface. If scraping the surface of the metal shows weakness beneath, the vehicle will fail.

☐ 52. Note that the security of doors and other openings must also be assessed, including the hinges, locks and catches. Corrosion damage or other weakness in the vicinity of these

items can mean failure. All doors must latch securely. It must be possible to open both front doors from inside and outside the vehicle and rear doors from the outside only.

Exterior Bodywork

☐ 53. Look out for surface rust, or accident damage, on the exterior bodywork, which leaves sharp/jagged edges and which may be liable to cause injury. Ideally, repairs should be carried out by welding in new metal, but for non-structural areas, riveting a plate over a hole, bridging the gap with glass fibre/body filler or even taping over the gap can be legally acceptable, at least as far as the MoT test is concerned.

Fuel System

☐ 54. Another recent extension of the regulations brings the whole of the fuel system under scrutiny, from the tank to the engine. The system should be examined with and without the engine running, and there must be no leaks from any of the components. The tank must be securely mounted, and the filler cap must fit properly - 'temporary' caps are not permitted.

Emissions

☐ 55. In almost every case, a proper 'engine tune' will help to ensure that your vehicle is running at optimum efficiency, and there should be no difficulty in passing the test, unless your engine or its ancillaries are well worn.

All petrol engines are subject to the 'visual smoke emission' test. The engine must be fully warmed up, allowed to idle, then revved slightly. If smoke emitted is regarded by the examiner as being 'excessive', the vehicle will fail. Often smoke emitted during this test is as a result of worn valve stem seals, allowing oil into the combustion chambers during tickover, to be blown out of the exhaust as 'blue smoke' when the engine is revved. In practice, attitudes vary widely between MoT stations on this aspect of the test.

☐ 56. For diesel-engined vehicles a 'smoke' test also applies. Again, the engine must be fully warmed up, and allowed to idle, before being revved to around 2,500 rpm for 20 seconds (to 'purge' the system). If dense blue or black smoke is emitted for more than five seconds, the vehicle will fail. In addition, the exhaust smoke is tested. Problems will require **SPECIALIST SERVICE**.

GETTING THROUGH THE MOT

FACT FILE: VEHICLE EMISSIONS

PETROL ENGINED VEHICLES WITHOUT CATALYSER

Vehicles first used before 1 August 1973
- visual smoke check only.

Vehicles first used between 1 August 1973 and 31 July 1986
- 4.5% carbon monoxide and 1,200 parts per million, unburned hydrocarbons.

Vehicles first used between 1 August 1986 and 31 July 1992
- 3.5% carbon monoxide and 1,200 parts per million, unburned hydrocarbons.

PETROL ENGINED VEHICLES FITTED WITH CATALYTIC CONVERTERS

Vehicles first used from 1 August 1992 (K-registration on).

All have to be tested at an MoT Testing Station specially equipped to handle cars fitted with catalytic converters whether or not the vehicle is fitted with a 'cat'. If the test, or the garage's data, shows that the vehicle was not fitted with a 'cat' by the manufacturer, the owner is permitted to take the vehicle to a Testing Station not equipped for catalysed cars, if he/she prefers to do so (up to 1998-only). Required maxima are - 3.5% carbon monoxide and 1,200 parts per million, unburned hydrocarbons. The simple emissions test (as above) will be supplemented by a further check to make sure that the catalyst is maintained in good and efficient working order.

The tester also has to check that the engine oil is up to a specified temperature before carrying out the test. (This is because 'cats' don't work properly at lower temperatures - ensure *your* engine is fully warm!)

DIESEL ENGINES' EMISSIONS STANDARDS

The Tester will have to rev your engine hard, several times. If it is not in good condition, he is entitled to refuse to test it. This is the full range of tests, even though all may not apply to your car.

Vehicles first used before 1 August, 1979

Engine run at normal running temperature; engine speed taken to around 2500 rpm (or half governed max. speed, if lower) and held for 20 seconds. FAILURE, if engine emits dense blue or black smoke for next 5 seconds, at tick-over. (NOTE: Testers are allowed to be more lenient with pre-1960 vehicles.)

Vehicles first used on or after 1 August, 1979

After checking engine condition, and with the engine at normal running temperature, the engine will be run up to full revs between three and six times to see whether your engine passes the prescribed smoke density test. (For what it's worth - 2.5k for non-turbo cars; 3.0k for turbo diesels. An opacity meter probe will be placed in your car's exhaust pipe and this is not something you can replicate at home.) Irrespective of the meter readings, the car will fail if smoke or vapour obscures the view of other road users.

IMPORTANT NOTE: The diesel engine test puts a lot of stress on the engine. It is IMPERATIVE that your car's engine is properly serviced, and the cam belt changed on schedule, before you take it in for the MoT test. The tester is entitled to refuse to test the car if he feels that the engine is not in serviceable condition and there are a number of pre-Test checks he may carry out.

CHAPTER 8 - FACTS & FIGURES

This Chapter serves two main purposes. In *Part I,* we aim to provide you with a guide to all the major production changes that have taken place, and second, we supply the 'Facts & Figures' you will need when servicing your car. In fact, *Part II* of this chapter, *Capacities and Settings,* will make essential reading when you come to carrying out servicing, since you will then need to know things like the correct spark plug gap, torque settings and a whole host of other adjustments and measurements.

PART I - MAJOR MILESTONES

Please note that there have been dozens of 'special models' of Fiesta produced over the years, some of them in very small numbers. It simply isn't possible to list them all.

Feb. 1977 - 'Mk I' Fiesta available in the U.K. (announced July '76) with 957 and 1117 cc engines and 3 doors. In September the 1300 S and Ghia were added.

Mar. 1979 - Millionth edition produced, with silver or black finish.

Dec. 1980 - 950 Popular and 950/1100 Popular Plus introduced.

Sep. 1981 - Deeper bumpers for all models; interior improvements.

Dec. 1981 - 1597cc XR2 introduced, with OHV engine.

Sep. 1983 - New Fiesta ('Mk II') introduced. New bonnet, tailgate, lights and details inc. fascia. 5-speed g-box option on 1100. 957 cc and 1117 cc engines still OHV, but 1295 cc and 1598 cc engines become overhead cam (CVH) engines, recognised by the wider cam cover and the grey timing belt cover on the left-hand side of the engine (viewed from standing in front of the engine). 1.6 Diesel also added to range.

May 1984 - High performance XR2 Sports available (with ex-Escort 1587 cc engine) and 957 cc models given servo-assisted brakes as standard.

Jan. 1986 - 1.4 CVH engine replaces the 1.3 CVH and electronic ignition used on 957 and 1117 cc OHV engines.

June 1987 - CTX (Continuously variable Transaxle) automatic transmission available on 1.1 litre and Ghia models.

Apr. 1989 - The New (again!) 'Mk III' Fiesta was introduced with a bigger body, wrap-around rear tail lamps, 5-door versions now available, and redesigned interior. New 999 cc HCS (High Compression Swirl) engine added. Anti-lock brakes available as option. Mk III petrol and Diesel vans introduced. 999, 1118 cc petrol and 1753 cc Diesel.

Oct. 1989 - XR2i became available. 'Cat' (unleaded only) available on some models. (Over next 3 years, catalyser standard on some models; optional on others - phased in haphazardly up to 1992.) 1.4 CFi (Cat.) engines available in Vans.

Jun. 1990 - RS Turbo added to the range with 1596 cc Turbo-chargd power plant. Trim improvements were made to many other Fiestas.

Sep. 1991 - 999 cc engine discontinued; replaced with 1.1.

Oct. 1991 - Courier ('high cube') van introduced, 1.3 petrol or 1.8 Diesel. December: Van petrol engines become 1118 cc or 1297 cc.

Feb. 1992 - 'New' XR2i 16v fuel injected Zeta 1.8 engine, with cat. (unleaded). RS1800, similar to XR2i but with rear spoiler, alloy wheels, Recaro seats, replaces RS Turbo.

Feb. 1994 - All Cars and Vans with driver's air bag, seat belt grabbers, side impact bars, immobiliser on petrol versions.

Sep. 1994 - 'Mk IV' launched: Similar body but better engines and suspension; airbags and side impact bars; anti-theft system; new 1.4 and 1.6 engines. To succeed the XR2i, the Si was added to the range. Power assisted steering on some models.

PART II - CAPACITIES AND SETTINGS

IMPORTANT NOTE: Is your car fitted with points or electronic ignition? See FACT FILE: IGNITION SYSTEMS in *Chapter 3, Servicing Your Car.*

ENGINES FROM 1986 TO 1983:

950 cc overhead valve:

Firing order - 1-2-4-3
Bore - 2.91 in (73.96 mm)
Stroke - 2.19 in (55.70 mm)
Cubic capacity - 957 cc (58.4 cu in)
Compression ratio:
low compression engines - 8.3: 1
high compression engines - 9.0 : 1
Compression pressure:
low - 137 to 166 psi (9.5 to 11.5kg/sg cm)
Compression pressure:
high - 159 to 188 psi (11 to 13kg/sg cm)
Idle speed - 775 to 825 rpm
CO percentage - 0.75 to 1.75
Spark plug type - Motorcraft AGRF 22
Spark plug gap - 0.030 in (0.8 mm)
Contact breaker points gap:
Bosch - 0.018 in (0.45 mm)
Ford - 0.025 in (0.64 mm)
Dwell angle - 48 to 52 degrees
Ignition timing - 10 degrees BTDC at 800 rpm

1100 cc overhead valve:

Firing order - 1-2-4-3
Bore - 2.91 in (73.96 mm)
Stroke - 2.56 in (64.98 mm)
Cubic capacity - 1117 cc (68.16 cu in)
Compression ratio - 9.0 : 1
Compression pressure - 159 to 188 psi (11 to 13 kg/sg cm)
Idle speed - 750 to 850 rpm
CO percentage - 0.75 to 1.75
Spark plug type - Motorcraft AGRF 22
Spark plug gap - 0.030 in (0.8 mm)
Contact breaker points gap:
Bosch - 0.018 in (0.45 mm)
Ford - 0.025 in (0.64 mm)
Dwell angle - 48 to 52 degrees
Ignition timing - 10 degrees BTDC at 800 rpm

1300 cc overhead valve:

Firing order - 1-2-4-3
Bore - 3.188 in (80.98 mm)
Stroke - 2.48 in (62.99 mm)
Cubic capacity - 1298 cc (79.21 cu in)
Compression ratio - 9.0 : 1 (9.2 : 1 1978 on)
Compression pressure:
high - 142 to 170 psi (10 to 12 kg/sg cm)
Idle speed - 775 to 825 rpm (750 to 850rpm 1978 on)
CO percentage - 1.25 to 1.75
Spark plug type - Motorcraft AGR 12
Spark plug gap - 0.025 in (0.6 mm)
Contact breaker points gap:
Bosch - 0.018 in (0.45 mm)
Ford - 0.025 in (0.64 mm)

Dwell angle - 48 to 52 degrees
Ignition timing - 6 degrees BTDC at 750 to 800 rpm

1600 cc overhead valve:

Firing order - 1-2-4-3
Bore - 3.188 in (80.98 mm)
Stroke - 3.06 in (77.62 mm)
Cubic capacity - 1598 cc (96.87 cu in)
Compression ratio - 8.5 : 1
Idle speed - 775 to 825 rpm
CO percentage - See engine decal
Spark plug type - Motorcraft AGPR 12c
Spark plug gap - 0.025 in (0.6 mm)
Ignition timing - 10 degrees BTDC at 800 rpm

XR2 models:

As above except:
Compression ratio - 9.0 : 1
Compression pressure - 159 to 174 psi (11 to 12 kg/sg cm)
Idle speed - 750 to 850 rpm
CO percentage - 1.25 to 1.75

Valve clearances: (all set with engine cold)

	Inlet
950 c	0.009 in (0.22 mm)
1100 cc	0.009 in (0.22 mm)
1300 cc	0.010 in (0.25 mm)
1600 cc	0.010 in (0.25 mm)

	Exhaust
950 cc	0.023 in (0.60 mm)
1100 cc	0.023 in (0.60 mm)
1300 cc	0.022 in (0.55 mm)
1600 cc	0.022 in (0.55 mm)

ENGINES FROM 1983 TO 1988:

1.0 litre:

Firing order - 1-2-4-3
Bore - 73.96 mm (2.91 in)
Stroke - 55.70 mm (2.19 in)
Cubic capacity - 957 cc (58.4 cu in)
Compression ratio - 8.5 : 1
Compression pressure - 137 to 166 psi (9.5 to 11.5 kg/sg cm)
Idle speed - 750 to 850 rpm
CO percentage - 0.5 to 1.5
Spark plug type - Motorcraft AGRF 22
Spark plug gap - 0.030 in (0.75 mm)
Contact breaker points gap - 0.016 to 0.020 in (0.4 to 0.5 mm)
Dwell angle - 48 to 52 degrees
Ignition timing - 12 degrees BTDC

1.1 litre:

Firing order - 1-2-4-3
Bore - 73.96 mm (2.91 in)
Stroke - 64.98 mm (2.56 in)
Cubic capacity - 1117 cc (68.16 in)
Compression ratio - 9.5 : 1
Compression pressure - 189 to 217 psi (13.3 to 15.3 kgf/cm2)
Idle speed - 750 to 850 rpm
CO percentage - 0.5 to 1.5

Spark plug type - Motorcraft AGRF 22
Spark plug gap - 0.030 in (0.75 mm)
Contact breaker points gap - 0.016 to 0.020 in (0.4 to 0.5 mm)
Dwell angle - 48 to 52 degrees
Ignition timing - 6 degrees BTDC

1.3 litre CVH:
Firing order - 1-3-4-2
Bore - 79.96 mm (3.15 in)
Stroke - 64.52 mm (2.54 in)
Cubic capacity - 1296 cc (79.09 cu in)
Compression ratio - 9.5 : 1
Compression pressure - 159 to 210 psi (11.2 to 14.8 kg/sg cm)
Idle speed - 775 to 825 rpm
CO percentage - 1 to 2
Spark plug type - Motorcraft AGPR 22 C
Spark plug gap - 0.030 in (0.75 mm)
Ignition timing (tick-over) - 12 degrees BTDC

1.4 litre CVH:
As 1.3 litre except:
Bore - 77.24 mm (3.04 in)
Stroke - 74.30 mm (2.93 in)
Cubic capacity - 1392 cc
Spark plug type - Motorcraft Super AGPR 22C

1.6 litre CVH:
Firing order - 1-3-4-2
Bore - 79.96 mm (3.15 in)
Stroke - 79.52 mm (3.13 in)
Cubic capacity - 1597 cc (97.46 cu in)
Compression ratio - 9.5 : 1
Compression pressure - 159 to 210 psi (11.2 to 14.8 kg/sg cm)
Idle speed - 775 to 825 rpm
CO percentage - 1 to 2
Spark plug type - Motorcraft AGPR 12 C
Spark plug gap - 0.030 in (0.75 mm)
Ignition timing (tick-over) - 12 degrees BTDC

1.6 litre diesel
Firing order - 1-3-4-2
Bore - 80.0 mm (3.15 in)
Stroke - 80.0 mm (3.15 in)
Cubic capacity - 1608 cc (98.09 cu in)
Compression ratio - 21.5 : 1
Compression pressure - 28 to 34 bar (406 to 493 lbf/ft2)
Idle speed - 850 to 910 rpm

Valve clearances, petrol: (all set with engine cold)

1.0 and 1.1 litre
Inlet - 0.20 to 0.25 mm (0.008 to 0.010 in)
Exhaust - 0.56 to 0.61 mm (0.22 to 0.24 in)

Valve clearances, diesel: (all set with engine cold)
Inlet - 0.235 to 0.365 mm (0.009 to 0.014 in)
Exhaust - 0.435 to 0.565 mm (0.017 to 0.022 in)

ENGINES FROM 1989 TO 1994:

1.0 litre overhead valve:
Firing order - 1-2-4-3
Bore - 68.68 mm (2.71 in)
Stroke - 67.40 mm (2.66 in)
Cubic capacity - 999 cc (60.94 cu in)

Compression ratio - 9.5 : 1
Idle speed - 700 to 800 rpm
CO percentage - 0.5 to 1.5
Spark plug type - Champion RS9YCC or RS9YC
Spark plug gap - 0.040 in (1.0 mm)
Ignition timing - No data available

1.1 litre overhead valve:
Firing order - 1-2-4-3
Bore - 68.68 mm (2.71 in)
Stroke - 75.48 mm (2.98 in)
Cubic capacity - 1118 cc (68.2 cu in)
Compression ratio - 9.5 : 1
Idle speed - 700 to 800 rpm
CO percentage - 0.5 to 1.5
Spark plug type - Champion RS9YCC or RS9YC
Spark plug gap - 0.040 in (1.0 mm)
Ignition timing - No data available

1.3 litre overhead valve:
Bore - 73.94 mm (2.91 in)
Stroke - 75.48 mm (2.97 in)
Cubic capacity - 1297 cc (79.1 cu in)
Compression ratio (CFi) - 8.8 : 1
Idle speed - 700 to 800 rpm
CO percentage - 0.5 to 1.5
Spark plug type - Champion RC7YCC or RC7YC
Spark plug gap - 0.040 in (1.0 mm)
Ignition timing - 8 to 12 degrees BTDC nominal
Compression pressure:
All OHV (HCS) engines - 13 to 16 bars

Valve clearances: (all set with engine cold)

1.0 and 1.1 litre
Inlet - 0.20 to 0.25 mm (0.008 to 0.010 in)
Exhaust - 0.30 to 0.35 mm (0.012 to 0.014 in)

1.3 litre
Inlet - 0.20 mm (0.008 in)
Exhaust - 0.30 mm (0.012 in)

1.4 litre CVH:
As 1.3 litre CVH except:

1.4 (not CFi)
Compression ratio - 9.5 : 1
Idle speed - 700 to 800 rpm
CO percentage - 0.5 to 1.5
Spark plug type - Champion RC7YCC or RC7YC
Spark plug gap:
RC7YCC - 0.032 in (0.8 mm)
RC7YC - 0.028 in (0.7 mm)
Ignition timing - Controlled by ignition module

1.4 CFi
Compression ratio - 8.5 : 1
Idle speed - 850 to 950 rpm
CO percentage - Closed loop control, not adjustable
Spark plug type - Champion RC7YCC or RC7YC
Spark plug gap:
RC7YCC - 0.040 in (1.0 mm)
Ignition timing - 10 degrees BTDC nominal (Set by manufacturer)

1.6 litre CVH:

As previous 1.6 litre CVH specifications except:

1.6 (not EFi)

Compression ratio - 9.5 : 1
Idle speed - 850 to 950 rpm
CO percentage - 1.25 to 1.75
Spark plug type - Champion RC7YCC or RC7YC
Spark plug gap:
RC7YCC - 0.032 in (0.8 mm)
RC7YC - 0.028 in (0.7 mm)
Ignition timing - No adjustment possible

1.6 EFi

Compression ratio - 9.75 : 1
Idle speed - 700 to 800 rpm
CO percentage - 0.55 to 1.05
Spark plug type - Champion RC6YC or C6YCC
Spark plug gap:
RC6YC - 0.028 in (0.7 mm)
C6YCC - 0.032 in (0.8 mm)
Ignition timing - No adjustment possible

1.6 litre EFi turbocharged

Compression ratio - 8.0 : 1

COMPRESSION PRESSURES

All CVH engines - 12 to 14 bar

TORQUE WRENCH SETTINGS

The torque wrench settings shown here are, in the main, only applicable to this Service Guide. If you do more complex work on the car, requiring further dismantling, refer to a workshop manual.

From 1976 to 1983

	950 and 1100 cc		1300 and 1600cc	
	lbf ft	kgf m	lbf ft	kgf m
Sump drain plug	18	2.4	22	3.0
Spark plugs	13	1.7	25	3.5
Rocker cover	3.3	0.45	3.3	0.45
Distributor clamp	2.6	0.35	2.6	0.35
Alternator mounting	15-18	2.07-3.5	15-18	2.07-3.5
Brake caliper to suspension unit	40	5.5	40	5.5
Wheel bolts	74	10.0	74	10.0

From 1983 to 1988

	1.0 and 1.1 litre		1.3,1.4 & 1.6 litre	
	lbf ft	kgf m	lbf ft	kgf m
Sump drain plug	14	1.9		
Spark plugs	14	1.9	20	2.7
Rocker cover	3	0.4	6	0.8
Distributor clamp	3	0.4	5	0.7
Brake caliper to suspension unit	41	5.6	41	5.6
Wheel bolts	74	10.0	74	10.0

From 1989 to 1994

	1.0 and 1.1 litre		1.4 and 1.6 litre	
	lbf ft	kgf m	lbf ft	kgf m
Sump drain plug	6-9	0.8-1.2	15-21	2.1-2.8
Spark plugs	10-15	1.4-2.0	20	2.7

Rocker cover	3-4	0.4-0.5	4-6	0.6-0.8
Brake caliper to suspension unit	37-49	5.0-6.6	37-49	5.0-6.6
Wheel bolts	52-74	7.0-10.0	52-74	7.0-10.0

1.3 litre HCS

This uses the same figures as the 1.1 litre HCS version except for the following:

	lbf ft	kgf m
Modified rocker cover bolts	3.5	0.5

1.6 litre diesel models

	lbf ft	kgf m
Sump drain plug	16-21	2.1-2.8
Glow plugs to head	18-20	2.5-3.0
Fuel pipe to pump union	12-15	1.6-2.0

CAPACITIES:

Engine oil including filter:

	Imp. pints	litres
1.0 & 1.1 litre	5.7	3.25
1.3 & 1.4 litre	6.2	3.50
1.6 litre	6.2	3.50
DOHC 16-valve	7.5	4.25

Cooling System:

	Imp. pints	litres
1.0 & 1.1 litre engines	9.7	5.5
1.3 & 1.4 litre engines	11.1	6.3
1.6 litre engines	14.1	8.0
DOHC engines	12.3	7.0
Diesel engines	15.0	8.5

Transmission:

Four-speed	4.9	2.8
Five-speed	5.5	3.1
CTX automatic	6.2	3.5

Fuel tank:

All models 1989-on	9.25 gals (42 litres)
Pre-1989 (except XR2)	7.5 gals (34 litres)
XR2 before 1989	8.4 gals (38 litres)

Brake fluid:

All models   Universal Brake & Clutch Fluid

Tyre pressures:

The is an enormous number of different tyre sizes, specifications and pressures that are applicable to the Fiesta range and we recommend that you first look at your Ford Operator's Handbook. If you are in doubt about the correct tyre pressure to use, consult your local tyre specialist.

CHAPTER 9 - TOOLS & EQUIPMENT

Although good tools are not cheap, if you reckon their cost against what you would otherwise spend on professional servicing and repairs, your arithmetic should show you that it doesn't take long to recoup your outlay - and then to start showing a profit!

In fact, there is no need to spend a fortune all at once - most owners who do their own servicing acquire their implements over a long period of time. However, there are some items you simply cannot do without in order to properly carry out the work necessary to keep your car on the road. Therefore, in the following lists, we have concentrated on those items which are likely to be valuable aids to maintaining your car in a good state of tune, and to keep it running sweetly and safely and in addition we have featured some of the tools that are 'nice-to-have' rather than 'must have' because as your tool chest grows, there are some tools that help to make servicing just that bit easier and more thorough to carry out.

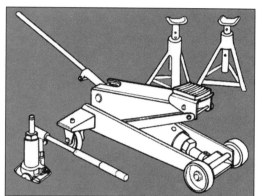

Two vital points - firstly always buy the best quality tools you can afford. 'Cheap and cheerful' items may look similar to more expensive implements, but experience shows that they often fail when the going gets tough, and some can even be dangerous. With proper care, good quality tools will last a lifetime, and can be regarded as an investment. The extra outlay is well worth it, in the long run.

Over the years, there have been various nut/bolt/spanner designations. For many years British cars standardised on 'AF', a designation referring to the measurement 'across the flats' of the hexagon nut or bolt head, while the 'foreigners' were 'Metric'. While there are still many 'AF' cars around, all modern cars are 'Metric' of course, apart from American cars. (For the record, 'metric' sizes are also measured across their flats!). Be sure you know which designation applies to your car before you start buying. Your local motor accessory store should be able to advise, or you could all your local main dealer to make sure, if necessary.

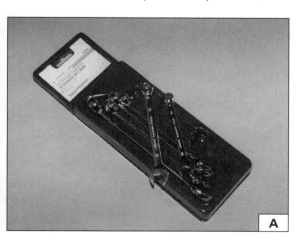

SPANNERS:

A. The two common types of spanner are the ring and the open-ended. The ring spanner grips practically all round the bolt, and is preferable where the bolt is really tight, for an open-ended spanner, merely straddling two flats of the bolt, could slip. On the other hand, the open-end is often quicker and easier to use - so this set of 'Combination' spanners, a ring at one end, open-ended the other, is a nice compromise!

All the tools featured here are available from your local High Street auto-accessory store or Super Store. Any special tools needed for your car are referred to in Chapter 3.

B. While the 'flatness' of the combination spanners (or of a conventional open-ended spanner) is often useful, there are occasions when only the offset, or 'swan neck' of the conventional ring spanner will do the job - like when having to operate over the top of one bolt in order to undo another.

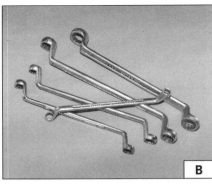

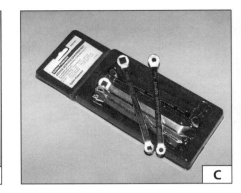

Unlike the combination spanners, the conventional ring and open-ended spanners will have a different size at each end. Usually, the AF sizes will rise in sixteenths of an inch, and the metrics by one millimetre - the following sizes will probably cover most of your needs:
AF - 3/8 x 7/16, 1/2 x 9/16, 5/8 x 11/16, 13/16 x 7/8
Metric - 10 x 11, 12 x 13, 14 x 15, 16 x 17

C. The sturdy specialist brake spanner used, for brake adjusters or bleed nipples, is undeniably a wise buy, as mentioned in the brake servicing text. You might not need the set as shown here, but you can choose individual sizes to suit your car, such as 1/4 in. square x 11/32 in. square or 1/4 in. hexagonal x 5/16 in. AF, or perhaps 8 x 10mm hexagonal - there are others.

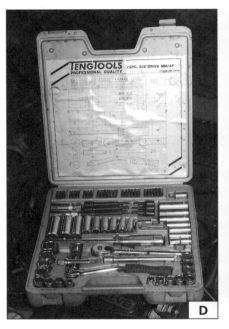

D. A basic socket set should figure highly on your shopping list, for it will cover your basic spanner sizes and can often solve difficult access or extra-leverage problems. This one is a fairly sophisticated set, and includes a number of useful extras, such as spark plug spanners and Allen key and screwdriver bits. Don't buy more than you need, however, and don't be tempted by cheap, nasty - and often dangerous - market stall socket sets.

E. A torque wrench was also once a luxury, but nowadays it's practically essential, with specific torque settings quoted for many of the nuts and bolts used in modern car engineering. The example shown will cater for most applications, including adjustable wheel-bearing hub nuts, but even the next size up (30-150 lb/ft) in the DIY range will still fall short of the 200-odd lb/ft specified for some hub nuts!

F. If you still need a plug spanner, and particularly if your engine features deep-set spark plugs, this Sykes-Pickavant 'extra long plug wrench', combining both 10mm and 14mm sizes, could be a boon. Some plugs are set deeper than the average length of a socket-set spark plug spanner, and if the socket set's extension bar is prone to leaving the spanner socket stuck on the plug, then you could have a problem ...

SCREWDRIVERS:

G. You will need a selection of screwdrivers, both flat-bladed and cross-headed, long ones, short ones, slim ones, fat ones ...

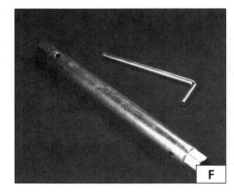

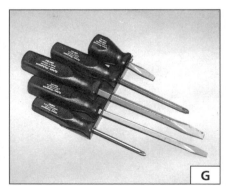

TOOLS & EQUIPMENT

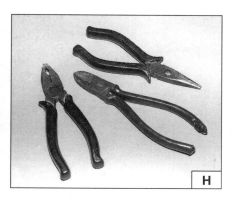

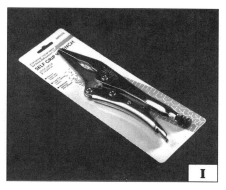

PLIERS:

H. Ordinary combination (or 'engineers') pliers are needed for general work, while a long-nosed pair are handy where access is tight. Their cutting edges are useful for stripping cable insulation, or for snipping wire or trimming split-pin lengths, but you might prefer a pair of specialist side-cutter pliers for such work.

I. Jolly useful as an extra pair of hands, or for gripping such as a rusty nut or bolt really tightly, is a self-grip wrench. This is a long-nose example, but there are also ordinary straight-jaw and round jaw versions.

SUNDRIES:

J. You'll need hammers, including the useful 1lb ball-pein type, plus a hefty copper hammer and maybe a soft (plastic-headed) hammer, too.

K. The wire brush should have brass bristles and as well as an ordinary set of feeler gauges, an 'ignition set' covers most plug and points gap sizes, and includes a points file and a spark plug gap setting tool.

L. You may need a grease gun (although virtually no modern cars have grease points) but you *will* want an oil can, and an oil funnel, and a container of sufficient capacity into which the engine oil can be drained.

M. You may also need a drain plug 'key' suitable for your car unless all the drain plugs are 'bolt'-type hexagons.

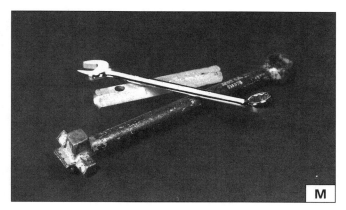

TOOLS & EQUIPMENT

N. Well worthwhile, since some oil filters can be cussedly tight, is some sort of oil filter wrench - this chain-type is a nice example. In extreme cases, even these wrenches can fail to get a grip, in which case, drive an old screwdriver right through the filter and twist it loose.

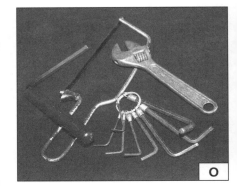

O. A separate set of hand-held Allen keys is a good idea (they come in metric or Imperial sizes), and an adjustable spanner and a 'Junior' hacksaw will have their uses.

P. For your weekly maintenance checks, you'll need a tyre pressure gauge, tyre tread depth gauge and a footpump - which might, like the example here, have an integral pressure gauge. And whether you're wheel-changing at home or roadside, you will welcome the extremely useful Sykes-Pickavant 'Wheelmaster' wrench, which can be extended to give enough leverage to shift those wheel nuts or bolts that the average car-kit wheelbrace wouldn't even look at - see the wheel-change routine at the start of Chapter 3. Remember to carry the extendable wrench with you in the car!

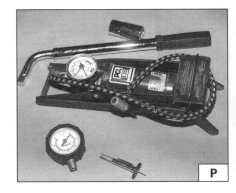

LIFTING:

Q. While the jack supplied with the car *might* be OK for emergency wheel-changes, you would soon tire of trying to use it for servicing operations. Here, you need a good trolley jack, and one of the latest on the market is this 2-ton lifting capacity 'Lift and Lock' example which, as its name suggests, has a built-in fail-safe locking device in the event of hydraulic failure.

R. No matter what sort of jack you use, it is ESSENTIAL that you should not venture beneath a car supported on a jack alone. Having raised it, you need to support it safely and securely. What you need now is definitely NOT house bricks (or any other such potentially dangerous items!) but rather axle stands or wheel-ramps. Adjustable-height stands are essential and both axle stands and ramps should be produced by a 'name' manufacturer, for safety's sake. If you don't need the wheels off, it can be argued that the ramps offer better stability - though you'll benefit from some assistance when it comes to driving upon them. See the start of *Chapter 3*.

TUNING AIDS:

S. As we have said earlier in this chapter and within the servicing sections, the tuning aids that are now available to the DIY market have become practically invaluable 'musts' for the dedicated home mechanic. Any of the Gunson's collection shown here would soon prove their worth. Top of the tree, of course, is their 'Gastester Professional' - don't let its designation suggest that it's not for DIY use, for although it's expensive a group of friends sharing its cost would find their outlay well worth the benefits offered by the unit's Exhaust Gas 'CO' functions, plus its Voltage, Dwell and RPM modes. If it's pure 'multi-meter' you're after, then their 'Digimeter 320' is a tidy little hand-held unit, with clear digital read-outs for such as Volts (DC and household AC) and Amps, Ohms, rpm, and Dwell (degrees and per cent), and its sophistication extends to Frequency, Period and Pulsewidth testing (handy for fuel injection systems), as well as Diode, Resistance and Continuity testing. Also by Gunson's is the powerful 'Timestrobe' xenon timing light, the now not so new, but still novel 'Colortune' and (not shown) the 'Carbalancer'. The latter two devices are virtually invaluable when it comes to carburettor tuning.

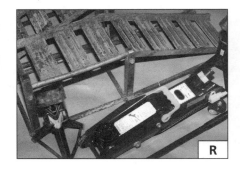

APPENDIX 1
RECOMMENDED CASTROL
LUBRICANTS

ENGINE

PETROL ENGINES

Pre 1987
Castrol GTX (20W/50):

1987 on
Castrol GTX3 Lightec (10W/40): Specially formulated for multi-valve, high-technology engines, including turbos, where a light viscosity oil has been recommended.

DIESEL ENGINES
Castrol GTD (15W/40): Specially formulated for the particular demands of all diesel engines, including turbo-charged.

GEARBOX OIL

MANUAL TRANSMISSION
Castrol Syntrax Universal

AUTOMATIC TRANSMISSION
All models:
Castrol TQ Dexron R III
MTX 75 Gearbox - Castrol FMT

IMPORTANT NOTE: For CTX models, use only Ford fluid available through your Ford dealership.

BRAKE FLUID
Castrol Universal Brake & Clutch Fluid

BRAKE MECHANISM
Areas of metal-to-metal contact
Proprietary brand of high melting point brake grease such as Castrol PH Grease - not conventional high point melting grease.

CV JOINTS
Castrol Moly Grease

WHEEL BEARINGS
Castrol LM Grease

LOCKS AND HINGES
Castrol Everyman Oil (in a can)

HANDBRAKE CABLE AND LINKAGE
Castrol LM Grease

ELECTRICAL CONNECTIONS
Castrol DWF

NUT AND BOLT RELEASE
Castrol Easing Oil

COOLING SYSTEM
Castrol Antifreeze and Summer Coolant

CASTROL ANTIFREEZE: Recommended for use in petrol or diesel engine cooling systems, with aluminium or cast engines. Its formulation of mono ethylene glycol and corrosion inhibitors makes it suitable for all-year-round use, and because it contains no phosphate it is reckoned that the problems of deposits in some modern uprated engines are eliminated. A 33 per cent concentration will protect down to minus 17 degrees C.

SPECIALISTS & SUPPLIERS

APPENDIX 2
SPECIALISTS & SUPPLIERS
FEATURED IN THIS BOOK

All of the products and specialists listed below have contributed in various ways to this book. All of the consumer products used are available through regular high street outlets or by mail order from specialist suppliers.

Castrol (UK) Ltd., Burmah House, Pipers Way, Swindon, Wiltshire, SN3 1RE. Tel: 01793 452222
Contact Castrol's Consumer Technical Department Help Line on the above number for advice on lubrication recommendations.

Dinol (GB) Ltd., Dinol House, 98 Ock Street, Abingdon, Oxford, OX14 5DH. Tel: 01235 530677
Suppliers of Dinitrol rust proofing fluids, and are equipped to carry out rustproofing on vehicles.

Gunson Ltd., Coppen Road, Dagenham, Essex, RM8 1NU. Tel: 0181 984 8855
Electrical and electronic engine tuning equipment.

HPI Autodata, HP Information plc, Dolphin House, P O Box 61, New Street, Salisbury, Wiltshire, SP1 2TB. Tel: 01722 422422
Before buying any used car, check it out with HPI Autodata.

Moff Motors Ltd., Castle Cary, Somerset, BA7 7PF. Tel: 01963 350310

NGK Spark Plugs (UK) Ltd., 7-8-9 Garrick Industrial Centre, Hendon, London, NW9 6AQ. Tel: 0181 202 2151
Top quality spark plugs.

SP Tyres UK Ltd., Fort Dunlop, Birmingham, B24 9QT. Tel: 0121 384 4444
Manufacturers of Dunlop tyres.

Sykes-Pickavant Group plc, Kilnhouse Lane, Lytham St Annes, Lancs, FY8 3DU. Tel: 01253 721291
Wide range of hand tools and specialist equipment, some of which were used in this book.

Waste Oil Disposal
There are 1,300 listed waste oil disposal sites in the UK alone. PLEASE don't foul the environment by tipping waste oil into the drains or the ground. Find your nearest oil disposal point by running the National Rivers Authority on FREEPHONE 0800 663366.

APPENDIX 3
SERVICE HISTORY

This Chapter helps you keep track of all the servicing carried out on your vehicle and can even save you money! A vehicle with a Service History is always worth more than one without, and you can make full use of this section, even if you have a garage or mechanic carry out the work for you. It enables you to specify the jobs you want to have carried out to your vehicle and, of course, it enables you to keep that all-important Service History. And even if your vehicle doesn't have a 'history' going back to when it was new, keeping this Chapter complete will add to your vehicle's value when you come to sell it. Mind you, it obviously won't be enough to just to tick the boxes: keep all your receipts when you buy oil, filters and other consumables or parts. That way, you'll also be able to return any faulty parts if needs be.

Buying Parts

Before carrying out a service on your car, you will need to purchase the right parts. Please refer to **Chapter 2, Buying Guide** for information on how to buy the right parts at the right prices and for information on how to find your car's 'identity numbers'; information that you will need in order to buy the right parts, first time!

Month, whichever comes first, is repeated at each one of the following Service Intervals. The same applies to the **6,000 Miles or Six Months** interval: much of it is repeated at **12,000 Miles or Twelve Months.** Every time a Job or set of Jobs is 'repeated' from an earlier Interval, we show it in a tinted area on the page. You can then see more clearly which jobs are unique to the level of Service Interval that you are on.

The Job Lists

Wherever possible, the Jobs listed in this section have been placed in a logical order or placed into groups that will help you make progress on the car. We have tried to save you too much in the way of unnecessary movement by grouping jobs around areas of the car. Therefore, at each Service Interval, you will see the work grouped into Jobs that need carrying out in The Engine Bay, Around The Car or Under The Car.

You'll also see space at each Service Interval for you to write down the date, price and seller's name every time you buy consumables or accessories. And once again, do remember to keep your receipts! There's also space for you to date and sign the Service Record or for a garage's stamp to be applied.

As you move through the Service Intervals, you will notice that the work carried out at say, **1,500 Miles or Every**

You will also find that all the major Intervals, right up to the 'longest', contain Jobs that are unique to that Service Interval. That's why we have continued this Service History right up to the **36,000 Miles or every Three Years** interval. So now, you will be able to service your car and keep a full record of the work, in the knowledge that your car has been looked after as well as anyone could wish for!

Important Note!

The Service Jobs listed here are intended as a check list and a means of keeping a record of your vehicle's service history, *not* as a set of instructions for working on your car. It is most important that you refer to **Chapter 3, Servicing Your Car** for full details of how to carry out each Job listed here and for essential SAFETY information and, see also, **Chapter 1, Safety First!**.

EVERY 500 MILES, WEEKLY OR BEFORE A LONG JOURNEY

This list is shown, complete, only once. It would have been a bit much to have provided the list 52 times over for use once a week throughout the year! Each job is, however, included with every longer Service list from 3,000 miles/Three Months-on so that each of the 'weekly' Jobs is carried out as part of every service.

Every 500 Miles - The Engine Bay

☐ Job 1. Engine oil level.

☐ Job 2. Check coolant level.

☐ Job 3. Brake fluid level.

☐ Job 4. Check windscreen wash level.

☐ Job 5. Check battery electrolyte level.

Every 500 Miles - Around the Car

☐ Job 6. Check tyre pressures.

☐ Job 7. Check front lights.

☐ Job 8. Check side repeater indicators (if fitted).

☐ Job 9. Check rear lights.

☐ Job 10. Check number plate light.

☐ Job 11. Check interior lights.

☐ Job 12. Check horn.

☐ Job 13. Windscreen wipers.

☐ Job 14. Check screen washers.

☐ Job 15. Check heater blower/demist.

EVERY 1,500 MILES - OR EVERY MONTH, WHICHEVER COMES FIRST

These Jobs are similar to the 500 Mile Jobs but don't need carrying out quite so regularly. Once again, these Jobs are not shown with a separate listing for each 1,500 miles/1 Month interval but they are included as part of every 3,000 miles/Three Months Service list and for every longer Service interval.

Every 1,500 Miles - Around the Car

☐ Job 16. Check tyres.

☐ Job 17. Check spare tyre.

☐ Job 18. Wash bodywork.

☐ Job 19. Touch-up paintwork.

☐ Job 20. Lubricate aerial.

☐ Job 21. Valet interior.

☐ Job 22. Improve visibility.

☐ Job 23. Clean mirrors.

Every 1,500 Miles - Under the Car

☐ Job 24. Clean mud traps.

EVERY 3,000 MILES - OR EVERY THREE MONTHS, WHICHEVER COMES FIRST

All the Service Jobs in the tinted area have been carried forward from earlier service intervals and are to be repeated at this service.

Every 3,000 Miles - The Engine Bay

First carry out all Jobs listed under earlier Service intervals as applicable.

☐ Job 1. Engine oil level.

☐ Job 2. Check coolant level.

☐ Job 3. Brake fluid level.

☐ Job 4. Check windscreen wash level.

☐ Job 5. Check battery electrolyte level.

☐ Job 25. Check alternator drive belt.

☐ Job 26. Check oil filler cap.

☐ Job 27. **DIESEL ENGINES ONLY** Drain fuel filter.

☐ Job 28. Check brake and fuel lines.

Every 3,000 Miles - Around The Car

First carry out all Jobs listed under earlier Service intervals as applicable.

☐ Job 6. Check tyre pressures.

☐ Job 7. Check front lights.

☐ Job 8. Check side repeater indicators (if fitted).

☐ Job 9. Check rear lights.

☐ Job 10. Check number plate light.

☐ Job 11. Check interior lights.

☐ Job 12. Check horn.

☐ Job 13. Windscreen wipers.

☐ Job 14. Check screen washers.

☐ Job 15. Check heater blower/demist.

☐ Job 16. Check tyres.

☐ Job 17. Check spare tyre.

☐ Job 18. Wash bodywork.

☐ Job 19. Touch-up paintwork.

☐ Job 20. Lubricate aerial.

☐ Job 21. Valet interior.

☐ Job 22. Improve visibility.

☐ Job 23. Clean mirrors.

☐ Job 29. Check wheel nuts/bolts.

☐ Job 30. Check handbrake adjustment.

☐ Job 31. Check door and tailgate seals.

☐ Job 32. Check rear view mirrors.

☐ Job 33. Check windscreen.

Every 3,000 Miles - Under the Car

First carry out all Jobs listed under earlier Service intervals as applicable.

☐ Job 24. Clean mud traps.

☐ Job 34. Check exhaust system and mountings.

☐ Job 35. Check brake and fuel lines.

☐ Job 36. Check fuel tank for leaks.

☐ Job 37. Check steering rack gaiters.

☐ Job 38. Check drive shaft gaiters.

☐ Job 39. Check steering ball joints.

☐ Job 40. Check suspension joints and bushes.

☐ Job 41. Check underside for leaks.

☐ Job 42. Check ABS braking (where fitted).

Every 3,000 Miles - Road Test

☐ Job 43. Clean controls.

☐ Job 44. Check instruments and controls.

☐ Job 45. Check throttle and choke action.

☐ Job 46. Check clutch action.

☐ Job 47. Road test of brakes and steering.

Date serviced:...

Carried out by:...
Garage Stamp or signature:

Parts/Accessories purchased (date, parts, source) ....

....

....

....

....

EVERY 6,000 MILES - OR EVERY SIX MONTHS, WHICHEVER COMES FIRST

All the Service Jobs in the tinted area have been carried forward from earlier service intervals and are to be repeated at this service.

Every 6,000 Miles - The Engine Bay

First carry out all Jobs listed under earlier Service intervals as applicable.

☐ Job 2. Check coolant level.

☐ Job 3. Brake fluid level.

☐ Job 4. Check windscreen wash level.

☐ Job 5. Check battery electrolyte level.

☐ Job 25. Check alternator drive belt.

☐ Job 26. Check oil filler cap.

☐ Job 27. **DIESEL ENGINES ONLY** Drain fuel filter.

☐ Job 28. Check brake and fuel lines.

☐ Job 48. Change engine oil.

☐ Job 49. Change oil filter.

☐ Job 50. Clean and check spark plugs.

☐ Job 51. Clean and check ignition components.

☐ Job 52. Check/set C.B. points/dwell angle.

☐ Job 53. Contact breaker points renewal.

☐ Job 54. Check ignition timing.

☐ Job 55. Check/lubricate wiper mechanism.

☐ Job 56. Check battery electrolyte.

☐ Job 57. Clean radiator.

☐ Job 58. Check water pump.

☐ Job 59. Check CVH camshaft belt.

☐ Job 60. Check manual gearbox oil.

☐ Job 61. Check automatic transmission fluid.

☐ Job 62. Check steering column couplings.

☐ Job 63. Check/adjust valve clearances.

☐ Job 64. Lubricate carburettor linkages.

☐ Job 65. **NOT FUEL INJECTION ENGINES** Adjust carburettor.

☐ Job 66. **FUEL INJECTION PETROL ENGINES** Check idle speed.

☐ Job 67. **DIESEL ENGINES ONLY** Check idle speed.

☐ Job 68. Check exhaust emission.

Every 6,000 Miles - Around the Car

First carry out all Jobs listed under earlier Service intervals as applicable.

☐ Job 6. Check tyre pressures.

☐ Job 7. Check front lights.

☐ Job 8. Check side repeater indicators (if fitted).

☐ Job 9. Check rear lights.

☐ Job 10. Check number plate light.

☐ Job 11. Check interior lights.

☐ Job 12. Check horn.

☐ Job 13. Windscreen wipers.

☐ Job 14. Check screen washers.

☐ Job 15. Check heater blower/demist.

☐ Job 16. Check tyres.

☐ Job 17. Check spare tyre.

☐ Job 18. Wash bodywork.

☐ Job 19. Touch-up paintwork.

☐ Job 20. Lubricate aerial.

☐ Job 21. Valet interior.

☐ Job 22. Improve visibility.

☐ Job 23. Clean mirrors.

☐ Job 29. Check wheel nuts/bolts.

☐ Job 30. Check handbrake adjustment.

☐ Job 31. Check door and tailgate seals.

☐ Job 32. Check rear view mirrors.

☐ Job 33. Check windscreen.

Every 6,000 Miles - Under the Car

☐ Job 24. Clean mud traps.

☐ Job 34. Check exhaust system and mountings.

☐ Job 35. Check brake and fuel lines.

☐ Job 36. Check fuel tank for leaks.

☐ Job 37. Check steering rack gaiters.

☐ Job 38. Check drive shaft gaiters.

☐ Job 39. Check steering ball joints.

☐ Job 40. Check suspension joints and bushes.

☐ Job 41. Check underside for leaks.

☐ Job 42. Check ABS braking (where fitted).

Every 6,000 Miles - Road Test

☐ Job 43. Clean controls.

☐ Job 44. Check instruments and controls.

☐ Job 45. Check throttle and choke action.

☐ Job 46. Check clutch action.

☐ Job 47. Road test of brakes and steering.

EVERY 9,000 MILES - OR EVERY NINE MONTHS, WHICHEVER COMES FIRST

All the Jobs at this Service Interval have been carried forward from earlier Service Intervals and are to be repeated at this service.

Every 9,000 Miles - The Engine Bay

☐ Job 1. Engine oil level.

☐ Job 2. Check coolant level.

☐ Job 3. Brake fluid level.

☐ Job 4. Check windscreen wash level.

☐ Job 5. Check battery electrolyte level.

☐ Job 25. Check alternator drive belt.

☐ Job 26. Check oil filler cap.

☐ Job 27. **DIESEL ENGINES ONLY** Drain fuel filter.

☐ Job 28. Check brake and fuel lines.

☐ Job 69. Check seat belts and mountings.

☐ Job 70. Check fuel filler seal.

☐ Job 71. **NOT HIGH SECURITY LOCKS** Lubricate locks, check straps and hinges.

☐ Job 72. Lubricate bonnet release.

☐ Job 73. Check seat mountings.

☐ Job 74. Check shock absorber action.

☐ Job 75. Check/renew front brake pads.

☐ Job 76. Check/renew rear brake shoes.

Date serviced:..

Carried out by:..
Garage Stamp or signature:

Parts/Accessories purchased (date, parts, source) ....
....
....
....
....

Every 9,000 Miles - Around The Car

- [ ] Job 6. Check tyre pressures.
- [ ] Job 7. Check front lights.
- [ ] Job 8. Check side repeater indicators (if fitted).
- [ ] Job 9. Check rear lights.
- [ ] Job 10. Check number plate light.
- [ ] Job 11. Check interior lights.
- [ ] Job 12. Check horn.
- [ ] Job 13. Windscreen wipers.
- [ ] Job 14. Check screen washers.
- [ ] Job 15. Check heater blower/demist.
- [ ] Job 16. Check tyres.
- [ ] Job 17. Check spare tyre.
- [ ] Job 18. Wash bodywork.
- [ ] Job 19. Touch-up paintwork.
- [ ] Job 20. Lubricate aerial.
- [ ] Job 21. Valet interior.
- [ ] Job 22. Improve visibility.
- [ ] Job 23. Clean mirrors.
- [ ] Job 29. Check wheel nuts/bolts.
- [ ] Job 30. Check handbrake adjustment.
- [ ] Job 31. Check door and tailgate seals.
- [ ] Job 32. Check rear view mirrors.
- [ ] Job 33. Check windscreen.

Every 9,000 Miles - Under the Car

- [ ] Job 24. Clean mud traps.
- [ ] Job 34. Check exhaust system and mountings.
- [ ] Job 35. Check brake and fuel lines.
- [ ] Job 36. Check fuel tank for leaks.
- [ ] Job 37. Check steering rack gaiters.
- [ ] Job 38. Check drive shaft gaiters.
- [ ] Job 39. Check steering ball joints.
- [ ] Job 40. Check suspension joints and bushes.
- [ ] Job 41. Check underside for leaks.
- [ ] Job 42. Check ABS braking (where fitted).

Every 9,000 Miles - Road Test

- [ ] Job 43. Clean controls.
- [ ] Job 44. Check instruments and controls.
- [ ] Job 45. Check throttle and choke action.
- [ ] Job 46. Check clutch action.
- [ ] Job 47. Road test of brakes and steering.

Date serviced: ....

Carried out by: ....
Garage Stamp or signature:

Parts/Accessories purchased (date, parts, source) ....

....

....

....

....

EVERY 12,000 MILES - OR EVERY TWELVE MONTHS, WHICHEVER COMES FIRST

All the Service Jobs in the tinted area have been carried forward from earlier service intervals and are to be repeated at this service.

Every 12,000 Miles - The Engine Bay

First carry out all Jobs listed under earlier Service intervals as applicable.

- [ ] Job 4. Check windscreen wash level.
- [ ] Job 5. Check battery electrolyte level.
- [ ] Job 25. Check alternator drive belt.
- [ ] Job 26. Check oil filler cap.
- [ ] Job 27. **DIESEL ENGINES ONLY** Drain fuel filter.
- [ ] Job 28. Check brake and fuel lines.
- [ ] Job 48. Change engine oil.
- [ ] Job 49. Change oil filter.
- [ ] Job 51. Clean and check ignition components.
- [ ] Job 52. Check/set C.B. points/dwell angle.
- [ ] Job 53. Contact breaker points renewal.
- [ ] Job 54. Check ignition timing.
- [ ] Job 55. Check/lubricate wiper mechanism.
- [ ] Job 56. Check battery electrolyte.
- [ ] Job 57. Clean radiator.
- [ ] Job 58. Check water pump.
- [ ] Job 59. Check CVH camshaft belt.
- [ ] Job 60. Check manual gearbox oil.
- [ ] Job 61. Check automatic transmission fluid.
- [ ] Job 62. Check steering column couplings.
- [ ] Job 63. Check/adjust valve clearances.
- [ ] Job 64. Lubricate carburettor linkages.
- [ ] Job 65. **NOT FUEL INJECTION ENGINES** Adjust carburettor.
- [ ] Job 66. **FUEL INJECTION PETROL ENGINES** Check idle speed.
- [ ] Job 67. **DIESEL ENGINES ONLY** Check idle speed.
- [ ] Job 68. Check exhaust emission.

☐ Job 77. Change air filter element.

☐ Job 78. Clean air filter housing.

☐ Job 79. Check air intake control valve.

☐ Job 80. **DIESEL ENGINES ONLY** Check valve clearances.

☐ Job 81. Renew fuel filter.

☐ Job 82. Check vacuum hoses.

☐ Job 83. Check/renew crankcase hoses and valves.

☐ Job 84. Check cooling system hoses.

☐ Job 85. Replace coolant.

☐ Job 86. **PETROL ENGINES** Renew spark plugs.

☐ Job 87. **DIESEL ENGINES** Clean glow plugs.

☐ Job 88. Clean battery terminals.

☐ Job 89. Check wiring and terminals.

☐ Job 90. Check door light switches.

Every 12,000 Miles - Around the Car

First carry out all Jobs listed under earlier Service intervals as applicable.

☐ Job 6. Check tyre pressures.

☐ Job 7. Check front lights.

☐ Job 8. Check side repeater indicators (if fitted).

☐ Job 9. Check rear lights.

☐ Job 10. Check number plate light.

☐ Job 11. Check interior lights.

☐ Job 12. Check horn.

☐ Job 14. Check screen washers.

☐ Job 15. Check heater blower/demist.

☐ Job 16. Check tyres.

☐ Job 17. Check spare tyre.

☐ Job 18. Wash bodywork.

☐ Job 19. Touch-up paintwork.

☐ Job 20. Lubricate aerial.

☐ Job 21. Valet interior.

☐ Job 22. Improve visibility.

☐ Job 23. Clean mirrors.

☐ Job 29. Check wheel nuts/bolts.

☐ Job 30. Check handbrake adjustment.

☐ Job 31. Check door and tailgate seals.

☐ Job 32. Check rear view mirrors.

☐ Job 33. Check windscreen.

☐ Job 69. Check seat belts and mountings.

☐ Job 70. Check fuel filler seal.

☐ Job 71. **NOT HIGH SECURITY LOCKS** Lubricate locks, check straps and hinges.

☐ Job 72. Lubricate bonnet release.

☐ Job 73. Check seat mountings.

☐ Job 74. Check shock absorber action.

☐ Job 75. Check/renew front brake pads.

☐ Job 76. Check/renew rear brake shoes.

☐ Job 91. Clean tailgate electrical contacts.

☐ Job 92. Check tool kit and jack.

☐ Job 93. Lubricate window and sunroof runners.

☐ Job 94. Renew wiper blades.

☐ Job 95. Check hub bearings.

☐ Job 96. Check steering and suspension.

☐ Job 97. Check floors.

☐ Job 98. Renew alarm sender unit batteries.

Every 12,000 Miles - Under the Car

First carry out all Jobs listed under earlier Service intervals as applicable.

☐ Job 24. Clean mud traps.

☐ Job 34. Check exhaust system and mountings.

☐ Job 35. Check brake and fuel lines.

☐ Job 36. Check fuel tank for leaks.

☐ Job 37. Check steering rack gaiters.

☐ Job 38. Check drive shaft gaiters.

☐ Job 39. Check steering ball joints.

☐ Job 40. Check suspension joints and bushes.

☐ Job 41. Check underside for leaks.

☐ Job 42. Check ABS braking (where fitted).

☐ Job 99. Inspect underside.

☐ Job 100. Clear drain holes.

☐ Job 101. Renew brake fluid.

☐ Job 102. Check engine and gearbox mountings.

☐ Job 103. Lubricate handbrake linkage.

Every 12,000 Miles - Road Test

☐ Job 43. Clean controls.

☐ Job 44. Check instruments and controls.

☐ Job 45. Check throttle and choke action.

☐ Job 46. Check clutch action.

☐ Job 47. Road test of brakes and steering.

Date serviced:...

Carried out by:...
Garage Stamp or signature:

Parts/Accessories purchased (date, parts, source) ....
....
....
....
....

EVERY 15,000 MILES - OR EVERY FIFTEEN MONTHS, WHICHEVER COMES FIRST

All the Jobs at this Service Interval have been carried forward from earlier Service Intervals and are to be repeated at this service.

Every 15,000 Miles - The Engine Bay

- [ ] Job 1. Engine oil level.
- [ ] Job 2. Check coolant level.
- [ ] Job 3. Brake fluid level.
- [ ] Job 4. Check windscreen wash level.
- [ ] Job 5. Check battery electrolyte level.
- [ ] Job 25. Check alternator drive belt.
- [ ] Job 26. Check oil filler cap.
- [ ] Job 27. **DIESEL ENGINES ONLY** Drain fuel filter.
- [ ] Job 28. Check brake and fuel lines.

Every 15,000 Miles - Around The Car

- [ ] Job 6. Check tyre pressures.
- [ ] Job 7. Check front lights.
- [ ] Job 8. Check side repeater indicators (if fitted).
- [ ] Job 9. Check rear lights.
- [ ] Job 10. Check number plate light.
- [ ] Job 11. Check interior lights.
- [ ] Job 12. Check horn.
- [ ] Job 13. Windscreen wipers.
- [ ] Job 14. Check screen washers.
- [ ] Job 15. Check heater blower/demist.
- [ ] Job 16. Check tyres.
- [ ] Job 17. Check spare tyre.
- [ ] Job 18. Wash bodywork.
- [ ] Job 19. Touch-up paintwork.
- [ ] Job 20. Lubricate aerial.
- [ ] Job 21. Valet interior.
- [ ] Job 22. Improve visibility.
- [ ] Job 23. Clean mirrors.
- [ ] Job 29. Check wheel nuts/bolts.
- [ ] Job 30. Check handbrake adjustment.
- [ ] Job 31. Check door and tailgate seals.
- [ ] Job 32. Check rear view mirrors.
- [ ] Job 33. Check windscreen.

Every 15,000 Miles - Under the Car

- [ ] Job 24. Clean mud traps.
- [ ] Job 34. Check exhaust system and mountings.
- [ ] Job 35. Check brake and fuel lines.
- [ ] Job 36. Check fuel tank for leaks.
- [ ] Job 37. Check steering rack gaiters.
- [ ] Job 38. Check drive shaft gaiters.
- [ ] Job 39. Check steering ball joints.
- [ ] Job 40. Check suspension joints and bushes.
- [ ] Job 41. Check underside for leaks.
- [ ] Job 42. Check ABS braking (where fitted).

Every 15,000 Miles - Road Test

- [ ] Job 43. Clean controls.
- [ ] Job 44. Check instruments and controls.
- [ ] Job 45. Check throttle and choke action.
- [ ] Job 46. Check clutch action.
- [ ] Job 47. Road test of brakes and steering.

Date serviced:......................................

Carried out by:....................................
Garage Stamp or signature:

Parts/Accessories purchased (date, parts, source)...
....
....
....
....

EVERY 18,000 MILES - OR EVERY EIGHTEEN MONTHS, WHICHEVER COMES FIRST

All the Jobs at this Service Interval have been carried forward from earlier Service Intervals and are to be repeated at this service.

Every 18,000 Miles - The Engine Bay

- [ ] Job 2. Check coolant level.
- [ ] Job 3. Brake fluid level.
- [ ] Job 4. Check windscreen wash level.
- [ ] Job 5. Check battery electrolyte level.
- [ ] Job 25. Check alternator drive belt.
- [ ] Job 26. Check oil filler cap.
- [ ] Job 27. **DIESEL ENGINES ONLY** Drain fuel filter.
- [ ] Job 28. Check brake and fuel lines.
- [ ] Job 48. Change engine oil.
- [ ] Job 49. Change oil filter.
- [ ] Job 50. Clean and check spark plugs.
- [ ] Job 51. Clean and check ignition components.
- [ ] Job 52. Check/set C.B. points/dwell angle.
- [ ] Job 53. Contact breaker points renewal.
- [ ] Job 54. Check ignition timing.
- [ ] Job 55. Check/lubricate wiper mechanism.
- [ ] Job 56. Check battery electrolyte.
- [ ] Job 57. Clean radiator.
- [ ] Job 58. Check water pump.
- [ ] Job 59. Check CVH camshaft belt.
- [ ] Job 60. Check manual gearbox oil.
- [ ] Job 61. Check automatic transmission fluid.
- [ ] Job 62. Check steering column couplings.
- [ ] Job 63. Check/adjust valve clearances.
- [ ] Job 64. Lubricate carburettor linkages.
- [ ] Job 65. **NOT FUEL INJECTION ENGINES** Adjust carburettor.
- [ ] Job 66. **FUEL INJECTION PETROL ENGINES** Check idle speed.
- [ ] Job 67. **DIESEL ENGINES ONLY** Check idle speed.
- [ ] Job 68. Check exhaust emission.

Every 18,000 Miles - Around the Car

- [ ] Job 6. Check tyre pressures.
- [ ] Job 7. Check front lights.
- [ ] Job 8. Check side repeater indicators (if fitted).
- [ ] Job 9. Check rear lights.
- [ ] Job 10. Check number plate light.
- [ ] Job 11. Check interior lights.
- [ ] Job 12. Check horn.
- [ ] Job 13. Windscreen wipers.
- [ ] Job 14. Check screen washers.
- [ ] Job 15. Check heater blower/demist.
- [ ] Job 16. Check tyres.
- [ ] Job 17. Check spare tyre.
- [ ] Job 18. Wash bodywork.
- [ ] Job 19. Touch-up paintwork.
- [ ] Job 20. Lubricate aerial.
- [ ] Job 21. Valet interior.
- [ ] Job 22. Improve visibility.
- [ ] Job 23. Clean mirrors.
- [ ] Job 29. Check wheel nuts/bolts.
- [ ] Job 30. Check handbrake adjustment.
- [ ] Job 31. Check door and tailgate seals.
- [ ] Job 32. Check rear view mirrors.
- [ ] Job 33. Check windscreen.
- [ ] Job 69. Check seat belts and mountings.
- [ ] Job 70. Check fuel filler seal.
- [ ] Job 71. **NOT HIGH SECURITY LOCKS** Lubricate locks, check straps and hinges.
- [ ] Job 72. Lubricate bonnet release.
- [ ] Job 73. Check seat mountings.
- [ ] Job 74. Check shock absorber action.
- [ ] Job 75. Check/renew front brake pads.
- [ ] Job 76. Check/renew rear brake shoes.

Every 18,000 Miles - Under the Car

First carry out all Jobs listed under earlier Service intervals as applicable.

- [ ] Job 24. Clean mud traps.
- [ ] Job 34. Check exhaust system and mountings.
- [ ] Job 35. Check brake and fuel lines.
- [ ] Job 36. Check fuel tank for leaks.
- [ ] Job 37. Check steering rack gaiters.
- [ ] Job 38. Check drive shaft gaiters.
- [ ] Job 39. Check steering ball joints.
- [ ] Job 40. Check suspension joints and bushes.
- [ ] Job 41. Check underside for leaks.
- [ ] Job 42. Check ABS braking (where fitted).

Every 18,000 Miles - Road Test

- [ ] Job 43. Clean controls.
- [ ] Job 44. Check instruments and controls.
- [ ] Job 45. Check throttle and choke action.
- [ ] Job 46. Check clutch action.
- [ ] Job 47. Road test of brakes and steering.

Date serviced:...

Carried out by: ....
Garage Stamp or signature:

Parts/Accessories purchased (date, parts, source) ....
....
....
....
....

EVERY 21,000 MILES - OR EVERY TWENTY ONE MONTHS, WHICHEVER COMES FIRST

All the Jobs at this Service Interval have been carried forward from earlier Service Intervals and are to be repeated at this service.

Every 21,000 Miles - The Engine Bay

- [ ] Job 1. Engine oil level.
- [ ] Job 2. Check coolant level.
- [ ] Job 3. Brake fluid level.
- [ ] Job 4. Check windscreen wash level.
- [ ] Job 5. Check battery electrolyte level.
- [ ] Job 25. Check alternator drive belt.
- [ ] Job 26. Check oil filler cap.
- [ ] Job 27. **DIESEL ENGINES ONLY** Drain fuel filter.
- [ ] Job 28. Check brake and fuel lines.

Every 21,000 Miles - Around the Car

- [ ] Job 6. Check tyre pressures.
- [ ] Job 7. Check front lights.
- [ ] Job 8. Check side repeater indicators (if fitted).
- [ ] Job 9. Check rear lights.
- [ ] Job 10. Check number plate light.
- [ ] Job 11. Check interior lights.
- [ ] Job 12. Check horn.
- [ ] Job 13. Windscreen wipers.
- [ ] Job 14. Check screen washers.
- [ ] Job 15. Check heater blower/demist.
- [ ] Job 16. Check tyres.
- [ ] Job 17. Check spare tyre.
- [ ] Job 18. Wash bodywork.
- [ ] Job 19. Touch-up paintwork.
- [ ] Job 20. Lubricate aerial.
- [ ] Job 21. Valet interior.
- [ ] Job 22. Improve visibility.
- [ ] Job 23. Clean mirrors.
- [ ] Job 29. Check wheel nuts/bolts.
- [ ] Job 30. Check handbrake adjustment.
- [ ] Job 31. Check door and tailgate seals.
- [ ] Job 32. Check rear view mirrors.
- [ ] Job 33. Check windscreen.

Every 21,000 Miles - Under the Car

- [ ] Job 24. Clean mud traps.
- [ ] Job 34. Check exhaust system and mountings.
- [ ] Job 35. Check brake and fuel lines.
- [ ] Job 36. Check fuel tank for leaks.
- [ ] Job 37. Check steering rack gaiters.
- [ ] Job 38. Check drive shaft gaiters.
- [ ] Job 39. Check steering ball joints.
- [ ] Job 40. Check suspension joints and bushes.
- [ ] Job 41. Check underside for leaks.
- [ ] Job 42. Check ABS braking (where fitted).

Every 21,000 Miles - Road Test

- [ ] Job 43. Clean controls.
- [ ] Job 44. Check instruments and controls.
- [ ] Job 45. Check throttle and choke action.
- [ ] Job 46. Check clutch action.
- [ ] Job 47. Road test of brakes and steering.

Date serviced:...

Carried out by: ....
Garage Stamp or signature:

Parts/Accessories purchased (date, parts,

source) ....

....

....

....

....

EVERY 24,000 MILES - OR EVERY TWO YEARS, WHICHEVER COMES FIRST

All the Service Jobs in the tinted area have been carried forward from earlier service intervals and are to be repeated at this service.

Every 24,000 Miles - The Engine Bay

First carry out all Jobs listed under earlier Service intervals as applicable.

- [ ] Job 4. Check windscreen wash level.
- [ ] Job 5. Check battery electrolyte level.
- [ ] Job 26. Check oil filler cap.
- [ ] Job 27. **DIESEL ENGINES ONLY** Drain fuel filter.
- [ ] Job 28. Check brake and fuel lines.
- [ ] Job 48. Change engine oil.
- [ ] Job 49. Change oil filter.
- [ ] Job 51. Clean and check ignition components.
- [ ] Job 52. Check/set C.B. points/dwell angle.
- [ ] Job 53. Contact breaker points renewal.
- [ ] Job 54. Check ignition timing.
- [ ] Job 55. Check/lubricate wiper mechanism.
- [ ] Job 56. Check battery electrolyte.
- [ ] Job 57. Clean radiator.
- [ ] Job 58. Check water pump.
- [ ] Job 59. Check CVH camshaft belt.
- [ ] Job 60. Check manual gearbox oil.
- [ ] Job 61. Check automatic transmission fluid.
- [ ] Job 62. Check steering column couplings.
- [ ] Job 63. Check/adjust valve clearances.
- [ ] Job 64. Lubricate carburettor linkages.
- [ ] Job 65. **NOT FUEL INJECTION ENGINES** Adjust carburettor.
- [ ] Job 66. **FUEL INJECTION PETROL ENGINES** Check idle speed.
- [ ] Job 67. **DIESEL ENGINES ONLY** Check idle speed.
- [ ] Job 68. Check exhaust emission.
- [ ] Job 77. Change air filter element.
- [ ] Job 78. Clean air filter housing.
- [ ] Job 79. Check air intake control valve.
- [ ] Job 80. **DIESEL ENGINES ONLY:** Check valve clearances.
- [ ] Job 81. Renew fuel filter.
- [ ] Job 82. Check vacuum hoses.
- [ ] Job 83. Check/renew crankcase hoses and valves.
- [ ] Job 84. Check cooling system hoses.
- [ ] Job 85. Replace coolant.
- [ ] Job 86. **PETROL ENGINES** Renew spark plugs.
- [ ] Job 87. **DIESEL ENGINES** Clean glow plugs.
- [ ] Job 88. Clean battery terminals.
- [ ] Job 89. Check wiring and terminals.
- [ ] Job 90. Check door light switches.

- [ ] Job 104. Renew coolant expansion tank cap.
- [ ] Job 105. Renew alternator drive belt.

Every 24,000 Miles - Around the Car

Every 24,000 Miles - Under the Car

- [ ] Job 6. Check tyre pressures.
- [ ] Job 7. Check front lights.
- [ ] Job 8. Check side repeater indicators (if fitted).
- [ ] Job 9. Check rear lights.
- [ ] Job 10. Check number plate light.
- [ ] Job 11. Check interior lights.
- [ ] Job 12. Check horn.
- [ ] Job 14. Check screen washers.
- [ ] Job 15. Check heater blower/demist.
- [ ] Job 16. Check tyres.
- [ ] Job 17. Check spare tyre.
- [ ] Job 18. Wash bodywork.
- [ ] Job 19. Touch-up paintwork.
- [ ] Job 20. Lubricate aerial.
- [ ] Job 21. Valet interior.
- [ ] Job 22. Improve visibility.
- [ ] Job 23. Clean mirrors.
- [ ] Job 29. Check wheel nuts/bolts.
- [ ] Job 30. Check handbrake adjustment.
- [ ] Job 31. Check door and tailgate seals.
- [ ] Job 32. Check rear view mirrors.
- [ ] Job 33. Check windscreen.
- [ ] Job 69. Check seat belts and mountings.
- [ ] Job 70. Check fuel filler seal.
- [ ] Job 71. **NOT HIGH SECURITY LOCKS** Lubricate locks, check straps and hinges.
- [ ] Job 72. Lubricate bonnet release.
- [ ] Job 73. Check seat mountings.
- [ ] Job 74. Check shock absorber action.
- [ ] Job 75. Check/renew front brake pads.
- [ ] Job 76. Check/renew rear brake shoes.
- [ ] Job 91. Clean tailgate electrical contacts.
- [ ] Job 92. Check tool kit and jack.
- [ ] Job 93. Lubricate window and sunroof runners.
- [ ] Job 94. Renew wiper blades.
- [ ] Job 95. Check hub bearings.
- [ ] Job 96. Check steering and suspension.
- [ ] Job 97. Check floors.
- [ ] Job 98. Renew alarm sender unit batteries.

Every 24,000 Miles - Road Test

- Job 24. Clean mud traps.
- Job 34. Check exhaust system and mountings.
- Job 35. Check brake and fuel lines.
- Job 36. Check fuel tank for leaks.
- Job 37. Check steering rack gaiters.
- Job 38. Check drive shaft gaiters.
- Job 39. Check steering ball joints.
- Job 40. Check suspension joints and bushes.
- Job 41. Check underside for leaks.
- Job 42. Check ABS braking (where fitted).
- Job 99. Inspect underside.
- Job 100. Clear drain holes.
- Job 101. Renew brake fluid.
- Job 102. Check engine and gearbox mountings.
- Job 103. Lubricate handbrake linkage.

- Job 43. Clean controls.
- Job 44. Check instruments and controls.
- Job 45. Check throttle and choke action.
- Job 46. Check clutch action.
- Job 47. Road test of brakes and steering.

EVERY 27,000 MILES - OR EVERY TWENTY SEVEN MONTHS, WHICHEVER COMES FIRST

All the Jobs at this Service Interval have been carried forward from earlier Service Intervals and are to be repeated at this service.

Every 27,000 Miles - The Engine Bay

- Job 1. Engine oil level.
- Job 2. Check coolant level.
- Job 3. Brake fluid level.
- Job 4. Check windscreen wash level.
- Job 5. Check battery electrolyte level.
- Job 25. Check alternator drive belt.
- Job 26. Check oil filler cap.
- Job 27. **DIESEL ENGINES ONLY** Drain fuel filter.
- Job 28. Check brake and fuel lines.

Date serviced:...

Carried out by: ....
Garage Stamp or signature:

Parts/Accessories purchased (date, parts, source) ....
....
....
....
....

Every 27,000 Miles - Around the Car

- [ ] Job 6. Check tyre pressures.
- [ ] Job 7. Check front lights.
- [ ] Job 8. Check side repeater indicators (if fitted).
- [ ] Job 9. Check rear lights.
- [ ] Job 10. Check number plate light.
- [ ] Job 11. Check interior lights.
- [ ] Job 12. Check horn.
- [ ] Job 13. Windscreen wipers.
- [ ] Job 14. Check screen washers.
- [ ] Job 15. Check heater blower/demist.
- [ ] Job 16. Check tyres.
- [ ] Job 17. Check spare tyre.
- [ ] Job 18. Wash bodywork.
- [ ] Job 19. Touch-up paintwork.
- [ ] Job 20. Lubricate aerial.
- [ ] Job 21. Valet interior.
- [ ] Job 22. Improve visibility.
- [ ] Job 23. Clean mirrors.
- [ ] Job 29. Check wheel nuts/bolts.
- [ ] Job 30. Check handbrake adjustment.
- [ ] Job 31. Check door and tailgate seals.
- [ ] Job 32. Check rear view mirrors.
- [ ] Job 33. Check windscreen.

Every 27,000 Miles - Under the Car

- [ ] Job 24. Clean mud traps.
- [ ] Job 34. Check exhaust system and mountings.
- [ ] Job 35. Check brake and fuel lines.
- [ ] Job 36. Check fuel tank for leaks.
- [ ] Job 37. Check steering rack gaiters.
- [ ] Job 38. Check drive shaft gaiters.
- [ ] Job 39. Check steering ball joints.
- [ ] Job 40. Check suspension joints and bushes.
- [ ] Job 41. Check underside for leaks.
- [ ] Job 42. Check ABS braking (where fitted).

Every 27,000 Miles - Road Test

- [ ] Job 43. Clean controls.
- [ ] Job 44. Check instruments and controls.
- [ ] Job 45. Check throttle and choke action.
- [ ] Job 46. Check clutch action.
- [ ] Job 47. Road test of brakes and steering.

EVERY 30,000 MILES - OR EVERY THIRTY MONTHS, WHICHEVER COMES FIRST

All the Jobs at this Service Interval have been carried forward from earlier Service Intervals and are to be repeated at this service.

Every 30,000 Miles - The Engine Bay

- [ ] Job 2. Check coolant level.
- [ ] Job 3. Brake fluid level.
- [ ] Job 4. Check windscreen wash level.
- [ ] Job 5. Check battery electrolyte level.
- [ ] Job 25. Check alternator drive belt.
- [ ] Job 26. Check oil filler cap.
- [ ] Job 27. **DIESEL ENGINES ONLY** Drain fuel filter.
- [ ] Job 28. Check brake and fuel lines.
- [ ] Job 48. Change engine oil.
- [ ] Job 49. Change oil filter.
- [ ] Job 50. Clean and check spark plugs.
- [ ] Job 51. Clean and check ignition components.
- [ ] Job 52. Check/set C.B. points/dwell angle.
- [ ] Job 53. Contact breaker points renewal.
- [ ] Job 54. Check ignition timing.
- [ ] Job 55. Check/lubricate wiper mechanism.
- [ ] Job 56. Check battery electrolyte.
- [ ] Job 57. Clean radiator.
- [ ] Job 58. Check water pump.
- [ ] Job 59. Check CVH camshaft belt.
- [ ] Job 60. Check manual gearbox oil.
- [ ] Job 61. Check automatic transmission fluid.
- [ ] Job 62. Check steering column couplings.
- [ ] Job 63. Check/adjust valve clearances.
- [ ] Job 64. Lubricate carburettor linkages.
- [ ] Job 65. **NOT FUEL INJECTION ENGINES** Adjust carburettor.
- [ ] Job 66. **FUEL INJECTION PETROL ENGINES** Check idle speed.

Date serviced:..

Carried out by: ....

Garage Stamp or signature:

Parts/Accessories purchased (date, parts, source) ....

....

....

....

....

☐ Job 67. **DIESEL ENGINES ONLY** Check idle speed.

☐ Job 68. Check exhaust emission.

Every 30,000 Miles - Around the Car

☐ Job 6. Check tyre pressures.

☐ Job 7. Check front lights.

☐ Job 8. Check side repeater indicators (if fitted).

☐ Job 9. Check rear lights.

☐ Job 10. Check number plate light.

☐ Job 11. Check interior lights.

☐ Job 12. Check horn.

☐ Job 13. Windscreen wipers.

☐ Job 14. Check screen washers.

☐ Job 15. Check heater blower/demist.

☐ Job 16. Check tyres.

☐ Job 17. Check spare tyre.

☐ Job 18. Wash bodywork.

☐ Job 19. Touch-up paintwork.

☐ Job 20. Lubricate aerial.

☐ Job 21. Valet interior.

☐ Job 22. Improve visibility.

☐ Job 23. Clean mirrors.

☐ Job 29. Check wheel nuts/bolts.

☐ Job 30. Check handbrake adjustment.

☐ Job 31. Check door and tailgate seals.

☐ Job 32. Check rear view mirrors.

☐ Job 33. Check windscreen.

☐ Job 69. Check seat belts and mountings.

☐ Job 70. Check fuel filler seal.

☐ Job 71. **NOT HIGH SECURITY LOCKS** Lubricate locks, check straps and hinges.

☐ Job 72. Lubricate bonnet release.

☐ Job 73. Check seat mountings.

☐ Job 74. Check shock absorber action.

☐ Job 75. Check/renew front brake pads.

☐ Job 76. Check/renew rear brake shoes.

Every 30,000 Miles - Under the Car

First carry out all Jobs listed under earlier Service intervals as applicable.

☐ Job 24. Clean mud traps.

☐ Job 34. Check exhaust system and mountings.

☐ Job 35. Check brake and fuel lines.

☐ Job 36. Check fuel tank for leaks.

☐ Job 37. Check steering rack gaiters.

☐ Job 38. Check drive shaft gaiters.

☐ Job 39. Check steering ball joints.

☐ Job 40. Check suspension joints and bushes.

☐ Job 41. Check underside for leaks.

☐ Job 42. Check ABS braking (where fitted).

Every 30,000 Miles - Road Test

☐ Job 43. Clean controls.

☐ Job 44. Check instruments and controls.

☐ Job 45. Check throttle and choke action.

☐ Job 46. Check clutch action.

☐ Job 47. Road test of brakes and steering.

EVERY 33,000 MILES - OR EVERY THIRTY THREE MONTHS, WHICHEVER COMES FIRST

All the Jobs at this Service Interval have been carried forward from earlier Service Intervals and are to be repeated at this service.

Every 33,000 Miles - The Engine Bay

☐ Job 1. Engine oil level.

☐ Job 2. Check coolant level.

☐ Job 3. Brake fluid level.

☐ Job 4. Check windscreen wash level.

☐ Job 5. Check battery electrolyte level.

☐ Job 25. Check alternator drive belt.

☐ Job 26. Check oil filler cap.

☐ Job 27. **DIESEL ENGINES ONLY** Drain fuel filter.

☐ Job 28. Check brake and fuel lines.

Date serviced: ....

Carried out by: ....
Garage Stamp or signature:

Parts/Accessories purchased (date, parts, source) ....

....

....

....

....

Every 33,000 Miles - Around The Car

- [ ] Job 6. Check tyre pressures.
- [ ] Job 7. Check front lights.
- [ ] Job 8. Check side repeater indicators (if fitted).
- [ ] Job 9. Check rear lights.
- [ ] Job 10. Check number plate light.
- [ ] Job 11. Check interior lights.
- [ ] Job 12. Check horn.
- [ ] Job 13. Windscreen wipers.
- [ ] Job 14. Check screen washers.
- [ ] Job 15. Check heater blower/demist.
- [ ] Job 16. Check tyres.
- [ ] Job 17. Check spare tyre.
- [ ] Job 18. Wash bodywork.
- [ ] Job 19. Touch-up paintwork.
- [ ] Job 20. Lubricate aerial.
- [ ] Job 21. Valet interior.
- [ ] Job 22. Improve visibility.
- [ ] Job 23. Clean mirrors.
- [ ] Job 29. Check wheel nuts/bolts.
- [ ] Job 30. Check handbrake adjustment.
- [ ] Job 31. Check door and tailgate seals.
- [ ] Job 32. Check rear view mirrors.
- [ ] Job 33. Check windscreen.

Every 33,000 Miles - Under the Car

- [ ] Job 24. Clean mud traps.
- [ ] Job 34. Check exhaust system and mountings.
- [ ] Job 35. Check brake and fuel lines.
- [ ] Job 36. Check fuel tank for leaks.
- [ ] Job 37. Check steering rack gaiters.
- [ ] Job 38. Check drive shaft gaiters.
- [ ] Job 39. Check steering ball joints.
- [ ] Job 40. Check suspension joints and bushes.
- [ ] Job 41. Check underside for leaks.
- [ ] Job 42. Check ABS braking (where fitted).

Every 33,000 Miles - Road Test

- [ ] Job 43. Clean controls.
- [ ] Job 44. Check instruments and controls.
- [ ] Job 45. Check throttle and choke action.
- [ ] Job 46. Check clutch action.
- [ ] Job 47. Road test of brakes and steering.

Date serviced:..

Carried out by:...
Garage Stamp or signature:

Parts/Accessories purchased (date, parts,
source) ....
....
....
....
....

EVERY 36,000 MILES - OR EVERY THREE YEARS, WHICHEVER COMES FIRST

All the Service Jobs in the tinted area have been carried forward from earlier service intervals and are to be repeated at this service.

Every 36,000 Miles - The Engine Bay

First carry out all Jobs listed under earlier Service intervals as applicable.

- [ ] Job 4. Check windscreen wash level.
- [ ] Job 5. Check battery electrolyte level.
- [ ] Job 26. Check oil filler cap.
- [ ] Job 27. **DIESEL ENGINES ONLY** Drain fuel filter.
- [ ] Job 28. Check brake and fuel lines.
- [ ] Job 48. Change engine oil.
- [ ] Job 49. Change oil filter.
- [ ] Job 51. Clean and check ignition components.
- [ ] Job 52. Check/set C.B. points/dwell angle.
- [ ] Job 53. Contact breaker points renewal.
- [ ] Job 54. Check ignition timing.
- [ ] Job 55. Check/lubricate wiper mechanism.
- [ ] Job 56. Check battery electrolyte.
- [ ] Job 57. Clean radiator.
- [ ] Job 58. Check water pump.
- [ ] Job 59. Check CVH camshaft belt.
- [ ] Job 60. Check manual gearbox oil.
- [ ] Job 61. Check automatic transmission fluid.
- [ ] Job 62. Check steering column couplings.
- [ ] Job 63. Check/adjust valve clearances.
- [ ] Job 64. Lubricate carburettor linkages.
- [ ] Job 65. **NOT FUEL INJECTION ENGINES** Adjust carburettor.
- [ ] Job 66. **FUEL INJECTION PETROL ENGINES** Check idle speed.
- [ ] Job 67. **DIESEL ENGINES ONLY** Check idle speed.
- [ ] Job 68. Check exhaust emission.
- [ ] Job 77. Change air filter element.

☐ Job 78. Clean air filter housing.

☐ Job 79. Check air intake control valve.

☐ Job 80. **DIESEL ENGINES ONLY**: Check valve clearances.

☐ Job 81. Renew fuel filter.

☐ Job 82. Check vacuum hoses.

☐ Job 83. Check/renew crankcase hoses and valves.

☐ Job 84. Check cooling system hoses.

☐ Job 85. Replace coolant.

☐ Job 86. **PETROL ENGINES** Renew spark plugs.

☐ Job 87. **DIESEL ENGINES** Clean glow plugs.

☐ Job 88. Clean battery terminals.

☐ Job 89. Check wiring and terminals.

☐ Job 90. Check door light switches.

☐ Job 106. Renew camshaft drive belt.

☐ Job 107. Renew HT leads, distributor cap and rotor arm.

Every 36,000 Miles - Around the Car

☐ Job 6. Check tyre pressures.

☐ Job 7. Check front lights.

☐ Job 8. Check side repeater indicators (if fitted).

☐ Job 9. Check rear lights.

☐ Job 10. Check number plate light.

☐ Job 11. Check interior lights.

☐ Job 12. Check horn.

☐ Job 14. Check screen washers.

☐ Job 15. Check heater blower/demist.

☐ Job 16. Check tyres.

☐ Job 17. Check spare tyre.

☐ Job 18. Wash bodywork.

☐ Job 19. Touch-up paintwork.

☐ Job 20. Lubricate aerial.

☐ Job 21. Valet interior.

☐ Job 22. Improve visibility.

☐ Job 23. Clean mirrors.

☐ Job 29. Check wheel nuts/bolts.

☐ Job 30. Check handbrake adjustment.

☐ Job 31. Check door and tailgate seals.

☐ Job 32. Check rear view mirrors.

☐ Job 33. Check windscreen.

☐ Job 69. Check seat belts and mountings.

☐ Job 70. Check fuel filler seal.

☐ Job 71. **NOT HIGH SECURITY LOCKS** Lubricate locks, check straps and hinges.

☐ Job 72. Lubricate bonnet release.

☐ Job 73. Check seat mountings.

☐ Job 74. Check shock absorber action.

☐ Job 75. Check/renew front brake pads.

☐ Job 76. Check/renew rear brake shoes.

☐ Job 91. Clean tailgate electrical contacts.

☐ Job 92. Check tool kit and jack.

☐ Job 93. Lubricate window and sunroof runners.

☐ Job 94. Renew wiper blades.

☐ Job 95. Check hub bearings.

☐ Job 96. Check steering and suspension.

☐ Job 97. Check floors.

☐ Job 98. Renew alarm sender unit batteries.

Every 36,000 Miles - Under the Car

☐ Job 24. Clean mud traps.

☐ Job 34. Check exhaust system and mountings.

☐ Job 35. Check brake and fuel lines.

☐ Job 36. Check fuel tank for leaks.

☐ Job 37. Check steering rack gaiters.

☐ Job 38. Check drive shaft gaiters.

☐ Job 39. Check steering ball joints.

☐ Job 40. Check suspension joints and bushes.

☐ Job 41. Check underside for leaks.

☐ Job 42. Check ABS braking (where fitted).

☐ Job 99. Inspect underside.

☐ Job 100. Clear drain holes.

☐ Job 101. Renew brake fluid.

☐ Job 102. Check engine and gearbox mountings.

☐ Job 103. Lubricate handbrake linkage.

☐ Job 108. Top-up rustproofing.

Every 36,000 Miles - Road Test

☐ Job 43. Clean controls.

☐ Job 44. Check instruments and controls.

☐ Job 45. Check throttle and choke action.

☐ Job 46. Check clutch action.

☐ Job 47. Road test of brakes and steering.

LONGER TERM SERVICING

Every 72,000 Miles - The Engine Bay

☐ Job 109. **DIESEL ENGINES** Renew glow plugs.

☐ Job 110. **FUEL INJECTION PETROL AND DIESEL ENGINES** Check and renew injectors (if necessary).

☐ Job 111. Change gearbox oil.

Date serviced:..

Carried out by:..
Garage Stamp or signature:

Parts/Accessories purchased (date, parts, source) ....

....

....

....

....

NOTES

You can learn a lot about the condition of an engine from looking at the spark plugs. The following information and photographs, reproduced here with grateful thanks to NGK, show you what to look out for.

1. Good Condition

If the firing end of a spark plug is brown or light grey, the condition can be judged to be good and the spark plug is functioning at its best.

4. Overheating

When having been overheated, the insulator tip can become glazed or glossy, and deposits which have accumulated on the insulator tip may have melted. Sometimes these deposits have blistered on the insulator's tip.

6. Abnormal Wear

Abnormal electrode erosion is caused by the effects of corrosion, oxidation, reaction with lead, all resulting in abnormal gap growth.

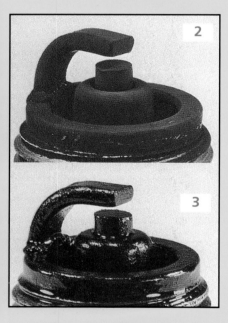

5. Normal Wear

A worn spark plug not only wastes fuel but also strains the whole ignition system because the expanded gap requires higher voltage. As a result, a worn spark plug will result in damage to the engine itself, and will also increase air pollution. The normal rate of gap growth is usually around 'half-a-thou.' or 0.0006 in. every 5,000 miles (0.01 mm. every 5,000 km.).

7. Breakage

Insulator damage is self-evident and can be caused by rapid heating or cooling of the plug whilst out of the car or by clumsy use of gap setting tools. Burned away electrodes are indicative of an ignition system that is grossly out of adjustment. Do not use the car until this has been put right.

2. Carbon Fouling

Black, dry, sooty deposits, which will eventually cause misfiring and can be caused by an over-rich fuel mixture. Check all carburettor settings, choke operation and air filter cleanliness. Clean plugs vigorously with a brass bristled wire brush.

3. Oil Fouling

Oily, wet-looking deposits. This is particularly prone to causing poor starting and even misfiring. Caused by a severely worn engine but do not confuse with wet plugs removed from the engine when it won't start. If the "wetness" evaporates away, it's not oil fouling.

Job 79. Check air intake control valve.

CARBURETTOR MODELS ONLY

79A. Make sure the vacuum-controlled flap in the air intake is functioning correctly.

79B. When cold and during warm-up the flap (A) is held open by vacuum so that only warm air drawn from round the exhaust manifold is admitted. When operating temperature is reached however, a bi-metallic valve shuts off the vacuum from the capsule and allows the valve to close, allowing cold air to enter the filter housing.

Check the operation of the valve by observing the flap through the end of the intake, first with the engine cold, then when it has reached operating temperature. If the valve fails to open when the engine is started, check the vacuum pipe from the inlet manifold to the vacuum capsule for signs of splitting or other damage. Otherwise, seek **SPECIALIST SERVICE** from your Ford dealer.

79A

Job 80. Check valve clearances.

DIESEL ENGINES ONLY

Both the 1.6 litre and 1.8 litre diesel engines fitted to the Fiesta are overhead cam designs with the valve clearances adjusted by shim washers. Special tools, and a supply of shim washers of various thicknesses are needed to adjust the clearances, and we strongly recommend that you seek **SPECIALIST SERVICE** and leave this job to your Ford dealer.

Job 81. Renew fuel filter

PETROL FUEL INJECTION MODELS ONLY

81A. On early fuel injection systems the fuel filter is located below the air filter housing. Slacken the fuel pipe unions slowly and have a large rag handy to catch the fuel spillage that will occur. Slacken the filter clamp screw and remove the filter from the car.

Fit the new filter ensuring that the arrows embossed on its casing point in the direction of the fuel flow, i.e. towards the injection metering system above the air filter. Tighten the clamp screw and reconnect the fuel pipe unions.

PETROL ENGINE CARS WITH CARBURETTOR ONLY

81B. If your Fiesta was not fitted with a fuel filter from new, you can add one to the fuel line leading to the carburettor, using the clips provided. Buy a proprietary filter from your local accessory store. Renew it at this interval.

DIESEL ENGINE MODELS ONLY

Three types of filter have been used on the 1.6 and 1.8 litre diesel engines fitted to the Fiesta, two with spin-off throw-away canisters and one with a renewal filter element inside the filter body. Sometimes, the system will need bleeding afterwards. If so, consult your workshop manual, or seek **SPECIALIST SERVICE**. If all the air is not bled from the system, the engine may refuse to start or, at best, run poorly.

79B

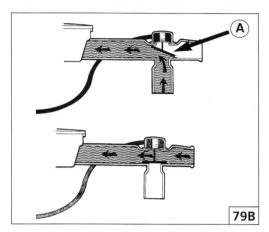
81A

81B

SAFETY FIRST!
Only a small amount of fuel is likely to be lost during this job, so have a large rag or small container positioned below the filter.

SAFETY FIRST!

i) Whenever you are dealing with diesel fuel, it's essential to protect your hands by wearing plastic gloves.

ii) Keep diesel fuel away from the clutch and brakes, the starter motor and any rubber components. Protect tarmac surfaces by putting down newspaper. IMPORTANT NOTE: Dirt is the enemy of fuel injection systems; even a microscopic quantity can be disastrous. Clean thoroughly around the filter before dismantling and work with clean lint-free rags to wipe every component clean before re-assembling.

The filter is located on the side of the engine block, above the clutch housing. Access is greatly improved if the air filter is removed. See *Job 27* for details of draining the filter - do so before dismantling.

81C. This is the earlier Bosch type of filter. Remove the body of the filter by unscrewing the canister, in a similar fashion to that for changing the engine oil filter - see below.

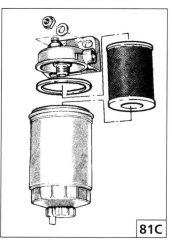

81C

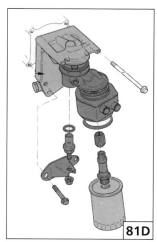

81D

81D. Some models have a disposable cartridge...

81E. ...for which you will need a filter removal strap or chain; the very one you use for your engine's oil filter, in fact!

81F. Others have a disposable body (A) sandwiched between the water bowls (B) and filter head (C). The Bosch clamp-fixing type is similar, and also has a through bolt disconnected from the top of the unit.

81G. The CAV unit looks different at the top but is, again similar in use. (Illustrations, courtesy Ford Motor Company Ltd)

81E

Always fit new seals (when they are separate) and lubricate fixed and separate seals with a smear of diesel fuel - don't re-assemble dry!

81H. This later type of Bosch filter is of the remove-and-throw-away type. You remove the pipes (B) and undo the clamps (A). Take care not to spill diesel fuel and dispose of waste fuel responsibly without pouring it into the ground or down the drain.

BLEEDING THE SYSTEM

Bosch filters are designed to be self-bleeding which means, in practice, that you'll have to crank the engine for ages until the fuel gets through. Speed things up by fitting the filter housing with fuel, as far as practicable, so less fuel has to be drawn through.

CAV filters have a priming pump (see arrow in *81G*), operated by pumping the black button on the top of the filter unit after first slackening the bleed screw. Pump until diesel fuel begins to flow.

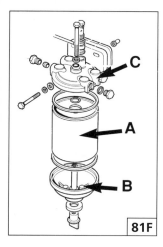

81F

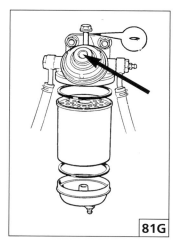

81G

81H

12,000 MILE SERVICE

☐ Job 82. Check vacuum hoses.

82A. Check the security of the vacuum hose from the inlet manifold on petrol engined cars (from the vacuum pump on diesel engines) to the brake servo. Bend it in your fingers. If it feels brittle, if you hear any signs of cracking, or the ends are split, the hose needs renewing.

82B. Check the condition and security of the vacuum pipes to the distributor advance and retard. Connected to or in these pipes there could be a fuel vapour trap valve, a spark sustain valve, a spark delay valve and a ported vacuum switch. All except the fuel vapour trap valve are part of the engine emission control system and control the distributor advance and retard, so that your engine produces the least harmful emissions at all throttle openings and engine loads. If your engine fails its exhaust emission test, and the carburettor is properly adjusted, it may be that one or more of these valves has failed. Checking them needs a specialist vacuum pump and gauges, so it is a job for **SPECIALIST SERVICE**.

82C. The exception is the fuel vapour trap valve, the one with a white end. The purpose of this is to prevent fuel being drawn into - and ruining - the distributor advance and retard diaphragm. It must be mounted either in a horizontal position or sloping down towards the inlet manifold, never sloping down towards the carburettor or, when you stop the engine, condensed liquid fuel in it could run down into the distributor and ruin the diaphragm. If you have to remove this valve to renew the hose, note that it is marked 'Dist' at one end and 'Carb' at the other. Make sure you replace it the correct way round.

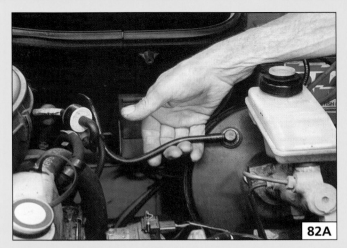

82A

82B

☐ Job 83. Check/renew crankcase hoses and valves.

83A. Check the condition and security of all the hoses and clips in the crankcase emission control system. Numerous types and layouts of crankcase emission valves and filters have been fitted to Fiesta engines over the years, and vary, depending on the type of engine, its capacity and its age. Refer to your workshop manual for full details if you can't follow the pipework by deduction alone.

Failure of one or more of the devices is often indicated by oil being drawn into the air cleaner housing. If this happens consistently, seek **SPECIALIST SERVICE** to determine which of the valves is at fault as it often needs specialist equipment to check them.

83B. However, on OHV engines, first check that the oil filler cap is not blocked (See *Job 26*).

INSIDE INFORMATION: On fuel injected CVH engines, the emission control system

82C

has been modified twice during the life of the Fiesta to prolong the life of the valves and avoid this problem of oil in the air filter. Ford dealers can update earlier systems to the later specification, but check on the cost first as it may involve changing the throttle body and could be an expensive operation.

83A

83B

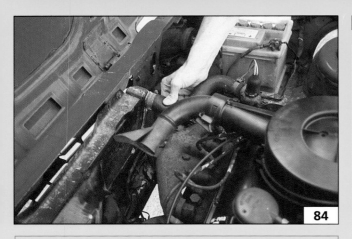

84

☐ **Job 84. Check cooling system hoses.**

SAFETY FIRST!
i) The coolant level should only be worked on WHEN THE ENGINE IS COLD. If you remove the pressure cap when the engine is hot, the release of pressure can cause the water in the cooling system to boil and spurt into the air with the risk of severe scalding. ii) Take care precautions to prevent antifreeze being swallowed or coming into contact with the skin or eyes and keep it away from children. If this should happen, rinse immediately with plenty of cold water, seek immediate medical help if necessary.

making it easy! *Sometimes when you buy a new hose, the rubber is so stiff that it is difficult to get it over the inlet pipe. A good tip is to put a smear of screen washer fluid on the tapered neck of an old wine or soft drink bottle and push this into the end of the hose, giving it a few twists, to spread the rubber and lubricate it. The hose usually goes on much more easily after this.*

84. Check all the coolant and heater hoses for security and leaks. Squeeze the larger hoses, and with the smaller hoses, bend the straights and straighten the bends, listening for cracking sounds. If you hear any 'internal' cracking sounds, or if the outside of any of the hoses is cracked, the hose needs renewing. Drain the cooling system, see *Job 85*.

☐ **Job 85. Replace coolant.**

85A

SAFETY FIRST!
Work on the cooling system only when the engine is cold. If you drain a system when the engine is hot, the remaining coolant inside can boil over and release scalding water and steam.

85A. Drain the cooling system by removing the expansion tank filler cap and undoing the bottom hose from the radiator. (On some models there is a drain plug on the bottom of the radiator, as here). If the old coolant looks like this, and shows signs of rust and sludge, flush the system out with a garden hose.

Clean out the coolant expansion tank with a small brush. Re-fit the drain plug or reconnect the hose. Re-fit the expansion tank and fill the system with the appropriate mixture of water and antifreeze, after first checking the quantity in *Chapter 8, Facts and Figures*. Check on the antifreeze container for the correct dilution - we recommend 50%.

85B. On early engines with push-on caps to the (non-pressurised) expansion tank, (see illustration *2A*) refill the system through the cap (A) on the radiator itself. Wait a few moment, and squeeze the radiator hose gently, until all the air bubbles have stopped, then top up to overflowing, re-fit the cap and top up the expansion tank to the level mark. Run the engine for a few minutes, wait for it to cool down, then finally top up the expansion tank.

85C. On models with a screw-on cap to the expansion tank, all filling is done through the expansion tank, not through the thermostat housing. Pour the fresh coolant into the header or expansion tank to give a 50-50 dilution; refer to *Chapter 8, Facts & Figures* for the capacity of your car's cooling system. Finally, add the required amount of fresh water, then start the engine and

85B

85C

check for leaks. After running the engine for a few minutes, switch off, leave to cool down and top up again. Do so again after the first time you use the car.

making it easy! Old hoses become very set in their ways, and should you need to renew one you may find that, even with its clips fully slackened off, it will be reluctant to budge.

Rather than employ too much force, particularly on a radiator, where there's a high risk of fracturing the hose stub, simply slide the clip out of the way and use a strong, sharp knife to slit the hose until you can open it up and peel it off the stub.

Thoroughly clean the stubs, carefully using a file and emery cloth if necessary, to remove the lumpy corrosion often found on elderly alloy cooling system components.

Position new clips (preferably of flat, 'worm-drive' type) on the new hose, ensuring their tightening screws are best placed for easy screwdriver access when the hose is fitted. A smear of washing-up fluid will help the hose slide fully home on the stubs. Tighten the clips firmly, but don't 'bury' them in the hose.

85D

SAFETY FIRST!
Keep your hands and clothing well away from the fan belt and fan when the engine is running. Do not wear loose clothing.

85D. INSIDE INFORMATION: In between coolant changes, you can check the specific gravity of the antifreeze with a hydrometer. This is similar to the hydrometer for checking battery acid but they are not interchangeable. Both types can be bought at most accessory shops. Follow the instructions and, if the specific gravity is too low, add more antifreeze.

INSIDE INFORMATION: Remember that antifreeze, even in diluted form, will attack paintwork. Be particularly careful when flushing especially if you have to disconnect the heater hoses. Any spilt antifreeze should be washed off immediately with plenty of cold water.

☐ Job 86. Renew spark plugs.

PETROL ENGINES

Some owners delay renewing spark plugs until they start to misfire, but this is a penny-wise, pound-foolish policy because worn plugs increase fuel consumption as well as detracting from the engine's performance. Always check the gap on new plugs before fitting them, see *Chapter 8, Facts and Figures*.

☐ Job 87. Clean glow plugs.

DIESEL ENGINES

87. Disconnect the battery, disconnect the electrical lead to the bus bar joining the glow plugs, removing the nuts and washers from the glow plugs (pointed out here) and remove the so-called bus (or 'connecting') bar. Unscrew each glow plug in turn with a deep socket and clean the carbon off the end with a non-fluffy rag and clean diesel fuel or proprietary carburettor cleaner. After cleaning and replacing the plugs, reconnect the bus bar, the cable and the battery connection.

87

SAFETY FIRST!
Whenever you are dealing with diesel fuel, it's essential to protect your hands by wearing plastic gloves.

making it easy! Because of the heat, and sometimes because of a previous owner's overtightening, spark plugs can be very tight to undo, so much so that you may have to use the long extension handle of your socket set and, even then, the insulation of the plug may break. To prevent this from happening in the future, put a smear of copper grease on the threads of the plugs before you screw them back in the cylinder head. Remember that taper-seat plugs, the sort with a taper instead of a sealing washer, must never be overtightened. See *Chapter 8, Facts and Figures*, for the correct tightening torque.

88

☐ Job 88. Clean battery terminals.

> *making it easy!* If the terminals on your battery are showing signs of growing white or green fur or crystals, clean it off by pouring boiling water over the terminals. You'll be surprised at how easily it comes away! Be sure to wash the corrosive stuff right off your car's bodywork.

88. Dry the terminals off, check the tightness of the connections and coat the terminals with petroleum jelly (Vaseline) to prevent further attack. If they are badly corroded, unbolt, sand them clean and re-assemble.

SAFETY FIRST!
Be very careful to guard against 'short circuits' when working on battery terminals. The gas ensuing from the cells, particularly when the battery is being charged, is extremely explosive and ignition by a careless spark can cause a truly horrific battery explosion.

☐ Job 89. Check wiring and terminals.

89A. These are by no means only in the engine bay, of course, but this is where the majority will be found. Terminals hanging on by a thread could be a breakdown waiting to happen - or even a fire. Your local accessory shop will stock standard-sized terminals and a crimping tool for fitting them.

89B. INSIDE INFORMATION: Where the earlier Fiesta's wiring passes from the body to the hatch, there are two pieces of rubber trunking. Inside one is a bunch of wires; inside the other, the rear screenwash tube. Both are prone to breakage, because of all the bending that goes on. Pull back the sheath and if necessary, it may be **SPECIALIST SERVICE** time for an auto-electrician to renew some of the cables. On later models, electric current is passed through by spring loaded electrical contacts. See **Job 91**.

89C. You can even *add* wiring in one trouble spot, using the crimping tool shown in **89A.** Rear light units have to earth thought their mounting screws if they are to work properly. If your lights have minds of their own, try connecting a separate earth wire from the body of the light unit to the body of the car.

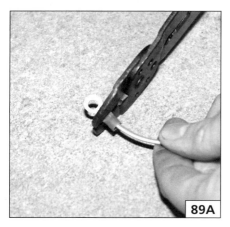

89A

☐ Job 90. Check door light switches.

90. Door light switches often fail because they corrode internally, or the wire breaks off the back. DON'T make a temporary twisted-wire repair - it could cause a fire. Crimp on a new connection or have **SPECIALIST SERVICE** attention. New switches are obtained from your Ford dealer. (Illustration, courtesy Ford Motor Company Ltd)

89B

89C

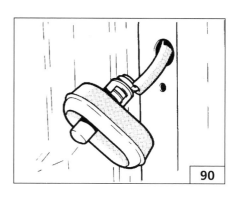

90

CHAPTER THREE

Every 12,000 Miles - Around the Car

First carry out the relevant jobs from the earlier service intervals.

☐ **Job 91. Clean tailgate electrical contacts.**

On later Fiestas, power for components fitted to the tailgate is transmitted to the tailgate through these spring loaded connectors.

91A. Clean the ends of the connectors, which are on the bottom of the tailgate near the catch, so that they make good contact with ...

91B. ... the connector plates just inside the luggage bay area. Make sure these are also clean and free of corrosion.

91A

☐ **Job 92. Check tool kit and jack.**

It is annoying, to say the least, to be caught out on the road with a puncture, a spare wheel, and no means of changing it. Lubricate the screw of the jack and check that it is working properly. Check that you have chocks to put under the wheels, and means to undo the wheel bolts.

91B

> *making it easy !* It is hard work undoing wheel bolts with the small spanner supplied by Ford, so you may like to supplement it with an extending wheel bolt spanner which you can buy at most accessory shops. If you carry an 'emergency kit' with a new fan belt and new bulbs, check that you have the necessary spanners and screwdrivers to fit these by the roadside.

☐ **Job 93. Lubricate window and sunroof runners.**

Spray silicone lubricant into the window and sunroof runners and you'll be surprised at how much more easily and smoothly they operate. You'll also be taking quite a load off the motors of electrically operated windows or sunroof.

☐ **Job 94. Renew wiper blades.**

94A

94A. Worn wiper blades can be a misery in the wet, as well as being an MoT failure. Renewing them is just a case of lifting the wiper arm from the screen, depressing the retaining catch (see *Job 13B*), unhooking the old blade and hooking the new one in position.

94B. Also, check the arms. If the springs are broken, renew the whole arm. Lift the hinged trim flap at the base of the arm, unscrew the nut and remove the arm.

☐ **Job 95. Check hub bearings.**

Raise the front of the car just sufficiently for the wheels to be clear of the ground. Grip the top and bottom of the wheel and try to rock it. If there is more than just the slightest suspicion of movement, **SPECIALIST SERVICE:** have the wheel bearings checked by a specialist. Do the same for the rear wheels.

94B

96A

96B

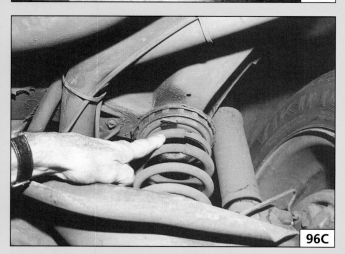

96C

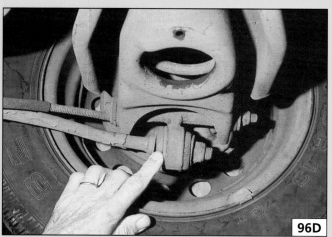

96D

☐ Job 96. Check steering and suspension.

96A. With the front wheels just clear of the ground, grasp the wheel at the sides and try to turn it from side to side. If you feel free play, put the car up on axle stands and get someone to turn the wheels while you investigate where the free play is occurring. If it is in one of the ball joints, these can be renewed, using your workshop manual, or seek **SPECIALIST SERVICE**. If the steering rack is worn, you can buy an exchange unit.

96B. With the front wheels still raised just clear of the ground, put a pry bar under the wheel and try to lever it upwards. If you get any free play it means wear in the suspension bushes or suspension strut. Seek **SPECIALIST SERVICE** advice.

96C. You will already have checked the front suspension as a part of *Job 40*. At the rear, check the springs for obvious breaks or sagging (measure the right height).....

96D. ... and the tie bar bushes for cracking, softness or wear. These are right on the limit!

SHOCK ABSORBERS

While you're in the area, check each shock absorber for leaks or corrosion, both of which mean a pair of shockers - both fronts or both rears - need replacing. (Don't replace them singly.)

☐ Job 97. Check floors.

97. Lift the carpets and check for signs of rust and wetness on the floor underneath, especially adjacent to the sills in the area shown here. If you find any, deal with it before any leaks are left for so long that you face the problem of seriously rusted metal as well. If you find any wetness, you will probably have to take the seats and the carpets right out to dry the carpets and any underfelt.

making it easy! Tracing leaks isn't the easiest of jobs, and sometimes the only way is to remove the carpets, dry the floor thoroughly and then get someone play a hose on the underside of the car, round the doors and over the bonnet while you look inside.

INSIDE INFORMATION: Leaks through spot-welded seams may be

just an indication of the original sealant having dried out and crumbled, in which case a new dose of mastic sealant will cure the problem. But it might just be the first sign of something more serious, like rusting. If you are in any doubt about the soundness of any part of the floor pan structure, seek SPECIALIST SERVICE advice.

97

☐ **Job 98. Renew alarm sender unit batteries.**

If your car is fitted with a remote control alarm system it is most galling to arrive at the car and find that the remote sender doesn't work and you can't get into your own car without setting off the alarm! Don't wait for the batteries to fail; renew them now.

> **SAFETY FIRST!**
> *Raise the car off the ground only after reading carefully the information at the start of this chapter on lifting and supporting the car. Wear goggles when carrying out any cleaning, painting or undersealing underneath the car.*

Every 12,000 Miles - Under the Car

First carry out the relevant service jobs from earlier service intervals.

☐ **Job 99. Inspect underside.**

99. Inspect the underside for rust and damage to the underbody sealant. Look particularly for loose, flaking sealant and, if necessary, scrape it off with a flat bladed paint scraper. If you expose the metal, treat the area with rust killer, then a good quality paint and finally a new coat of sealant. While you are doing this you may also find small jobs to do like renewing clips for wiring, pipe runs and so on, and check particularly the brake pipes for corrosion.

99

☐ **Job 100. Clear drain holes.**

100A. Make sure the drain holes at the bottom of each door are clear. Blocked drain holes here are often responsible for the unsightly rust you see at the bottoms of doors.

100B. Another vulnerable area for rust is the sills. Go along the bottom seam and use a small flat bladed screwdriver to make sure that all the slotted drain holes are clear.

100A

☐ **Job 101. Renew brake fluid.**

101. Over a period of time, brake fluid absorbs moisture from the air and, should the fluid at the calipers or wheel cylinders get very hot with prolonged braking, this water can boil and cause a vapour lock - in other words, completely useless brakes and a pedal that hits the floor! If this job is not carried out properly it can result in brakes which could let you down without warning.

Do not carry out this job unless you have been trained to do it, and do not attempt it without the workshop manual as procedures differ on different models of car, particularly if optional ABS braking is fitted. We strongly recommend that you regard this as a **SPECIALIST SERVICE** job and leave it to your Ford dealer or have a trained mechanic check your work before using the car, if you decide to do it yourself.

☐ **Job 102. Check engine and gearbox mountings.**

102A. Check each of the engine and gearbox mountings to make sure that oil leaks have not caused the rubber to become soggy or swollen. Check the tightness of the mounting bolts and use a pry bar to check that the sandwich of the mounting does not gape when you try to separate it.

100B

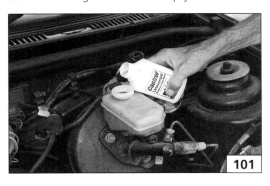
101

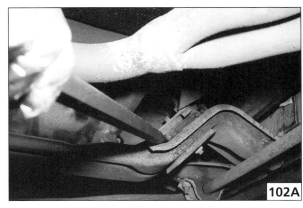
102A

102B

making it easy! 102B. All the mountings can be inspected from underneath, but you may find that one of the front engine mountings, where the engine support bracket is mounted on the subframe, is easier to check visually from under the bonnet.

☐ Job 103. Lubricate handbrake linkage.

103A. This is how the Fiesta's handbrake mechanism works. Only one part of the cable is exposed (see *103B*) but it's a good idea to place a blob of grease where the cable enters each 'outer' (G). (Illustration, courtesy Ford Motor Company Ltd)

103B. Apply grease liberally to the brake cable equaliser where the cable runs round a groove in the sector plate.

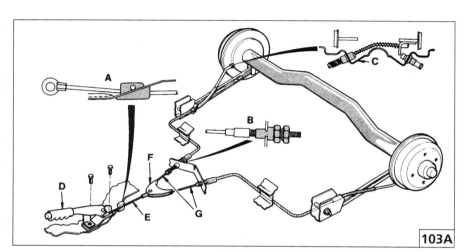

103A

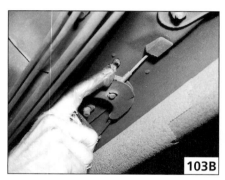

103B

Every 24,000 Miles, or Every Two Years - whichever comes first

Every 24,000 Miles - The Engine Bay

First carry out the relevant service jobs from earlier service intervals.

☐ Job 104. Renew coolant expansion tank cap.

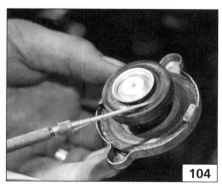

104

104. The cooling system is under pressure when the engine is hot. This raises the boiling point of the coolant so that the engine can run at its most efficient temperature. If the expansion tank cap does not hold pressure, the coolant can boil and form steam pockets inside the engine with local overheating and damage. Renew the cap, even if it looks good. The rubber hardens over time and the spring behind it weakens over time.

☐ Job 105. Renew alternator drive belt.

Renew the alternator drive belt (the fan belt to most people), see *Job 25* for details. A broken fan belt would at the very least be inconvenient, since you won't be able to continue your journey; at the worst, it could be catastrophic for your engine. Change it regularly, at this interval for complete peace of mind.

Every 36,000 Miles, or Every Three Years - whichever comes first

These are extra jobs to be carried out every time your car covers another 36,000 miles.

☐ Job 106. Renew camshaft drive belt.

Renewing the camshaft drive belt is a job for experienced fitters only. We strongly advise that you leave this job to **SPECIALIST SERVICE**. Replacement at this stage is much less expensive than what could easily be a written-off engine, if the belt breaks.

☐ Job 107. Renew HT leads, distributor cap and rotor arm.

PETROL ENGINES ONLY

107. Even though the HT leads, distributor cap and rotor arm may look OK on inspection, they can deteriorate with age. To ensure trouble free starting and running, it pays to renew them every six years.

> *making it easy!* *Mark the old cap and leads with typists' correction fluid to indicate which lead goes to which plug, remove the old cap and leads from the distributor and use the markings as a guide to fitting the new leads.*

☐ Job 108. Top-up rustproofing.

Renew and top-up the wax coating to the sills, box sections, insides of doors and underside of car. See *Chapter 5, Rustproofing*, for full details.

Every 72,000 Miles, or Every Six Years - whichever comes first

These are extra jobs to be carried out every time your car covers another 72,000 miles.

☐ Job 109. Renew glow plugs.

DIESEL ENGINES

Renew the glow plugs, see *Job 87* for details. Be sure to tighten to the correct torque - consult your main dealer when you buy the replacements to be sure you've got the correct figure for your engine.

☐ Job 110. Check and renew injectors (if necessary).

FUEL INJECTION PETROL AND DIESEL ENGINES

110. In time, and even with detergent fuels, injectors become carboned and do not work at their full efficiency. This may show up as poor starting or on an MoT exhaust emission test. Checking the spray pattern of injectors calls for specialist equipment, so this is a job for **SPECIALIST SERVICE**. (Illustration, courtesy V L Churchill)

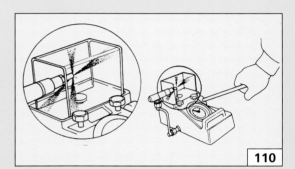

☐ Job 111. Change gearbox oil.

111. This is not part of the Ford service schedule but common sense dictates that fresh lubricant at this stage will allow components to last longer.

AUTOMATIC TRANSMISSION ONLY

To drain the old oil it is necessary (in the absence of a drain plug) to unbolt the oil pan. Remove all the bolts (but two, left loose); this will allow the plate to maintain its seal with the gasket until a drip tray can be positioned beneath it, when a sharp tap from a soft-faced hammer or block of wood, struck sideways, will free the plate and allow the oil to drain. This can be messy! The oil strainer should also be removed and washed in white spirit then dried before replacing it. IT IS ABSOLUTELY ESSENTIAL that no trace of dirt - not even fluff from a cloth - is allowed to get into the auto. transmission unit. This is the ATX unit; the CTX type is similar in principle - but DON'T touch the hydraulic control system found beneath the oil pan.
Always use a new gasket when re-fitting the plate, after draining is complete.

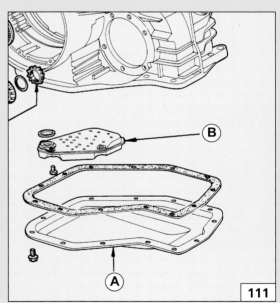

MANUAL TRANSMISSION ONLY

INSIDE INFORMATION: There is no means of drawing the oil through the gearbox casing, but note that most of the oil is lost when a driveshaft gaiter is removed. Make a mental note that, next time a gaiter needs replacing, you should ask the mechanic to tip the car to one side with the driveshaft out (it has to be removed to change the gaiter), drain as much oil as possible and renew it.

Top-up the gearbox with the recommended fluid. (See *Appendix 1, Recommended Castrol Lubricants*.)

CHAPTER 4 - BODYWORK

In this Chapter, we show you how to make your car look its best. First, we demonstrate that your car's appearance can be improved beyond recognition by a couple of hours of work on a Sunday morning. Then, just in case a passing gate post should leap out at you, we explain how to carry out simple bodywork repairs at home.

PART I: THE BODY BEAUTIFUL

Have you ever looked in amazement at the condition of cars on a dealer's forecourt and wondered why your car doesn't look like that? Well, it can! It's all a matter of know-how and a bit of hard work - and using the techniques described in this Chapter, you'll find that your car can be made to look almost like new again, without using too many cans of elbow grease!

☐ I.1 Apply a thin coat of modern car polish, to give a far longer-lasting shine than old-fashioned waxes (though we've yet to find one that lasts as long as claimed!). Cover just one section of the car at a time and then, as soon as the wax dries to a haze, buff off for a superb shine. You'll see the dull paint and oxides come off on the cloth as you buff.

I.1

making it easy! • As you polish, keep turning the cloth, always presenting a clean face to the surface of the paint - that's the secret of obtaining a clear shine with no rub marks. You'll need several clean cloths for polishing a whole car!

• Try removing a bug splat with a kitchen abrasive pad - the gentler sort made for non-stick pans - but only on glass and chrome; it'll ruin the shine on paintwork.

☐ I.2 Weekend trips in your car are likely to be cursed by the 'bugs on the bumper' syndrome, as well as black tar on the bodywork. Soak all the bug-splatted areas with soapy water first, while you wash the rest of the car, then come back later, when they've been softened. Rub off with cloth, rather than a sponge. Use a proprietary brand of tar remover to wipe off tar splash.

SOFT-TOP SPORTS CARS: If your vinyl soft-top has ingrained dirt, scrub it gently all over with a nail brush and soapy water. When dry, apply a good quality vinyl cleaner to bring the appearance back like new. Fabric soft-tops should only be washed, not scrubbed, but can be hosed off to shift the dirt.

I.2

☐ I.3 It's easy to forget that around a fifth of your car's 'bodywork' is in fact glass. Use purpose-made glass cleaner, or a clean wash leather, for sparkling results. Clouding on the inside (said to be the vapour from upholstery plastics!) cleans off in the same way.

I.3

I.4

☐ I.4 Tyres are one of the most 'visual' parts of your car. There are proprietary tyre polishes and paints available, but be warned that the improvement in appearance goes the first time you drive on a wet road! A good cleaning with the wash sponge - *after* you've washed the rest of the car - is usually enough. Alloy wheels need a spray-on alloy wheel cleaner to shift stuck-on brake dust.

☐ *I.5 INSIDE INFORMATION: Many people just don't know what to do about dull plastic bumpers. Use a colourless trim cleaner and you'll find that just wiping it on will bring about a magical improvement. Several coats may be needed. (The old, black-coloured bumper polish makes a real mess of your hands, by the way!)*

I.5

☐ I.6 Even when an engine bay is clean, it often looks dirty. Use a spray-on cleaner to remove the heavy dirt and grease - best if you let it soak in to the worst areas. Use an old paintbrush in nooks and crannies. A vinyl protectant will then bring up a wonderful sheen to all of your hoses and pipes as well as all underbonnet paintwork.

making it easy! If your engine is very oily, ask a local garage with a steam cleaner to hose off the worst of the 'grunge' before starting to clean up the engine bay. Paint any bare metal exposed by the steam cleaning, before it starts to rust.

☐ I.7 Choose a vinyl cleaner designed to put back the suppleness into vinyl and protect it from fading, as well as to remove dirt and grime and restore the appearance. If you hate the 'tacky' high gloss shine produced by some of them, look out for the low-gloss variety, giving a more natural finish.

INSIDE INFORMATION: If you can't get hold of low-gloss vinyl cleaner, try wiping over with a damp cloth before the cleaner has fully dried. This also 'wipes' away the worst of the gloss.

Rubber seals will last far longer if they are protected against the elements, by regular treatments with vinyl and rubber protectant. Scrape out dirt and grit from around the lower door seals then treat them all with several coats.

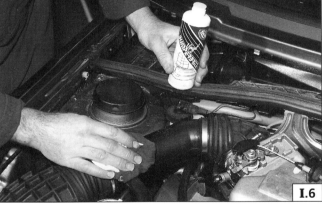

I.6

☐ I.8 Fabric seats and carpets will certainly benefit from cleaning with a proprietary brand of spray-on car upholstery cleaner - or a household upholstery cleaner. Follow the instructions carefully, take care not to soak cloth trim (it could cause shrinking) and the result will be carpets and cloth seats that look like new.

You can make leather more supple, and keep it cleaner and longer lasting by using a purpose-made brand of leather care. After use, the leather will feel soft and supple, because of the lanolin and moisturisers that you will have added. At first, you may be surprised to see the colour of your leather go much darker but don't worry; that will pass as the leather cleaner dries out naturally.

I.7

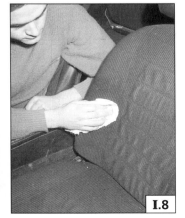

I.8

PART II: REPAIRING BODYWORK BLEMISHES

However well you look after your car, there will always be the risk of car park accident damage - or even worse! The smallest paint chips are best touched up with paint purchased from your local auto. accessory shop. If your colour of paint is not available, some auto. accessory shops offer a mixing scheme (including aerosols, in some cases) or you could look for a local paint factor in Yellow Pages. Take your car along to the paint factor and have them match the colour and mix the smallest quantity of cellulose paint that they will supply you with. Larger body blemishes will need the use of body filler.

SAFETY FIRST!
Always *wear plastic gloves when working with body filler, before it has set. Always wear a face mask when sanding filler and wear goggles when using a power sander.*

☐ II.1 The rear of this car's bodywork has sustained a nasty gash, the sort of damage for which you will certainly need to use body filler. The first stage is to mask off. Try to find "natural" edges such as body mouldings or styling stripes and wherever you can, mask off body trim rather than having to remove it.

☐ II.2 Remove all paint from the damaged area and for about 25mm (1 in.) around the damaged area. Roughen the bare metal or surface with coarse abrasive paper - a power sander is best. Wipe over the area with white spirit (mineral spirit) and then wash off with washing-up liquid in water - *not* car wash detergent.

INSIDE INFORMATION: Rub the surrounding paintwork with cutting compound so that the new paint has a better chance of matching the old.

☐ II.3 Mix the filler and hardener, following the instructions on the can. It's best to use a piece of plastic or metal rather than cardboard because otherwise, the filler will pick up fibres from the surface of the card. Mix thoroughly until the colour is consistent and no traces of hardener can be discerned.

☐ II.4 You can now spread the filler evenly over the repair. If the damage is particularly deep, apply the paste in two or more layers, allowing the filler to harden before adding the next layer. The final layer should be just proud of the level required, but do not overfill as this wastes paste and will require more time to sand down.

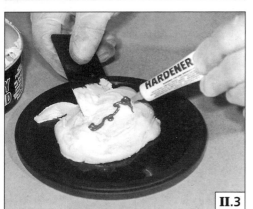

☐ II.5 It is essential when sanding down that you wrap the sanding paper around a flat block. You can see from the scratch marks that this repair has been sanded diagonally in alternate directions until the filler has become level with the surrounding panel, but you have to take care not to go deeply into the edges of the paint around the repair.

INSIDE INFORMATION: There will invariably be small pin holes even if the right

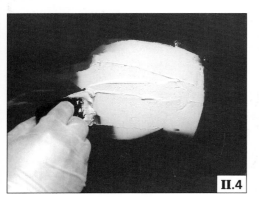

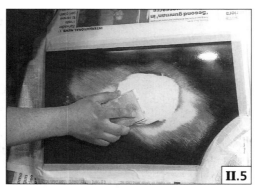

amount of filler was applied first time. Use a tiny amount of filler scraped very thin over the whole repair, filling in deep scratches and pin holes and then sanding off with a very fine grade of sand paper - preferably dry paper rather than wet-or-dry because you don't want to get water on to the bare filler.

☐ II.6 You can now use an aerosol primer to spray over the whole area of the repair but preferably not right up to the edges of the masking tape...

☐ II.7 ...and now use wet-or-dry paper, again on a sanding block, to sand the primer paint.

INSIDE INFORMATION: Don't sand fresh primer paint - leave it up to a day to harden off.

The filler is now protected from the water by the paint. If you do apply paint right up to the edge of the tape, be sure to 'feather' the edges of the primer, so that the edges blend in smoothly to the surrounding surface, with no ridges.

II.6

SAFETY FIRST!
Always wear an efficient mask when spraying aerosol paint and only work in a well-ventilated area, well away from any source of ignition, because spray paint vapour, even that given off by an aerosol, is highly flammable. Ensure that you have doors and windows open to the outside when using aerosol paint but in cool or damp weather, close them when the vapour has dispersed, otherwise the surface of the paint will "bloom", or take on a milky appearance. In fact, you may find it difficult to obtain a satisfactory finish in cold or damp weather.

II.7

☐ II.8 Before starting to spray, ensure that the nozzle is clear. Note that the can must be held with the index finger well back on the aerosol button. If you let your finger overhang the front of the button, a paint drip can form and throw itself on to the work area as a paint blob.

making it easy! • One of the secrets of spraying paint which doesn't run, is to put a very light coat of spray paint on to the panel first, followed by several more coats, allowing time between each coat for the bulk of the solvent to evaporate.

• *Alternate coats should go on horizontally, followed by vertical coats as shown on the inset diagram.*

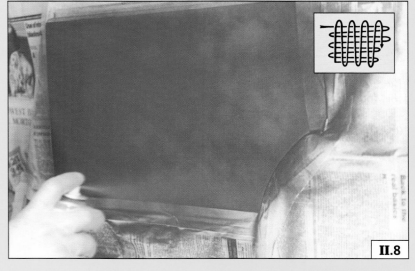
II.8

☐ II.9 After allowing about a week for the paint to dry, you will be able to polish it with a light cutting compound, blending the edges of the repair into the surrounding paintwork.

*INSIDE INFORMATION: Do note that if your repairs don't work out first time and you have to apply more paint on top of the fresh paint that you have already used, allow a week to elapse otherwise there is a strong risk of pickling or other reactions to take place. Also note that a prime cause of paint failure is the existence of silicones on the surface of the old paint before you start work. These come from most types of polish and are not all that easy to remove - they **won't** sand off!. Thoroughly wipe the panel down with white spirit before starting work and wash off with warm water and washing-up liquid to remove any further traces of the polish and the white spirit - but don't use the sponge or bucket that you normally use for washing the car otherwise you will simply introduce more silicones onto the surface!*

II.9